PSYCHIC
PHENOMENA

clairvoyance

ghosts

precognition

telekinesis

telepathy

G. C. BARNARD

SENATE

Psychic Phenomena

First published in 1933 as *The Supernormal* by
Rider & Company, London

This edition first published in 1997 by Senate,
an imprint of Random House UK Ltd,
Random House, 20 Vauxhall Bridge Road,
London SW1V 2SA

ISBN 1 85958 511 6

Printed and bound in Guernsey by
The Guernsey Press Co Ltd

CONTENTS

PART ONE

CHAPTER   PAGE

I. SCIENCE AND THE SUPERNORMAL . . 7

II. HYPNOTISM 20

III. PERSONALITY AND THE UNCONSCIOUS MIND 36

PART TWO

IV. TELEKINESIS 61

V. MATERIALIZATIONS 79

VI. IDEOPLASTICITY 94

VII. MEDIUMSHIP AND ITS INVESTIGATION . . 105

VIII. FOUR-DIMENSIONAL PHYSICS . . 120

PART THREE

IX. CRYPTÆSTHESIA 139

X. TELEPATHY 152

XI. PRECOGNITION 171

XII. CLAIRVOYANCE 196

PART FOUR

XIII. THE SURVIVAL OF THE PERSONALITY . . 210

XIV. TRANSCENDENTAL CONSCIOUSNESS . . 236

INDEX OF PROPER NAMES . . . 253

SUBJECT INDEX 255

THE SUPERNORMAL

PART ONE

CHAPTER ONE

SCIENCE AND THE SUPERNORMAL

" What is now proved was once only imagined."
W. BLAKE.

THERE is a natural tendency, which is shared by all who are not unduly credulous or superstitious, to dismiss as absurd, and obviously impossible, any highly unusual idea and any testimony as to the experience of highly unusual phenomena. Without this tendency, indeed, we should readily become the prey of every unsubstantial figment of our imaginations, as, in fact, some unfortunates are. It is to be observed, however, that the common objections to such phenomena rest ultimately on an appeal to everyday experience, so that we argue that a thing is impossible when it seems to contradict our own, or most other people's, experience. This, of course, is a useful practical test, but it is philosophically unsound, because the new facts, whose claim to admission we thus deny, are themselves an extension of human experience.

It behoves us, therefore, if we propose to examine any alleged phenomena, to reflect that the term " impossible " has an extremely limited field of useful application. Many things which clever men once labelled impossible are nevertheless true, and are now

7

universally recognized as being true. The record of the orthodox champions of science in this matter is not wholly spotless, as many well-known stories attest. When Harvey proclaimed the fact of the circulation of the blood, Venetian doctors ridiculed the idea. When Galvani discovered electric currents he was set down by the scientists of his day as being " The Frog's Dancing Master." Aviation was proved, over and over again, to be contrary to mathematical physics ; Hypnotism was opposed for a century. And so it is without much value to dismiss modern Psychic science on the mere ground that some scientists disbelieve in it. On the contrary, when one hears Flammarion's story of Dr. Bouillard and the Phonograph, one is inclined to credit anything which such scientists deny. When Edison's invention was first demonstrated at the Académie des Sciences in Paris, the worthy Dr. Bouillard rose angrily and denounced the demonstrator as a ventriloquizing cheat. Further than this, he had the hardihood later on to write that, after giving this supposed invention a thorough investigation, he had convinced himself that there was nothing in it but ventriloquism !

Now these examples of what we can recognize as the blind folly of pseudo-scientists are not rare or in any degree unusual ; they typify a state of mind which is extremely common, even amongst present-day scientists, and which has retarded the development of Psychic science not a little. We must, therefore, agree at the outset that nothing be deemed impossible except such propositions as involve a necessary contradiction in terms ; the proposition, for instance, that a triangle having only two sides can exist, or that a material object may be moved without the application of any external force. Perhaps there will be some readers who will object even to this limited use of the word, and maintain that " contraries may be equally true," as in William Blake's state called Beulah. In fact, to a mystic such a proposition is but natural, and mystics have, from the days of Lao-Tse to Ouspensky, maintained that logical contradictions may be true, that the part may equal the whole, and that A may be both A and Not-A. But these are considerations of greater subtlety than is required for our purpose here; we can learn quite enough about the elements of Pyschic science if we allow the impossibility of anything that involves a logical contradiction in terms.

Granting now that much of what has hitherto been deemed to be impossible, and therefore unworthy of investigation and discussion, is by no means so in reality, let us see what is the proper attitude to adopt in an inquiry into the supernormal and occult regions. Are we to throw the methods of science on one side and cultivate an emotional state of faith, or are we to submit everything to the test of experimental research and reason? It all depends on our personal temperament and on our aim. If we wish to *experience* the workings of occult forces, to see forms and phantasms, and to hear mysterious voices, then we must cultivate our own latent powers in these directions, or at least cultivate our faith in their reality; and this is most efficiently done by becoming a Spiritualist and joining a circle of believers. But if our object is to *know* and *comprehend intellectually* whatever may be true, then we must follow the same methods that we follow in any exact science; we must examine critically (which does not mean distrustfully) and we must devise experiments to test our hypotheses. And in this connection we may well bear in mind the following passage in which Freud (one of the greatest analytic minds of any age) discusses the evidence on which some of his own conclusions are based. He says:

(*Introductory Lectures on Psycho-analysis*, p. 39): " It is a mistake to believe that a science consists of nothing but conclusively proved propositions, and it is unjust to demand that it should. It is a demand made only by those who feel a craving for authority in some form and a need to replace the religious catechism by something else, even if it be a scientific one. Science in its catechism has but few apodeictic precepts; it consists mainly of statements which it has developed to varying degrees of probability. The capacity to be content with these approximations to certainty and the ability to carry on constructive work despite the lack of final confirmation are actually a mark of the scientific habit of mind.''

The best scientists, of course, are generally the least dogmatic. They recognize that few of the most widely-accepted scientific "laws" or even facts can be conclusively proved, in the sense that a theorem of Euclid's can be proved. Consequently it is with no little wonder that we find many of these same scientists, who in Physics or Chemistry or Biology show such an appreciation of the difference between a mathematical and an "evidential" proof, demanding the most impossible degree of logical rigidity before they will consent to discuss the evidence for a psychic fact. The most unquestioned facts of, say, Chemistry, rest ultimately on human testimony; we accept the evidence as given by a quite limited number of men, whose word we trust because, in the main, they all agree, and because their statements enable us to co-ordinate a large number of other facts. But if we attempted to verify any one chemical generalization without assuming the truth of most of the others we should soon get so lost in the maze of interrelated hypotheses and alleged facts that we should quickly realize the practical impossibility of our task. It is then unfair, and indeed ridiculous, to expect a psychic phenomenon to occur in such a manner that it is susceptible of absolutely rigid, cavil-proof demonstration. On the contrary we should study the evidence which has accumulated, using our discretion in judging which witnesses are reliable, and out of this mass of evidence we should select what seems capable of experimental proof, and of repetition under diverse conditions, and should attempt to develop it.

That there is something to develop, something to test, and something by which we may extend our knowledge of this world (I shelve the question of our knowledge of the next) is, I think, not to be disputed. One fact is striking, and needs explanation ; namely, that there is a group of men, a group containing many of the greatest modern scientists, who have deliberately given their testimony to the reality of supernormal phenomena. De Morgan, Crookes, Zollner, Lombroso, Morselli, Richet, Flammarion, W. James, and Lodge are perhaps the chief scientists of international renown who have devoted a considerable portion of their time to patient experimental investigation of psychic phenomena ; and they have all staked their reputations on the existence of facts unknown to the orthodox sciences. In the face of this important fact, what is the average man to think ? He may lightly say that all these men, be they never so eminent, are mad, and therefore irresponsible for what they have written. A noteworthy phenomenon, indeed, and one that would lead us to suppose that anyone else whom we chose was mad ; for these men have carried on all their other work with as much sanity as anyone else could claim.

Another hypothesis, which has often been suggested, is that these men have deceived the public, and written books full of falsehoods. But if scientists of standing, men who have achieved their eminence precisely because of their unusual fidelity to the exact truth, are to be thus accused when they proclaim new discoveries, our whole outlook on humanity, and our whole attitude to positive science in particular, must be changed. If Crookes' researches into Spiritualism are impugned, what ground have we for believing in his researches on Electrons ? One will say that the latter have been corroborated and expanded by the work of other scientists ; but so have the former also, and in some instances by the very same scientists !

The third hypothesis, that the investigators have been hallucinated or hypnotized by clever mediums, is equally ridiculous. Hallucination (by which is not meant mere mal-observation, a fault which would keep any scientist in a very obscure back row) is a very unusual thing outside the mad-house, and the simultaneous and identical hallucination of two or more persons is so rare that I doubt if a single authentic case has ever been recorded. We feel that if two or more persons were simultaneously to see the same non-existent object, the object would really be there ! As to hypnotism, which we may take here to include illusions induced by suggestion, it is usually the medium who is hypnotized, not the person conducting the research. Finally, one cannot hallucinate or hypnotize the self-registering instruments, cameras, cinematographs, phonographs, or recording needles, which have been used repeatedly to confirm the objectivity of various phenomena.

And so it is to the fourth hypothesis, namely fraud on the part of the medium, that all objectors turn eventually. This, indeed, is an easy postulate, and a medium is considered fair game. It is a fact admitted and deplored by all those who investigate or believe in supernormal occurrences that a large number of mediums do cheat in one way or another[1] ; some habitually ; some only occasionally ; some deliberately ; and some while in a trance, and therefore not conscious (with their normal waking personality) of their actions. And, moreover, this is quite natural and easy to understand. There are religious, personal, and financial motives sufficiently strong to make many people try to impress

[1] Nevertheless Sir O. Lodge, in the witness-box during a recent case, stated : " I have heard about fraudulent mediums, but I have not come across them." He was, presumably, only referring to deliberate conscious frauds ; but still his opinion is significant and suggests that he demands a rigorous *proof* of fraud before he will accept it as an explanation, whereas many people are satisfied with the bare demonstration of its *possibility*.

others with their supernormal powers, or to convince them that " spirits " are communicating. Moreover, the most genuine and honest medium may, while uncon- scious, produce physical phenomena (raps, levitations, etc.) which are supposed to be due to spirits, but which are in fact due to normal physical means. This is easily explained, for, adopting for a moment the theory that a genuine medium is able to materialize a kind of extra limb and raise a table by means of this, we may suppose that such a procedure will only occur on account of some *desire* on the part of the medium to lift the table. But if the entranced medium desires to move an object, is it not natural for him to attempt this by normal muscular action, such as is habitual to his organism, if it is possible, rather than embark on the hazardous enterprise of materializing a pseudo-limb ? In general we might expect that if a medium can move an object by normal means he will do so, and that supernormal methods will only be used when the habitual physical mechanisms are inapplicable. This, of course, is not universally and rigidly true, but it seems a useful point to bear in mind. As a corollary (and also from the observations of many investigators) we must admit that the proved occurrence of fraud in any one instance has very little relevance to the question of the genuineness of other instances. It is only when fraud is deliberate and consciously contrived that its discovery should seriously affect our attitude towards the medium.

Moreover, even if a medium is shown to be consciously fraudulent, we cannot always conclude that he is thereby shown to be incapable of genuine phenomena ; for we have to consider the facts of the individual case. Sup- pose, for one moment, that a young girl is subject to trances and that in these states she speaks strangely and moves objects unaccountably ; that, in a word, some genuine supernormal phenomena do occur. Is it not probable that she will soon be regarded as a medium for spiritualist purposes, and become a person of importance in a certain circle ? Will she not be pressed to produce more phenomena, and, finding that they are entirely beyond her voluntary control and often refuse to occur, will she not be tempted to supplement them by simple fraud ? In most spiritualistic séances such fraud would be undiscovered, because no one would try to look for it. I should say that every medium must sometimes find circumstances are tempting her to help on, or to counterfeit, phenomena ; and thus many may become fraudulent.

But it is to be observed that all this must be based on a real power of mediumship, without which it would never start at all ! If you or I, for example, were to put forward claims as to clairvoyance or the power to materialize a spirit, our friends might perhaps say, " Well, we will see what you can do." But unless in the first instance we could produce some phenomena which not merely aroused interest, but convinced people of our powers, we should be at once discredited.

Moreover, we cannot suppose that a medium who thus supplemented her genuine powers by amateur trickery would be able thus to produce any of those numerous phenomena in which the force exerted is quite beyond the normal muscular power of even strong men ; nor would such trickery deceive capable investigators who specially set out to look for and to prevent it, and who imposed their own conditions on the medium. Nor, indeed, would such a medium submit to the rigid investigation demanded.

If, therefore, fraud is to be postulated to explain the feats of such mediums as Eusapia Palladino, Eva C (Marthe Beraud), Kluski, and similar people, it must be conscious, well-rehearsed, skilled fraud of such a kind as to baffle the prolonged and searching scrutiny of the most competent scientists in the world. In short, it must be far and away superior to anything which we know to be producible by a Houdini, a Maskelyne, or a

Devant. And yet most mediums have demonstrably no particular technical skill, or conjuring ability, of this order.

Only those who take the trouble to read the detailed records of some of the researches[2] in this field can appreciate the difficulty of controlling conditions, of observing, and of recording phenomena in such a way that, not those present at the time, but the outside reader can say with certainty that fraud could not enter. Perhaps it is impossible, but in so far as it is humanly possible it has been done. That is to say, the probability of fraud in these cases has become smaller than the probability of genuineness. When we find that a medium is medically examined before and after the sitting, the examination including all the natural orifices and extending so far, in one instance, as the administration of an emetic to ensure that no objects were produced by regurgitation or disposed of by swallowing; when the medium is completely stripped and then sewn up in a specially designed costume; when the investigator has his own special séance-room, to which the medium has no previous access; when a cinematograph record is made of the phenomena of materialization; when the process of extrusion of a substance from and reabsorption into the body is both watched and photographed; when all this and yet more is done, and the séance conducted in light up to 100 candle-power, it becomes rather imbecile to cling irrationally to the conviction that it was all fraud. The evidence for the analysis of water into Oxygen and Hydrogen is no stronger than Schrenck-Notzing's evidence for the production of ectoplasm.

We thus arrive at the position that we admit the occurrence of genuine supernormal phenomena, and wish to sort them out, classify them, and attempt to " explain " them. And here we may consider the meaning of the word *supernormal*. It does not imply

[2] e.g. Dr. Schrenck-Notzing's work, *Phenomena of Materialization*.

any more than that the phenomena in question are highly unusual, and take place under conditions and through agencies of whose nature we are ignorant. No scientist can admit the existence of *supernatural* phenomena or any *contrary* to the laws of nature. If a fact appears to be contrary to our statement of a natural law, and yet the fact is proved, then it is not the fact which is above nature, but our statement of a law which is false. No fact can be outside nature. It is necessary to accept this view, however much one may prefer the frankly mystical philosophy which admits the supernatural, if one is to consider the field of psychic *science* and attempt to co-ordinate and interpret the facts ; if our object, that is to say, is to gain an intellectual comprehension of this subject. But I freely grant that perhaps this is a vain endeavour, because our intellect may be incapable of dealing with the facts ; incapable of escaping from the hypothesis of Causation, which may be a chimera. It is here that the Spiritualist and the scientist may reasonably differ. The former has no faith in, and no desire to establish, intellectual representations of the mechanisms by which supernormal phenomena occur ; to him it is intellectually sufficient to assume the existence of spirits and their power of acting at will on the objects and minds in this world. He does not hesitate, on occasion, to allow them something approaching omnipotence, and omniscience and consequently he has no need to formulate a science. What is the use of observing, of classifying, of experimenting, if a spirit may wilfully do anything at any moment and invalidate all your conclusions ? Nothing need ever happen twice in the same way, for all is (or can be) at the mercy of caprice. The most thorough Spiritualists, perhaps, recognize the irrationality of their philosophy, and do not enter into arguments ; they simply make assertions.

A scientist, however, has different intellectual needs. He must study the conditions under which phenomena

occur, and interpret their mechanism or perish.   He
cannot bear to live in a world where nothing is orderly,
nothing is predictable, and everything happens through
the caprices of demi-gods—where tables rise in the air
because the spirits have suspended the laws of gravity ;
and where fire will burn him on one occasion and not
on another, because the spirits have set up vibrations
which nullify the heat vibrations ; where a hostile spirit
may knock him on the head at any moment, or a moral
spirit prevent him from placing a bet on the Derby
winner.   It is therefore incumbent on him, when he is
faced with facts of a psychic nature, to examine them
and attempt to interpret them as he would those belonging to any other category.   This, be it observed, is a
very different thing from denying them without any
examination, which is a usual attitude of scientists
to-day.

The investigation of the supernormal, however, is not
a task to be undertaken by any man, however eminent
he may be in any department, without some preparation, or without guidance from his precursors.   Would
a chemist consider himself qualified to undertake a
research on Cancer, without making himself as familiar
as possible with all that previous workers had done in
this field, and without undergoing any training in
medicine and surgery ?   No more can he, or anyone
else, expect to do good work in psychic research without
preliminary study.   And yet one constantly hears of
men, frequently quite untrained individuals, who investigate the subject for a few days or weeks, and then,
having discovered nothing, " expose " it as a delusion
and a fraud !   In any science the first task is to observe,
to note what happens, and to record the conditions
under which it happens.   Then one may attempt to
find out which of the many conditions are essential,
and so arrive at some judgment as to the inner nature
of the phenomena.   But this takes time and needs
patience unbounded.   Yet the first thing these amateur

" exposers " do is to impose their own conditions ; and when an experiment brings no result they stop investigating, having really succeeded in achieving their secret aim, which was to be able to go back and say : " There's nothing in it ! "

In this book we will not be put off by such people, nor shall we consider the mass of dramatic and really touching material which has been provided in abundance by enthusiastic Spiritualists and bereaved parents who have none of the patient reserve of judgment, none of the sceptical critical faculty, nor the familiarity with such psychological or pathological factors as may be operative in any given instance—none of the mental qualifications, in short, which are necessary in this field. We shall base our survey only on such cases as have been fully observed and well reported by reliable men, whose observations have been checked and corroborated by others. In taking this course we shall necessarily limit our scope, and exclude many interesting phenomena—some will say, exclude all the most interesting ones !—because our criterion relates to the observer, not to the phenomenon. But the main object of the book is not to review everything that may pertain to the field of Psychic Science, but only to set forth the chief phenomena which have definitely and unquestionably been verified, and in this way to lay out the foundations of ascertainable fact on which the scientific superstructure may be built. If for any reason we depart from this course, and refer to more doubtful cases, this will be indicated. Spiritualists will doubtless note, and deplore, the fact that we cite authors like Schrenck-Notzing, Flournoy, Richet, Mrs. Sidgwick, and Osty, in preference to the champions of Spiritualism, and we will certainly admit that in our opinion the definite statements and observations of these and similar more sceptical writers carry more weight, other things being equal, than those of the Spiritualists ; though we have no hesitation in accepting the observations of men like

Zollner, Sir O. Lodge, Dr. Crawford, and any others whose work reveals a similar care and exactitude of observation. If the fundamental tenets of Spiritualism are capable of scientific proof, which is greatly to be doubted, it is only through the work of men like these that the proof will be attained, and not through the melodramatic accounts of séances published by laymen.

In my own case, I started with the desire to get at the basic established facts, and to see where they necessarily led. The further I went, the more clear it became to me that the popular spirit theory is not by any means satisfactorily proved, and is usually based on quite insufficient arguments ; though this may, of course, be due to my own sceptical or agnostic prejudices. The reader will have to judge, during the course of the book, whether the facts seem to be capable of a naturalistic interpretation on the whole, or whether there is yet any definite and positive proof that discarnate souls communicate with people on this earth. Possibly he will arrive at a negative conclusion in respect to both propositions ; but at least he will, I think, see that a large portion of the phenomena usually adduced as proof of spirit survival are no proof of it at all, since they are equally capable of interpretation in terms of the living personality.

CHAPTER TWO

HYPNOTISM

1

THE subject of Hypnotism forms a natural, and indeed indispensable, link between the more or less systematic sciences of medicine and experimental psychology on the one hand, and the study of occult phenomena on the other. Fifty years ago hypnotism was not regarded differently from clairvoyance or prevision; it was still all humbug in the eyes of the scientific authorities. To-day it has been adopted into official medical practice, and the man who boldly denied the possibility of inducing " sleep " would be regarded as an ignoramus. Yet hypnotism still remains essentially occult, and still presents the same transcendental problems; only our present-day practitioners tacitly agree to pay no attention to these.

The history of hypnotism is so instructive that no one who is interested to see the kind of fate which awaits new discoveries in a scientific age should omit to study it. Mesmer, who was born in 1734 and graduated at Vienna (that home of epoch-making discoveries, which in our generation has given us Rejuvenation and Psycho-analysis) in 1776, learned from a Jesuit named Hehl that magnetized plates affected the human body; and from another cleric, Gassner, that " passes " made by moving the hands downwards also had an influence. From these hints he discovered that he could influence patients profoundly, relieving them of pain and inducing sleep in them, by these apparently magical methods. In 1778, being turned out of Vienna, where his methods were regarded as charlatanism and sorcery, he went to

Paris, where he met with considerable success. Eventually he settled in Spa, and died there in 1815.

Needless to say, Mesmer's success in curing patients of all descriptions led to the adoption of his methods by some disciples, of whom the Marquis de Puységur, who seems to have discovered the so-called somnambulistic stage, was one of the most important. But in the main his success only provoked the doctors to hostility. A commission was appointed by the Royal Academy of Medicine to investigate Mesmer's work, and it reported in effect that his results were due to the imagination of his patients. A second commission, in 1825, investigated the subject for six years and then reported favourably, confirming all the main claims of the mesmerists, including the fact of clairvoyance during the mesmeric trance. But this report was never printed, and the Academy appointed a further committee, composed of open antagonists of mesmerism, which, in 1837, reported unfavourably on the whole subject.

Meanwhile in England mesmerism was being practised by a few individuals ; Elliotson (the first physician to employ a stethoscope), Gregory (a Fellow of the Royal Society), Esdaile (an Anglo-Indian doctor), and James Braid were practically the sole protagonists for half a century.

Elliotson (1791–1868) was a professor at University College, London, and his mesmeric researches and demonstrations aroused so much hostility from his colleagues that he eventually resigned his appointment. We need not be surprised to learn that most of the doctors who condemned mesmerism out of hand refused also to attend any of Elliotson's demonstrations or see his experiments. It was the same, we remember, with the Paduan professors when Galileo invented a telescope ; they would not look through it, lest they should see what he said was in the sky, and be made to swallow their own dogmas. I cannot resist quoting the following facts, taken from Dr. Milne Bramwell's book, as they illustrate so perfectly the unfairness with which the subject was treated for a century.

"In Nottinghamshire, in 1842, Mr. Ward, surgeon, amputated a thigh during mesmeric trance ; the patient lay perfectly calm during the whole operation, and not a muscle was seen to twitch. The case, reported to the Royal Medical and Chirurgical Society, was badly received ; and it was even asserted that the patient had been trained not to express pain. Dr. Marshall Hall suggested that the man was an impostor, because he had been absolutely quiet during the operation ; for if he had not been simulating insensibility he should have had reflex movements in the other leg. Eight years afterwards Dr. Marshall Hall publicly stated at a meeting of the society that the patient had confessed that he had suffered during the operation. The doctor was promptly challenged to give his authority, and replied that he had received his information from a personal acquaintance, who, in his turn, had received it from a third party, but that he was not permitted to divulge their names, and would not give any further information on the subject. The man was still living, and signed a solemn declaration to the effect that the operation had been absolutely painless. Dr. Ashburner attended the next meeting and asked permission to read this statement in opposition to Dr. Marshall Hall's, but the society would not hear him."

This being the attitude of the medical profession, it is not surprising that hypnotism was so long in gaining ground. When people deliberately refuse to see experiments and listen to evidence, and when they content themselves with stories at third hand, they cannot possibly acquire new knowledge. The point, however, of this historical digression lies in its application to the present situation of the allied psychic sciences. We find to-day precisely the same refusal to look through the telescope, precisely the same preference for third-hand stories by the Cons over first-hand evidence by the Pros.

James Esdaile (1808–1859) adopted mesmerism in his practice when head of a native hospital in India. He was so successful that the Government gave him a small hospital in Calcutta, and appointed medical officers to report on his work, which they did very favourably. Nevertheless, and in spite of the numerous major operations which he performed painlessly, the medical journals attacked him and refused to publish his papers.

James Braid (*c.* 1795–1860) is in many ways the most important name in this field. Mesmer, Elliotson, and Esdaile had been wonderful practitioners, but had contributed little to the theoretical explanation of the subject. They believed that a vital fluid passed from the operator to the subject, and there explanation ceased. It was this semi-magical character of mesmerism that aroused all the hostility of the medical profession, for people of a rationalizing, but not truly scientific, turn of mind never will admit facts for which they can see no explanation. Braid, however, gradually abandoned the use of passes, concentrated gazing, and other physical means of inducing the trance, and substituted direct verbal suggestion for them. It is true that he only replaced one kind of magic by another, for the psychological action of " suggestion " is quite as baffling as any vital fluid or animal magnetism. But this emphasis on the mental rather than the physical aspect of the subject, combined with the invention of a new word, Hypnosis, gradually had its effect in diminishing prejudice ; and the fact that Braid disbelieved in clairvoyance, which had hitherto been so often affirmed by the mesmerists, made people the more ready to listen to him.

Since Braid's time a considerable number of men, notably Liébault, Charcot, Richet, Bernheim, Gurney, Janet, de Rochas, Schrenck-Notzing, Milne Bramwell, Boirac, and Alrutz have contributed to the theory and practice of hypnotism, but, as Bernard Hollander points

out, the majority of modern hypnotists, in discarding
the methods of the earlier mesmerists, have also failed
to reproduce many of their effects. It is an easy reply
to say that those effects, of clairvoyance, telepathy, or
prevision, were merely deceptive, and due to mal-
observation ; but the force of this retort is lessened
when we consider the evidence for these phenomena,
and notably for their spontaneous occurrence. It is at
least arguable, in view of the definite expressions of
opinion by many of the practitioners, that they have
not confirmed clairvoyance because they have taken
very good care not to look for it.

2

We must now turn to a study of the phenomena
involved in hypnotism, and to the psychological theories
to which these give rise ; and in view of the many
contradictory opinions and statements to be found in
the literature of the subject this is no light or straight-
forward task. In the first place there is little agreement
as to what are the best or most necessary methods of
inducing hypnosis. Mesmer and his followers used to
make passes over the body of the patient, and also
gazed fixedly into his eyes. Often also metallic plates
were applied, as the supposed magnetic virtue of these
was held to influence various diseases. James Braid at
first made his patients gaze slightly upwards at any
small bright object, but finding that this sometimes
caused eye-strain and conjunctivitis he gradually
abandoned the method, and relied on verbal suggestions.
This method was also followed by Liébault, who
practically founded in France the modern school of
hypnotism. From him Bernheim learnt the efficacy of
suggestion, and proceeded to explain the whole subject
by that one word. Wetterstrand and de Rochas, although
employing direct suggestion, combined it with magnetic
passes over the patient's body ; while Richet combined

suggestion with strong and steady pressure on the patient's thumbs. Almost all the advocates of the *Suggestion Theory*, according to which everything, from the induction of the hypnotic trance to the various phenomena produced during it, is sufficiently explained as the effect of suggestion, use in fact some physical modes of inducing hypnosis in addition to their verbal suggestions.

In support of the vital fluid theory Boirac[1] cites several observations and experiments which show that he could exert a real physical influence at a distance, independently of any suggestion. For example, by holding his right hand near any limb of a blindfolded, hypnotized subject, the latter soon felt that this limb was being attracted to something, and in fact the limb would move towards Boirac's hand. When the left hand was presented no attraction resulted, but a burning or prickly sensation was felt in the part covered by the hand. Ochorowicz has also described the same phenomenon. Boirac also verified Moutin's " pendulum " experiment, in which a blindfolded subject is irresistibly drawn sideways or backwards, to follow the operator's hand which is slowly moved away from the subject. He also confirmed the fact that the operator, by holding his hand over the (blindfolded) subject, can anæsthetize the part of the body covered by the hand. All these and other similar experiments have been done with definite exclusion of suggestion and have been confirmed by Drs. Barety and de Rochas.

The work of these French investigators has been confirmed by some very careful and scientifically devised experiments by Dr. Alrutz,[2] who set himself to show :

(1) That there exists a certain nervous effluence from the human body which can affect other human bodies provided that these are of a certain type and in a certain condition ;

[1] See his *Psychic Science*, p. 175, etc.
[2] Summarized by him in a paper, *Problems of Hypnotism*, in Part 83 (Vol. 32) of the Proceedings of the Society for Psychical Research.

(2) That this effluence can be absorbed by certain substances (e.g. cardboard, flannel) and is transmitted through other substances (e.g. glass and metals) ;

(3) That this effluence is not in the nature of a vibratory radiation, as light is, but is more analogous to a corpuscular or fluid emission. It can be conducted along rods and wires, as also Boirac had proved.

Dr. Alrutz's experiments are of particular value on two counts ; first, by reason of their precision, and, secondly, by reason of the precautions taken to exclude all suggestion, whether due to expectation, to auto-suggestion arising from faint sense perceptions (by the subject) of the operator's movements, or even to telepathically transmitted suggestions. Generally speaking, the subject was first lightly hypnotized, and then, his face being covered with a black cloth and his ears sometimes plugged, was submitted to experiment. In order to investigate the effect of passes, Dr. Alrutz enclosed the subject's two arms in light wooden boxes which had glass tops, and which were fixed on the arms of the chair in which he sat. One of these boxes might be wholly or partially covered with a sheet of metal, of cardboard, of paper, flannel, or of some other material. Under these conditions the subject was quite ignorant (*a*) as to which arm was being subjected to passes, (*b*) whether this arm was screened or not, (*c*) what substance was used as a screen, (*d*) whether the passes were up or down. In other experiments Dr. Alrutz arranged matters so that he himself did not know which arm was screened, nor which portion of it was screened ; and in still other cases, third parties, who were ignorant of the various results to be expected, did the actual process of making passes or of arranging the screens in the absence of Dr. Alrutz, who afterwards came in and investigated the subject's sensibility, deducing from this the nature of the screens and passes which had been used. In this way all possibility of telepathic suggestion was removed.

The results obtained by these experiments definitely showed that when downward passes were made the sensibility of the part thus " magnetized " was notably diminished ; while upward passes increased the sensibility. Also that screens of card, paper, flannel, etc., effectively cut off the effluence, while screens of glass or metal transmitted it.

Dr. Alrutz was able, by the use of passes, to anæsthetize one side of the patient while increasing the sensibility of the other side, and he investigated the degree of sensibility with regard to pain, warmth, cold, pressure, smell, and sight, as well as the knee-jerk reflex, using instrumental methods as far as possible. He found, what has also been found by other investigators, that in *light hypnosis* there is some degree of hyper-sensibility and hyper-irritability (with regard to the senses and muscles respectively), both of which may be increased by upward passes ; while in deep hypnosis there is diminution of the sensibility and iritability.

From all these observations and experiments we see that there is indubitably a physical influence which can be exerted by one person on another, without any direct contact between the two, and without the knowledge of the subject. The chief phenomena of hypnosis, namely hyper-æsthesia and anæsthesia, can certainly be produced by means of this influence, and in all probability the hypnotic state itself can be so produced. We may note also in this connection that the traditional methods adopted by the Indian Yogi to achieve a trance condition which is essentially analogous to hypnosis are very largely physical, although, of course, there is here plenty of auto-suggestion as well. The chief methods of Yoga appear to be control of the respiration, combined with a fixed " *Asana* " posture (usually involving the compression of some nerve centre) and concentration of the gaze either on the navel or on the tip of the nose —i.e. some form of squinting similar to that first used by Braid. All this is also to be accompanied by absolute concentration of thought, or, in advanced cases, by its deliberate obliteration.

Moreover, with regard to *gazing* (which Dr. Alrutz considers to have an influence similar to that of the passes made with the hands, since two large nerves terminate at the eyes) we may note that crystal-gazers commonly fall into a trance analogous to the hypnotic trance. The mystic, Jacob Boehme, experienced his first ecstasy, it is said, as a result of looking intently at the bright reflection of light from a metal bowl. These facts must be borne in mind when psychologists wish us to consider the claims of the Suggestionist school to give us the key to the mystery.

The Suggestion theory may be summarized somewhat as follows : " *The human mind is so constituted that any idea presented to it from outside tends to be accepted ; and any idea which is accepted tends to fufil itself, or expresses itself in reality.*" Thus, for example, the mere reiterated assertion of an idea (e.g., the idea that suggestion explains everything) tends to make people believe it.

Of course, it is manifest that in practice, owing to the enormous multitude of ideas presented to any one mind, any one specific suggestion will probably find that its tendency to acceptance and fulfilment is frustrated by the previous acceptance of numerous other suggestions. The individual, in fact, has such a train of mental prejudgments, habits of thought, memories, desires, and impulses, that a particular suggestion given now will not be accepted unless it can fit in without opposing this system. Thus we must modify the original statement, and say : " *Suggestions which in the light of the mind-content of the subject seem plausible or agreeable are likely to be accepted ; but those which oppose his present system of ideas and impulses will be rejected.*" Particularly strong are those suggestions which find a ready support and motive power in one of the main instincts, of self-preservation, sex, hunger, or gregariousness.

This, it will be seen, does not promise to carry us very

far towards an explanation of hypnosis. Any ordinary suggestion given to a man in his waking state may be accepted or rejected, according to the choice of the man concerned. But how does invoking the power of suggestion help us to explain why a subject, who is fully awake, and under the influence of convincing auto- and external suggestions to that effect, should nevertheless accept the manifestly untrue suggestion that he is falling asleep, his eyelids closing, his limbs feeling heavy, etc. ?

Moreover, it is a matter of common knowledge that a suggestion is the more readily accepted if the subject believes in its probability. Yet we find that Milne Bramwell says, in discussing susceptibility to hypnosis :

" Faith alone has apparently little effect on susceptibility. I have failed with subjects who firmly believed I could hypnotize them, and that they were specially susceptible. On the other hand I have succeeded with many who have been convinced that they could not be influenced."

He also quotes Forel and Liégeois as holding similar opinions.

A second point, which I have not seen discussed by the suggestionists, is this. Why, when it is suggested that a patient is drowsy and he is told to sleep, should he not sleep ? Why should he, instead of fulfilling the suggestion, pass into a quite different condition, and one which is only superficially akin to sleep ? When Liébault stretched forth his hands and said " Sleep," his patients did not sleep ; they became hypnotized instead. Moreover, when Mesmer, du Potet, Esdaile, and the rest first began their work in different places and at different times not one in a hundred, indeed at the commencement not one, not even Mesmer, knew what would happen—there was not the possibility of suggesting analgesia, hyperæsthesia, amnesia, enhanced memory, echolalia, catalepsy, rapport or increased suggestibility, in the initial cases, and even after all these manifestations had been noticed they reappeared spontaneously in the absence of any suggestions to excite them. Esdaile remarked that he could not have taught his Indian patients to produce the phenomena which they did produce, as he himself was ignorant of them until he had seen them appear.

All this, however, does not lead to the conclusion that the idea of suggestion is empty of meaning, but only that it has been applied too indiscriminately, and used to prevent thought. We must admit the fact that people do tend to accept some suggestions quite irrationally (see, for example, Trotter's well-known book on *Instincts of the Herd*) and that some people, notably children, are more suggestible than others. Moreover, we can take it as an agreed fact that everyone is much more suggestible when in an hypnotic trance than when awake, and that consequently suggestion can be used to increase the manifestation of any particular phenomenon during hypnosis. But this does not help us to understand how the state arises, nor why, in the face of many contradictory internal and external suggestions, a particular one should be accepted ; still less why certain typical suggestions—pain, absence of pain, anæsthesia, hyperæsthesia, catalepsy, and change of Personality—should be provoked so easily and so unerringly in almost every case.

To sum up the methods of inducing hypnosis, we may say that probably there may be a real physical influence which, emanating from the operator, can by itself cause hypnotic trance ; further, that " shock " methods, or loud noises, or bright lights (see e.g. Voisin's method, Charcot's, and others) can sometimes bring about the same result ; and finally, that pure suggestion—even telepathic suggestion (Janet, Ochorowicz, Gibert and Myers)—may sometimes be sufficient. In practice, however, it is obviously best to combine passes, gazing and suggestion, so as to get the maximum effect.[3]

[3] Boirac has argued that certain people are very susceptible to the physical " nervous effluence," while others are susceptible to suggestion and are little affected by the so-called " magnetic " influence.

3

It is not easy to define the characteristics of hypnosis, as here again the authorities, perhaps largely because they use different methods and wish to provoke different phenomena, disagree. There are certainly different shades or depths of hypnosis, from a light " fascination " stage, in which the subject has a somewhat increased sensibility and irritability but seems to have lost his alertness of mind, through stages of lethargy in which the subject is inert, and catalepsy, in which his muscles may be made rigid and there is general loss of sensibility, to somnambulism, in which the subject is more than usually alert in some ways, being capable of developing great hyperæsthesia and showing greatly increased intuition, but is *en rapport* with the operator, and retains no memory on awakening. But these stages are not in any way sharply marked, nor are they definitive in any sense, nor do they appear necessarily in the order given above. Generally speaking there is amnesia after hypnosis, perhaps because of a self-suggestion on the part of the patient (as Milne Bramwell thinks ; though the idea seems a little unnecessary), but the degree of forgetfulness varies according to the depth of the hypnosis. In any case during subsequent hypnosis all that happened during previous trances can be recalled.

It is difficult to know how far the subject is conscious during hypnosis, and what his consciousness comprises. Milne Bramwell maintains, with considerable show of reason, that during hypnosis the subject remains quite conscious, and has full will-power to refute any suggestions which are distasteful—e.g. immoral and criminal ones, or such as conflict with the subject's sense of fairness and decency. On the other hand Boirac insists on the absolute automatism of his subjects, and asserts that they have no power to resist the suggestions of the operator, however much these conflict with their moral sense. This contradiction is a beautiful example for the suggestionist school, seeing that each authority finds the phenomena which, as his writings show in many places, he was looking out for ! From a perusal of his book one can guess that Bramwell's patients felt that he wished to be able to affirm that a hypnotized subject can resist criminal suggestions ; while Boirac's subjects probably felt that he wished for absolute control.

If we survey the large number of different accounts by the various authorities, and put on one side all those cases in which the course of things has been deliberately interfered with by suggestion, it would seem that the natural effects of hypnosis, and their spontaneous progression, are usually as follows :

First State. Light Hypnosis (state of Fascination). The subject is inert and passive, but his general sensibility and muscular irritability are increased somewhat. He is in a peculiar condition of *rapport* with the operator, who can make him feel, or believe, or do almost anything by suggestion, although the subject still apparently retains his own will-power if he but choose to exert it. He generally does not remember what has been done during the trance when he wakes up.

Second State. Cataleptoid. (State of Waxy Rigidity.) General anæsthesia and insensibility appear spontaneously. Moreover, if his limbs are put into any posture, no matter how awkward or uncomfortable, they remain there with hardly any tendency to move ; while if a limb is pushed, the motion continues as if it were an ordinary lump of dead matter that moved. The subject does not reply, or scarcely replies, to questions.

Third State. Deep Hypnosis. (Somnambulistic state.) Here the phenomena of *rapport* are markedly strong. The operator has almost complete control over the subject's motor and nervous system, and can paralyse him, or produce great hyperæsthesia, or hallucinations, by simple verbal suggestion. Often a new, and deeper, mental content is revealed in this state, but there is

amnesia on awakening. Many experimenters, notably
Gurney and Milne Bramwell, have shown that in spite
of the apparent loss of memory of what occurs during
hypnosis, suggestions given in this state are remembered
subconsciously, and can and do affect the behaviour of
the subject when awake, although he is not in the least
conscious of them. Good examples of post-hypnotic
suggestions are given by these writers and also by Dr. S.
Wilkinson.[4] Their value lies in the fact that they
demonstrate the reality of unconscious processes involving memory, purpose, intelligent thought, mathematical calculation, imagination—in a word, everything
we associate with a conscious intelligence. They also,
incidentally, confirm Freud's analytical interpretation
of morbid, compulsive, and obsessive acts as having a
purely psychological, though unconscious, cause, since
the subject during his waking conscious life fulfils a
suggestion previously implanted in his mind without
being at all aware of its origin or its purpose, but feeling
that something inside him compels him to act thus.
They are, in fact, compulsive acts experimentally
produced.

When we sum up the main phenomena which charac-
terize hypnosis in its various degrees we find that, even
though some of them appear at first sight to be wholly
physiological, they may all be fundamentally psychological in origin. Hyperæsthesia, anæsthesia and
analgesia, together with diminished or increased muscular
irritability, are in general secondary effects, due to the
action of the subject's own will, although he may not
recognize the fact. We see clear examples of this in
hysteria, and it will suffice to quote one, taken from
Binet's *Alterations in Personality* (p. 133):

" Monocular blindness was suggested to a hysterical
patient—the suppression of the vision of the right eye.
The left eye of the patient was then closed, and a
book placed before her right eye, and although she

[4] See a paper in Part 69 of P.S.P.R.

declared she saw nothing, the pencil placed in her hand reproduced the words of the book. How could this automatic writing be possible if the monocular centre of vision, which alone is called upon to act in this experiment, were paralysed ? "

These alterations in sensibility, in fact, are one result of a much wider phenomenon which, though present in all living beings, is greatly intensified during hypnosis —namely, the control of the organism by the mind. It is on this that the whole medical value of hypnotism rests, since surgeons and physicians simply hypnotize a patient in order that he may dismiss a pain, recognize and repair diseased tissues, or restore the normal functioning of a morbid part. It is as if the consciousness of the hypnotized subject were in closer contact with his physical organism, and regained a primitive, voluntary control over it which has been lost in the development of the normal waking consciousness.

The other characteristics of hypnosis, namely, alteration of the available memory content, loss of memory on awakening, greatly increased suggestibility and *rapport* with the operator, are wholly psychological. The phenomenon of *rapport* is perhaps the most puzzling and the most important. As far as I am aware, the only attempt at a psychological explanation of it is that made by Freud. Arguing from the closely analogous *transference* which occurs during a certain stage of psycho-analysis, when the patient shows extraordinary esteem for and docility towards the analyst, and often ultimately falls in love with him, Freud suggested that in the condition of *rapport* the hypnotized subject had transferred his libido to the operator and voluntarily paid exclusive attention to him and obeyed his suggestions, while disregarding all other people. This explanation at least enables us to see why the suggestions of the operator should be adopted by the subject and embodied in his will, and it provides an explanation for their potency by allying them to the sex instinct. It also conforms to our knowledge of the very various powers of different hypnotists in producing effects on their patients. Sufficient attention has not yet been given to the operator in the literature of hypnotism, which tends to obscure the obvious fact that, while patience and practice will do much to cultivate one's hypnotic ability, there is also a purely personal and individual factor which enables one man to influence his subjects to a degree to which another never attains.

It remains for us now to attempt an investigation of the nature of the subject's personality during hypnosis, and in order to do this we must review briefly the main facts relating to the unconscious mind and alterations of personality.

BIBLIOGRAPHY

MOLL. Hypnotism.
MILNE BRAMWELL. Hypnotism; its History, Theory, and Practice.
BOIRAC. Psychic Science.
 The Psychology of the Future.
B. HOLLANDER. Hypnotism and Suggestion.
MYERS. Human Personality.
McDOUGALL. Abnormal Psychology (chap. on Hypnotism).
ALRUTZ. Problems of Hypnotism, P.S.P.R., Part 83.
WILKINSON. Recent Experiences in Hypnotic Practice, P.S.P.R., Part 69.

NOTE.—The initials P.S.P.R. are used to denote the Proceedings of the Society for Psychical Research.

CHAPTER THREE

PERSONALITY AND THE UNCONSCIOUS MIND

1

F. W. H. MYERS began his great work on *Human Personality* by pointing out the fundamental disagreement between two schools of thought—on the one hand that which regarded the personal ego as an indivisible entity which *has* thoughts, desires, etc., and on the other hand that to which experimental psychologists commonly belong, and which regards the apparent unity of the personality as the result of a " co-ordination of a certain number of states perpetually renascent and having for their sole common basis the vague feeling of our body " (Ribot). And Myers argued that both schools were in some degree right, and that their reconciliation was brought about through the introduction of a *subconscious* self, wider than our conscious personality. In a sentence pregnant with meaning he says : " *And I conceive also that no self of which we can here have cognisance is in reality more than a fragment of a larger self—revealed in a fashion at once shifting and limited through an organism not so framed as to afford it full manifestation.*" The concluding words of this sentence are of the highest importance.

Now we too must, if we are to avoid endless confusion, begin by trying to indicate our general conceptions, and in particular our use of such words as *self* and personality. We will admit that, behind every individual, there is a constant integrating principle or entity which unifies all the psychological components ; and we must also admit that what we apprehend as a *personality* is analysable into psychological constituents, many of which are not present to the consciousness of the individual. The personality of any individual may justly be regarded as the co-ordination of innate instincts and tendencies, together with acquired habits, memories and dispositions, into a synthetic whole which expresses itself by means of his organism. The conscious personality is that fraction of this system of which he is aware. It is clear that this definition makes of the personality something which in the first place is a complex structure, amenable to analysis; which in the second place is obviously ever-changing; and in the third place something which is necessarily incomplete at any moment— since the instincts, acquired dispositions, and habits must always conflict to a greater or lesser extent, and there is no one point in time at which all the memories and habits exist together.

But beyond the constituents of the personality, unifying and transcending them, we may postulate a Self, or Ego, or Soul. This entity, however, is not a subject for psychological analysis, nor can we treat of it in any scientific way, but only intuitively. Psychology can no more interpret the Psyche than Biology can interpret Life—it can only analyse its manifestations. When we study personality, therefore, it must clearly be grasped that we are not in any way analysing the soul, or the Ego, for that transcends our thought, as the whole transcends its parts. It is the failure to recognize this distinction which leads both materialists and spiritualists into such confusion. The former demonstrate that personality is of the earth earthy, and then write pæans in praise of the pursuit of " Truth, Beauty, and Goodness " (as Haekel did); and the latter, while proclaiming the ideals of spiritual existence, attribute the most mundane thoughts and desires to the departed, even finding it necessary to give an entirely materialistic picture of the next world lest they should be reproached with unreality ! Indeed, a good case might be made out for calling Vale Owen a complete materialist and Haeckel something of a spiritualist—his Monism really approaches the mysticism of Shelley, who said that :

> " Throughout this varied and eternal world
> Soul is the only element . . .
> And the minutest atom comprehends
> A world of loves and hatreds."

Our task here is the study of the personality, not of the soul, and we must begin by considering the chief facts relating to what is now commonly called the Unconscious. The conception that mental processes might go on without our being aware of them is not entirely new, although the experimental study of, and the accumulation of evidence for, such processes (whose outstanding pioneers have been Edmund Gurney, Pierre Janet, Binet, Freud, and Morton Prince) are the work of the past forty years.

The first important fact which was revealed in this study was the apparently limitless *Memory* of the unconscious mind. We all know that there are many facts in our memory which we can recall at will, or which come again into our consciousness when some associated idea is aroused ; and we have the general idea that these were somehow conserved somewhere. But it would appear from the evidence that there is no assignable limit to our memory, that every single fact and impression we have received is still preserved, somehow, though we may be totally unable to recall it. Of course, one cannot prove that *everything* is preserved in memory, but one can certainly not say of any given item that it is not. Many striking instances might be given of the extent of memory (the whole interpretation of psycho-neuroses, and their cure by psycho-analysis depends upon the conservation of apparently forgotten experiences), but we will confine ourselves, for the present, to the case given by G. Lowes Dickenson in P.S.P.R., Part 64. A certain Miss C., while in hypnotic trance, related a fictitious story in which many recondite details about people in the reign of Richard II were given. It was found that these details, genealogical data, etc., were correct, but were far beyond the normal knowledge of Miss C. Later, however, it was discovered that fourteen years previously, when she was only a child of eleven, her aunt had read a book to her, entitled *The Countess Maud*, in which these points were contained. Although she had completely forgotten all these facts, yet they emerged during hypnosis. It is part of the technique of psycho-analysis to recall to mind forgotten experiences which usually date from early childhood, and a study of the " automatic scripts " of a medium shows the most extensive conservation of trivial experiences, sufficient to justify the practical hypothesis that *everything* is conserved in memory, and could be recalled if the right stimulus and conditions were present.

But the Unconscious is far more than a storehouse of memories, and we can in no wise think of it as a static repository. It has dynamic, purposive elements, as Freud, in particular, has shown. This is hardly the place to dilate on Freud's interpretations of mistakes in speech, of dreams, or of hysterical symptoms, but we must mention them in passing. With the intuition of a true genius Freud discovered that at any rate dreams, mistakes, and hysterical symptoms have a psychological *meaning*, and are not purely accidental or wholly explicable in terms of physiology. Perhaps his finest example of the significance of errors is the case of a murderer, H., who, by representing himself as a bacteriologist, obtained dangerous germ-cultures with which he killed his victims. Once he wrote complaining of the ineffectiveness of one preparation, and instead of the expression : " in my experiments on mice (*Mausen*) and guinea-pigs (*Meerschweinchen*)," he put, for the last word, " ' men ' (*Menschen*) ! "

Of Freud's theory of dreams much has been written, for and against. What seems indisputable, however, is that a dream is frequently an hallucinatory wish-fulfilling phantasy, made up of elements of the previous day's experiences, which are used as symbols of other, more significant ideas. The difficulty of Freud's conception of a " *Censor* " who normally inhibits the expression of undesirable tendencies and wishes, and allows them during sleep a partial gratification by intricate symbolical phantasy, the difficulty, that is, of realizing that the incoherent and inconsequential episodes of the " manifest " dream are but substitutes for other ideas which constitute the real, latent dream, disappears when we realize the complexity of a personality.

> " Do I contradict myself ?
> Very well, then, I contradict myself.
> (I am large, I contain multitudes)."

Whitman's utterance is simply the first elementary truism about the Unconscious. In dreams we see the distorted results of psychological processes (mainly simple desires) of whose presence we are unaware in our waking life.

2

The Unconscious mind has been shown to possess an extraordinarily complete memory, and to have volition and purpose. It can also be demonstrated that it can reason and think imaginatively and constructively, not merely in a manner which reflects palely the powers of conscious thought, but to a degree that altogether surpasses them. Psychologists tend to use the term " *automatism*," implying that memories, etc., associate themselves automatically in new forms, and thus produce, by a sort of psychological reflex action, some utterance such as a delirious patient might produce. But, as a general rule, Unconscious thinking is by no manner of means analogous to any automatic process. As Geley has observed, an automatic action must be either innate (like the circulation of the blood) or acquired by constant repetition, forming a habit. In neither case does such a process innovate, or initiate new actions ; and yet it is this innovating, creative power which characterizes unconscious thinking. Moreover, the powers of the unconscious mind do not in any way correspond with the powers or development of the conscious mind, and they manifest themselves sporadically, and with a spontaneity which contradicts any notion of the origin in habits.

Perhaps the best example, out of many possible ones, which illustrates these points is that given by Myers, of the calculating prodigy. The gift of solving almost instantaneously complex arithmetical sums, without any conscious reasoning or calculation, occurs sporadically and quite at random, amongst stupid and non-mathematical children as well as amongst the intelligent. It usually shows itself between the ages of three and ten years, and it has no relation at all to previous arithmetical training. Generally it disappears again after a few years, though in a few men it persists. Dase was a good example of the calculating prodigy. His gift was shown in childhood, and he was a great dunce, even in mathematics, for " on one occasion Peterson tried in vain for six weeks to get the first elements of mathematics into his head. He could not be made to have the least idea of a proposition in Euclid. Of any language but his own he could never master a word." Yet this ignoramus made out tables of all the prime numbers and factors of the numbers between six million and nearly eight million, " a task," says Myers, " which probably few men could have accomplished without mechanical aid in an ordinary lifetime." Of Mr. Bidder, who was an intelligent man, it was said (by Mr. W. Pole, F.R.S.) : " He had an almost miraculous power of seeing, as it were, intuitively what factors would divide any large number, not a prime. Thus if he were given the number 17861 he would instantly remark that it was 337 times 53. He could not, he said, explain how he did this ; it seemed a natural instinct to him." (See Myers, Chap. 3.)

The unconscious mind, then, may have mathematical, or at any rate computative powers which considerably outrange those shown by any known conscious mind— for we must not forget that the speed with which these calculations are done counts in our estimate of the calculating ability. Nor is it only the calculating boy who can unconsciously compute figures, for many experiments with hypnotized persons show that they too can reckon accurately and swiftly, without the least conscious knowledge of the process. As an illustration we may cite one of Dr. Bramwell's experiments. While Miss D. was hypnotized he told her (at 3 p.m.) to make a cross on paper in 8650 minutes, and again in 8680 minutes and again in 8700 minutes. Six days later she spontaneously did this at 3.10 p.m. (correct), 3.40 p.m. (correct), and at 4 p.m. (correct). To complicate the arithmetic he again hypnotized her and said, " You are to repeat (all these experiments), but to-day you are to start from 2.55 instead of from 3 p.m. and to each suggestion you are to add 1440 minutes." That is, the arithmetic was made slightly harder, since she had to add 8650 plus 1440 minutes to 2.55 p.m. (Wednesday, May 13th) ; nevertheless she made the cross spontaneously at the correct time, 3.5 p.m. on Wednesday, May 20th.

But unconscious thinking is by no means limited to the calculation of arithmetical sums ; far more is it characterized by imagination, and the dramatist's power of creating fictitious characters and scenes, as we quickly see when we consider the " automatic " writings or speeches of mediums. Certainly it does not always, or even often, produce work better in quality than that produced by a good conscious intelligence, but these cases are the best to study at first, and the most interesting. Everyone knows of some instances of the unconscious creation of works of a very high order

—Coleridge's *Kubla Khan*, and large portions of William Blake's works, for example. And, though these have a marvellous degree of artistic value, they are no more wonderful than some of the by-products of pathology when considered from an intellectual point of view.

Myers quotes a fine example of imaginative constructive thought occurring in a normal man during sleep.[1] Dr. Hilprecht, professor of Assyrian at Pennsylvania University, was much occupied with the question of the nature and meaning of two fragments of agate, which were of different colour, and inscribed with defaced remnants of characters which he could not decipher. He had never seen the original fragments, which were found in a temple of Bel at Nippur, but worked from a sketch of them. One night, after correcting the proofs of a book in which he described them, he dreamt of a priest, who led him to the treasure chamber of a temple and told him that these two fragments were not really separate, nor parts of finger rings, as he had supposed, but that they were pieces of a votive cylinder offered by King Kurigalzu to Bel, and that this cylinder had subsequently been cut to make ear-rings. When he awoke, Professor Hilprecht found that the two pieces did belong together, and he deciphered the inscription thus : " To the god Ninib, son of Bel, his lord, has Kurigalzu, pontifex of Bel, presented this." Subsequently Professor Hilprecht saw the actual fragments, and verified the fact that they did belong together, although they had been so cut that one fragment was grey while the other was whitish. On a careful analysis it appeared that all the items of information given in the dream (I have only quoted the salient ones) were explicable as products of subconscious reasoning on the data present in Professor Hilprecht's mind, together with observations which he probably made, without realizing them consciously, as to the features of the two fragments. His subconscious mind, during sleep, put

[1] The original account is given in P.S.P.R., Part 30.

the various data together in a way that his waking mind had failed to do, and thus arrived at an interpretation which it proceeded to embody in an hallucinatory phantasy. It is important to notice that the information was conveyed, during his dream, under the form of a little story related by the priest; one more example of the propensity of the unconscious mind to personify and dramatize everything. It is this propensity, of course, which makes people interpret the results of sub-conscious activity as being the work of demons, spirits, etc.

3

The study of the unconscious, whether in dreams, in hysteria, in "automatic writing," or in the trance utterances of spiritualistic mediums, shows that there are numerous mental processes at work of which we are not aware. In extreme cases these unconscious elements, if they are powerful and insufficiently expressed in our waking life, may associate together to form one or more separate complex systems sufficiently coherent and stable to be recognized as distinct *personalities*. The ordinary man is aware of having different *moods* at different times, so that on one day he will behave and feel quite otherwise than he does on another day. There is no line of demarcation to be drawn between this normal phenomenon of alternations of mood and the abnormal one of alternations of personality, unless one takes the rather arbitrary criterion of memory as a test; otherwise, it is only a difference of degree, not of kind. The classical cases of multiple and alternating person-ality are those of Miss Beauchamp and of "B.C.A." studied by Dr. Morton Prince; of Léonie, by P. Janet; of Félida, by Dr. Azam; and of Helen Smith, by Prof. Flournoy. They are all cases of *Dissociation*; that is to say, certain memories, feelings and desires have been shut off from the conscious mind, and have grouped themselves together, growing and working without the patient's knowledge until (usually at the instance of some shock) they suddenly emerge and temporarily replace the normal personality, which in its turn is relegated to unconsciousness and displaced from its control of the organism.

Dr. Morton Prince studied Miss Beauchamp for a number of years, and noted the occurrence of three distinct personalities in her waking state, and two more in her hypnotized condition. Referring to these numerically for short, B1 was the Miss Beauchamp who came to Dr. Prince to be cured of her neurasthenic troubles. When hypnotized she changed to the personality B2. Spontaneously, after a time, a new personality, B3, appeared, and gave herself the name Sally. Again another, B4, appeared at intervals, while B5 was produced by hypnotizing B3 (Sally). As these various personalities, B1, B3, and B4, appeared spontaneously at odd times, and pursued different aims, each having its own separate self-consciousness, many complications arose. Dr. Prince found that B1 and B4 represented two different portions of the original normal conscious personality (which he had never seen) and that they had many elements in common. Each, when hypnotized, passed into the state B2, and hence he succeeded in re-integrating Miss Beauchamp by hypnotizing her when she was B4 and suggesting that she should, on awakening, know all about B1, and vice versa.

But B3 (Sally) was the most interesting personality, and had quite a different character, being very lively and childish, and inordinately fond of teasing B1. One of her jokes was to go out for a long ride into the country, and then " disappear " as Sally, and wake B1 up, who would then find herself without a penny and with six miles to walk home. She used to torment Miss Beauchamp in all manner of ways. One day, for example, she collected some snakes and spiders in a box, did them up in a parcel, and addressed them to Miss Beauchamp (B1) ; when the latter opened the parcel she had a terrible shock, as may be imagined ! It must be realized that Miss Beauchamp as Bl knew nothing about Sally and her doings ; whereas Sally knew the whole life of Bl, and all her thoughts, and was able to influence her actions at times to a certain extent—for example, she forced the very serious and prim Bl to sit with her feet on the mantelpiece, and Bl could not, in spite of herself, take her feet down ! Sally co-existed with Bl, and was conscious of Bl as of another person whom she disliked intensely, and her whole life ran parallel, though on entirely different lines, to that of Bl (and, later, of B4). But it was only occasionally that Sally got control of Miss Beauchamp's organism and displaced Bl or B4, who on these occasions became unconscious. Sally, in short, was a highly developed *subconsciousness* of Miss Beauchamp, which, at a certain date, awakened into independent life.

This case of Miss Beauchamp is exceedingly interesting, but very long and complex to outline here. We have said enough, perhaps, to show the points essential to our purpose ; namely, that groupings of desires, interests, and memories may take place subconsciously and may constitute a separate self-conscious personality which can replace the ordinary one.

A well-known case of duplication of personality is that of Félida X.[2] In what appeared to be her normal primary state (but what was probably in reality an hysterical modification of it) Félida was intelligent but melancholic and hypochondriacal. At the age of fourteen she occasionally felt pains in the head, fainted for a few minutes, and woke up in a new secondary state. In this state she was cheerful and healthy, behaved energetically, and seemed quite normal. Moreover she remembered all the events belonging to her primary sick state. But after a time she would relapse into the primary state, in which she was melancholic, and would have no memory for the events of her healthy

[2] See Binet's *Alterations of Personality*, pp. 6–21.

secondary state. After marriage her " attacks " became more frequent and lasted for longer periods, until eventually the secondary state became the predominant one and the primary state recurred for a few hours only at intervals of a month or more. In this case the second personality was in reality a more normal one, and more complete than the so-called primary one ; but whether it had ever really existed before she was fourteen—i.e. whether it was in truth the original personality—is conjectural.

One of the most interesting cases is that of the Rev. Thomas Hanna,[3] a capable young man who, at the age of twenty-five, was knocked unconscious by a fall. On awakening he had lost *all* his personality, and was like a newly born infant. He had no knowledge at all, either of things or words or the functions of his own body ; even distance and time had ceased to mean anything. But he learned anew very quickly, and thereby acquired a new personality with a totally fresh mental content. After a while the old personality of before the accident reasserted itself and began to alternate with the new one, which by now was quite well-developed and complete in itself. Mr. Hanna was born again, and born different ; and had he died at this stage it would puzzle one to decide which personality had earned immortality as a spirit. Fortunately, however, the two personalities were synthesized, so as to form a third and stable one which had all the memories of both the alternating ones.

These three cases of alternating personality are spontaneous ones, and, moreover, are unusually complete and have fortunately been well observed. But slighter examples of the same thing, and examples in which the two personalities co-exist and manifest simultaneously, have been artificially produced by suggestion, more especially with hysterical patients. One of the characteristic features of hysteria is insensibility over

[3] See Sidis and Goodhart, *Multiple Personality.*

a certain region, often an arm or hand. Binet has well shown the purely psychological nature of this insensibility, and its dependence upon mental dissociation. Suppose that we have a patient whose right arm is insensible, and that we screen this arm from his view, and also engage him in conversation to distract his attention. If now a third person places a pencil in the insensible hand, and whispers some questions which the patient does not consciously hear, the hand may write answers; and those often show that they arise in a system of memories, ideas, wishes, etc., of which the subject, who is meanwhile talking of other matters, is entirely unaware. Usually this system speaks in the first person, and refers to the patient as some stranger, and often claims to be another person with another name. This phenomenon of automatic writing can be easily cultivated by many people who are not obviously hysterical, by distracting their attention in one way or another while they hold a pencil to a piece of paper. It is in this manner that the majority of spirit communications are obtained, and although such a method of semi-involuntary writing must appear very like the intervention of external spirits to people who are ignorant of the phenomena of hysteria and mental dissociation, it is clear that such an interpretation can only be justified when the nature of the message itself is inexplicable otherwise.

A classical case of aiding and abetting in the creation of an elementary secondary personality is quoted by Binet (p. 147). Pierre Janet was studying the hysterical patient Lucie, and, while her normal self was conversing with a third person, Janet whispered : " Do you hear me ? " The insensible hand at once wrote " No." The conversation continued thus.—J : " But you must hear me in order to reply."—" Yes, of course."—" Then how is it ? "—" I do not know."—" There must certainly be someone who does hear me ? "—" Yes."—" Who is it ? "—" Someone else, not Lucie."—" Ah, indeed, another person ? Do you want to give this person a name ? "—" No."—" Yes, it will be more convenient." —" Very well—Adrienne."—" Then, Adrienne, do you hear me ? "—" Yes."

In cases of insanity we see more radical examples of dissociation with the creation of co-existent personalities. The secondary personality created, so to speak, out of the repressed desires and aims of the patient, may get control of certain parts of his organism, and may cause auditory and visual (or even tactile) hallucinations, in which it conveys its thoughts and purposes to the primary personality. A fine picture of this is given in *The Brothers Karamazov*, in the chapter where Ivan converses with the devil, whom he half recognizes as being only an hallucination, a projection of part of him-self—the worst and stupidest part—and yet cannot obliterate or treat as being unreal.   Ivan, however, was not then definitely insane, and consequently was not entirely convinced that the phantom was a separate entity. I cannot help feeling that Dostoevsky, by reason of his own personal experiences combined with his intuition and power of description, has as much right to be cited as an authority on insanity and allied condi-tions as anyone else ; but for the sake of orthodoxy I will also quote B. Hart (*Psychology of Insanity*, p. 125) : " Thus one patient, whose mode of life had wrecked both himself and his family, discussed his former experiences with revolting complacency. He com-plained bitterly, however, of the system of persecution to which he was subjected ; people concealed themselves in the ceiling and under his bed, and poured upon him a flood of abuse and threats, which rendered existence almost insupportable. Hallucinations of this kind may be regarded as literal examples of ' the small voice of conscience ' distorted by repression. It will be observed that such a patient has successfully avoided the sting of remorse, but he has exchanged Scylla for Charybdis and has sacrificed his mental integrity to obtain the hardly more desirable alternative of a constant persecution."

We thus see that it is by no means psychologically impossible for one personality to divide into two, each of which acts independently of and simultaneously with the other. Many Spiritualists urge that if the soi-disant spirit acts simultaneously with the medium it must be a separate entity, and not a sub-division of the medium's personality. Thus Bozzano in his recent criticism of Sudré's *Métapsychique Humaine* makes much of a case where four spirits and the medium were all manifesting intelligently together, and challenges his opponents to cite a single pathological example of dissociation into four simultaneously acting personalities. Such a thing, he declares, is a psychological impossibility, and every such case is therefore an incontrovertible proof of spiritism. Yet we have given examples of dissociation into two divisions, which in the case of the hysterical patient and of the insane patient manifested simultaneously, either by automatic writing or by auditory hallucination. The number two is not magical, and there is no theoretical limit to the possible personalities, but only a practical difficulty in obtaining them. A medium may have more opportunities than an hysterical patient in manifesting more than two subsidiary personalities ; the power of materializing a phantom or of speaking by the "direct voice" adds to the possibilities in this direction. There is also the question of incentive. Spontaneous dissociation occurs as a rule simply on account of mental conflict between two opposing tendencies and their associated system of ideas. The repressed system may organize itself into one new personality, but there is usually no cause for it to make more than this one. But a spiritualistic medium has an obvious motive to cause multiple and simultaneous personalities to be produced, and to manifest together, since this is considered a definite proof of the independent reality of spirits.

We may pass on now to the artificial alterations of personality produced by suggestion during hypnosis. These have been known for long enough, and Richet's cases will perhaps serve as a suitable illustration. I quote from Binet's book, as being the handiest reference. Richet hypnotized a patient, telling her with some decision that she was such and such a type of person. She at once adopted this suggestion and began to act, or rather to live, the part, losing entirely her own personal characteristics, memories, etc., and acquiring a fresh disposition, which was revealed not merely by speech and gesture, but also by an alteration of handwriting. As a sample we will quote the patient B . . . in two rôles :

" *As a General.* She goes, ' Hum, hum ! ' several times, assumes a severe manner, and speaks in an abrupt way. ' Let us go and have a drink ! Waiter, an absinthe ! Who is this coxcomb ? Here, let me pass. What do you want ? ' A piece of paper is handed her, which she seems to read. ' Who is it ? ' Answer : a man of the First. ' Ah, good ! There ! ' She scribbles something illegible. ' You will hand that to the Adjutant-Major. Now make yourself scarce. Well, that absinthe ? ' He is asked if he is a member of the Legion of Honour ? ' Of course ! ' Answer : ' There are stories abroad about you.' ' Ah, stories ! But ! But ! Sacrebleu, what stories ? Take care how you provoke me ! Who dare call me lazy ? ' She flies into a rage which almost ends in a nervous attack."

" Again, *as an old woman.* Someone said to her ' How do you do ? ' She bent her head and said ' Eh ! ' ' How are you ? ' Again she said, ' Eh ! Speak louder. I am a little hard of hearing.' She seated herself, still complaining, coughed, felt her chest and knees, saying to herself : ' Such pains ! O dear, O dear ! Ah ! bring me your child. She is a nice child. Kiss me, darling, and go and play. Have you a little tobacco ? ' "

We are now in a somewhat better position to

understand the psychological problems presented by hypnotism. It is clear that, in general, the process of hypnotizing a person thereby alters his personality for the time being, to a greater or less extent. As a rule this change seems one of diminution, as it chiefly involves a temporary loss of various factors which are normally active, without there being any corresponding appearance of new characteristics. To this extent it is analogous to sleep. But it would appear that the hypnotized subject is actually dimly conscious of all that is said or done, only that he does not pay any attention to anything except what he wishes—this usually being what the operator tells him to attend to. The subject usually retains his sense of identity, and also very often shows as good a memory of the events of waking life as, or even better than, his normal one. A patient of Bramwell's described the hypnotic condition thus : " I feel a kind of restfulness which I do not get in any other condition of life. I feel no fatigue. External sounds, other than your (the operator's) voice, I hear vaguely, as if in a dream, but pay no attention to them. I still feel that I am myself, and can reason just as well as if I were awake." On the other hand, the numerous experiments in which a suggestion given during hypnosis is afterwards " automatically " fulfilled during waking life prove that a subconscious layer has been reached, and that the self-consciousness of the waking personality is not identical or congruent with that of the hypnotized person. And in numerous cases a manifestly different personality creates itself in hypnosis ; for example, B2 and B5 in Morton Prince's case, and Janet's Léonie 2 and Léonie 3. The Léonie 1 of Janet's case was a timid, serious, sad peasant woman. When hypnotized lightly she became Léonie 2 and was noisy and impudent, but cheerful. On deeper hypnosis she became Léonie 3, who again was grave and serious. Léonie 3 knew all about the other two personalities, and felt them as being strangers, having nothing in common with her. She thought L1 was a good, stupid creature, and considered L2 a mad woman. In the same way L2, while ignorant of L3, knew all about L1, whom she regarded as a different person, just as Sally regarded Miss Beauchamp as another woman, and (like Sally) she apparently disliked L1 and used to find ways of tormenting her. Léonie 2 had her own " stream of consciousness," giving her the sense of identity, which was made up of the experiences and events of this state ; for the L2 condition occurred spontaneously, as well as during hypnosis, and that fairly frequently.

Of course a case of this sort is an extreme and abnormal one, and not typical of what occurs in hypnosis. But, taken together with the fact that fictitious personalities are so easily created at the suggestion of the operator, it suggests that the state of hypnosis is one in which the bands of waking personality are considerably loosened, so that psychic elements are set more or less free and are thus enabled, at the instance of suitable external or internal forces, to rearrange themselves, so that what was formerly latent becomes manifest, and what was consciously held by the ego is now held unconsciously. Hypnosis, then, involves a partial dissolution of the personality.

4

The tendency of dissociated groups of feelings and thoughts to integrate into a personality is one of the primary factors in life. On a small scale it is shown universally in children, who constantly occupy hours at a stretch in personificatory games in which they play fictitious parts. Why do children derive such enormous satisfaction out of pretending to be another personality —even a railway engine or a motor car ? A boy of five is hardly ever himself for long ; he is a Red Indian, a captain, a tram-conductor, a clergyman, a motor lorry —almost anything *but* himself ! And, on a larger scale,

we find the phenomenon of " spirit controls " ; often
perfect pieces of acting, involving a high degree of
histrionic ability, vast stores of memory, unconscious
perceptions, etc.   It is not often that we can definitely
trace the origin of the " spirit control " or demonstrate
its real nature, perhaps, but in simple instances the
thing has been done, and I will outline Flournoy's case
of M. Til as an example.[4]

M. Til, who was a normal man, tried automatic
writing, and having asked some questions of the spirits
relative to his children was informed by them that his
son Edward had stolen some cigarettes from his employer's box, had been detected, and was in danger of
dismissal, and he was ordered to go to his employer at
once.   M. Til was greatly perturbed, went to the office
and saw at first only an official, who gave him a very
good account of his son's conduct.   " I am wounded to
the core at the duplicity of this man," wrote the spirit !
Finally M. Til saw the employer, who assured him that
Edward was perfectly satisfactory.   Thereupon the
spirit wrote : " I have deceived you.   Michael, forgive
me ! "   What M. Til found most puzzling was that this
false spirit should not only make a false accusation,
but should insist on his seeing the employer, who should
prove that it was false !   But Flournoy notes some
important points.   In the first place, two or three weeks
before the automatic writing experiments, M. Til had
noticed that his son smoked much, and had reproached
him with it.   Edward replied that all the others did the
same, and that their employer allowed them to use his
cigarettes in the office.   M. Til hoped at the time that
Edward would not be indelicate enough to help himself.
Further, on the day of the automatic writing, a friend
casually said to M. Til : " By the way, has your son
left the bureau ?   I heard that M. Dupain was looking
for another employee ? "   M. Til, perplexed, asked if
M. Dupain was dissatisfied with Edward.   Returning

4 See *Spiritism and Psychology*, p. 194.

home, he told his wife of the conversation, and an hour
later the " bad spirit " wrote out the accusation.

" In this case of M. Til," said Flournoy, " we see an
example of a sort of small romance, subliminally
elaborated from memories and perceptions, under the
impulse of an emotional condition more or less intense,
by means of that curious faculty of dramatization and
personification which we see every day in the phenomena
of dreams."

It is, indeed, a very pretty example because it is
simple and typical, and it demonstrates the insufficiency
of a considerable portion of the evidence adduced for
spiritualistic beliefs.   There is, for example, no ground
for postulating the action of spirits merely to account
for the production of messages, etc. which seem independent of and alien to the medium's mind, and a case like
that of Stainton Moses, who held long theological
arguments with " Rector " and " Imperator," is sufficiently explained by dissociation, except in so far as
the messages show definite instances of supernormally
acquired information ; it is only this latter point which
remains at present a plausible argument for Spiritualism,
and we shall see later how far this argument will hold
good.   Meanwhile the mention of " Rector " leads us
to a discussion of the subject of " Spirit Controls " in
more detail ; for the spirit who misled M. Til, though
undoubtedly of the same essential nature as, say,
" Rector," would hardly be accepted as a sufficient
example of the phenomenon.   On the other hand it
would be difficult to find a more adequate " control "
than " Rector," who worked not only through Stainton
Moses but also through Mrs. Piper, and shewed considerable consistency all the time.

Almost all mediums have their habitual " Controls,"
or particular " spirits " who manifest themselves whenever the medium is in trance.   These controls are, of
course, taken by the medium and other believers to be
genuine spirits who have formerly lived on earth ;   and

their main functions are firstly to act as guide and protector, as guardian angel, to the medium, and secondly to act as intermediary between the consultants of the medium and the various spirits of departed friends with whom they wish to get in touch. That is to say, these various spirits (*Communicators*) inform the Control of what they wish him to make the medium say or write. To a spiritualist the Communicators are genuine spirits who cannot manifest themselves directly ; the Control is another genuine spirit who has obtained control over part or all of the medium's body and can thereby manifest himself by speech, writing, or gesture.

From the point of view of modern psychology, however, the Control is only a secondary personality of the medium's, and the Communicators are mere fleeting figments, fragmentary reconstructions based on hints given by the Consultants, on telepathic impressions, and occasionally on more recondite information obtained clairvoyantly. It is obvious that a medium gains greatly by a system which allows only one personality (or at most a very few) actually to manifest itself at the séances, especially if, as is so often the case, this Control is a person about whom there is little or no external information (e.g. " Rector," " Phinuit," or any of the numerous Oriental controls which are so popular). By this means (on our view) the medium in trance only acts one part, playing a rôle which suits him, and which he can elaborate and perfect, instead of having to enact on the spur of the moment the rôles of all the deceased friends of his consultants. Moreover, as Mrs. Sidgwick has pointed out : " Less is demanded from a spirit friend limited to communicating through another spirit, who may misunderstand what he is supposed to repeat, than from one purporting to talk with the sitter directly. As a matter of fact, the difficulty of this indirect communication is constantly adduced as an excuse for failure or confusion in the records before us."

The above passage occurs in Mrs. Sidgwick's masterly

analysis of Mrs. Piper's trance Phenomena (P.S.P.R., Part 71). In this lengthy work she has successfuly shown the inherent improbability that any of Mrs. Piper's Controls were other than subconscious creations of her own mind. In great detail she has traced the rise and fall of various Controls, and set forth their errors, their common memories and associations of ideas, etc. A few examples may cast light on the subject.

1. On January 19, 1897, the " George Pelham " control wrote : " *Yes, they two too. The verb too bothers me at times.* —— *to two too.*"

Next day, January 20, a totally different control, " George Eliot," wrote the line : " *Spirits are not finely touched but to two too fine issues.*"

Now neither the real George Pelham, nor George Eliot, would ever confuse the words *to*, *two*, and *too* ; nor, if one of them as a Spirit had lost some of his former facility for our grammar, would we expect the other one almost immediately to copy the error ; for G.P. and G.E. were supposedly totally separate and unconnected spirits. But Mrs. Piper herself was not a good grammarian, and it looks as if the two controls had her grammatical equipment in common.

2. A second grammatical error ; January 26, 1897, the Control G.P. said: " *I am plain George Pelham, and no angel as I know of* ; and on March 30, 1897, the control " George Eliot " said : " *I hardly know as there is enough light.*"

In both cases the use of " as " for " that " is characteristic of Mrs. Piper, and of her Controls, but not of the real persons in their lifetime.

3. The various Controls constantly protest against sitters using words denoting periods of time, such as a week, saying that they do not understand them, having lost all sense of time in their new life. On the other hand the same Controls frequently use these very expressions, showing that they know their meaning precisely. It seems, therefore, to be an adopted pose, which is

frequently forgotten in the excitement of communication.

4. An early Control, " Phinuit," who last appeared in 1897, had a special nickname, " The Captain," for Sir O. Lodge. Now on November 22, 1905, Hodgson, speaking to the Control " Rector," said : " I have an earnest request from Lodge, the friend of Myers and myself." Here " Rector " interrupted him saying : " *One moment, friend. We were told to give a message to you from Mrs. H. so called on our side, from a former reigning spirit known to us as Phinuit. The message was '—that I send my love to my old friend, the Captain ———.' "*

Clearly, therefore, when the name Lodge was mentioned it " reminded " Rector of a message to " The Captain "—i.e. Rector associated the two names together, just as Phinuit had done. And yet, later on, in 1906, " Sir Oliver had been present at a good many sittings before, on his inquiring about Phinuit and saying he was a friend of his, Rector asked : " *Could you by any possibility be the friend on earth whom he called Captain ?* " Therefore it seems improbable (to say the least !) that Phinuit had, in 1905, told Rector that he called Lodge the Captain. And hence it looks as if it were all the time an association of ideas in Mrs. Piper's mind, and that she simply never thought that Rector ought not to see the connection between Lodge and the Captain.

Mrs. Sidgwick concludes that Mrs. Piper's hypnotic self, or some part of it, successively personates a number of different characters ; " but I think that there is no divided-off part of Mrs. Piper which has assumed and permanently retains the character of, say, Rector, and is in that sense a secondary personality. Rector has no more persistent existence than Hamlet has. When the part of Rector is not being played he has no existence, just as Hamlet, however well the part is acted, ceases to exist as soon as the actor leaves the stage. That part of Mrs. Piper's mind which is used in acting as

Rector may act as a different Control when Rector's part ends, and is doing something else when the trance is over."

As the subject of Controls and the question as to their authenticity are of supreme importance I will mention one other case where some analysis has been undertaken.   Flournoy devotes a chapter of his book *From India to the Planet Mars* to a consideration of Helen Smith's control Leopold, who also claims to be Cagliostro (Joseph Balsamo).   Leopold manifested himself first in August 1892, but did not reveal the fact that he was really Cagliostro until later, and then under the following circumstances.   It appears that a certain Madame B. was one of Helen Smith's circle (called the N. group) and that she also frequented séances at another house, where the spirit of Cagliostro had appeared previously.   Madame B. once invited Helen to private séances at her house.

" At one of these, Helen having had a vision of Leopold, who pointed out to her with a wand a decanter, Mme. B. suddenly thought of a celebrated episode in the life of Cagliostro, and after the séance she proceeded to take from a drawer and show to Helen an engraving taken from an illustrated edition of Dumas, representing the famous scene of the decanter between Balsamo and the Dauphin at the chateau of Tavernay.   At the same time she gave utterance to the idea that the spirit who manifested himself at the table by means of Helen's hands was certainly Joseph Balsamo ; and she expressed her astonishment that Helen had given him the name Leopold, to which Helen had replied that it was he himself who had given that name.   Mme. B., continuing her deductions, told Mlle. Smith that perhaps she had formerly been the medium of the great magician, and consequently had been Lorenza Feliciani in a former life. Helen at once accepted the suggestion, and for several weeks considered herself to be the reincarnation of Lorenza, until one day a lady of her acquaintance remarked that it was impossible, Lorenza Feliciani having never existed save in the imagination and the romances of Alexandre Dumas *père*. Thus dispossessed of her supposed former existence Helen was not long in declaring through the table that she was Marie Antoinette. As to Leopold, a short time after Mme. B. had hypothetically identified him with Cagliostro, he himself confirmed that hypothesis at a séance of the N. group, dictating to the table that his real name was Joseph Balsamo."

Of course no analysis of this sort can *prove* for a certainty that a given control is not a genuine spirit; and in few actual instances has a laborious psychological analysis been made at all, since it demands great patience, much time, and rare insight. But what has been done will, I think, convince most sensible people that the very great weight of probability is against the spirit theory, and on the side of the view which regards these controls as more or less habitual personations, or secondary personalities, of the medium.

BIBLIOGRAPHY

F. W. H. Myers. Human Personality.
S. Freud. Introductory Lectures on Psycho-analysis.
M. Bramwell. Hypnotism.
M. Prince. Dissociation of a Personality.
  The Unconscious.
T. Flournoy. From India to the Planet Mars.
  Spiritism and Psychology.
A. Binet. Alterations of Personality.
B. Hart. Psychology of Insanity.
W. McDougall. Abnormal Psychology.
Mrs. Sidgwick. Psychology of Mrs. Piper's Trance
  Phenomena, P.S.P.R., Part 71.

PART TWO

CHAPTER FOUR

TELEKINESIS

THE development of Spiritualism as a distinct modern religious cult dates from the eighteen-forties, when Kate Fox, while still a child, had the wit to propose to the Hydesville ghost that it should answer questions by knocking in accordance with her code. From that date conversation with the soi-disant spirits could develop, and hence the religion of Spiritualism, which was based on the messages obtained from spirits, could arise. The original simple scheme by which one rap meant no and three raps yes, while two indicated doubt, was soon replaced by the more useful, though tedious device of calling out the letters of the alphabet one by one, and choosing those at which the spirit rapped. This was supplemented by the ouija board and planchette, as well as by automatic writing, in which a medium held a pencil and allowed his hand to write what it would, and also by trance-speaking, when, it was supposed, the spirit took control of the medium's vocal organs.

For some obscure, and probably quite unimportant reason, however, the production of raps or knocks by the seemingly spontaneous self-movement of tables, which tipped up at the right letter, became the fashionable mode of conversation on the part of the sitters, and as a consequence the movements of tables play quite a preponderating part in the records of psychic research.

It is very easy to understand that the sight of an untouched table spontaneously tipping up, or the sound of an unaccountable rap, at certain letters, producing at the end an intelligent, and often informative, series of words in response to questions asked, should of itself incline people to attribute the phenomenon to the action of spirits. It is also easy to see that the religious atmosphere which was thus induced, the desire of all sitters to converse with their own dear ones, the uncanny nature of such a procedure, the interest attaching to these messages, and the hostility which all this evoked in the sceptical outsider who was not of the spiritualist persuasion, should militate strongly against any detached and impartial investigation of the physical and mechanical processes involved in the actual production of the tilt or the rap. These were given as a miracle and it was felt that scientific investigation was an impertinence and a sacrilege. Moreover the various mediums, whose presence was necessary for spirit communications to take place, whether taken as a class or individually, had an obvious interest, emotional and sectarian as well as pecuniary, in obtaining messages, and were therefore especially tempted to simulate the phenomena fraudulently ; a proceeding which was all the easier because of the emotional and religious conditions of the séance, which, when added to the physical condition of almost complete darkness, made detection quite improbable.

On the other hand, hostile people asserted that the raps and table-tiltings were obviously produced by ordinary physical means, and were due to deliberate or unconscious muscular movements by the medium. Faraday and Chevreul both demonstrated the fact that small rhythmic muscular impulses, of which one is not aware, may impart motion to an object which is ever so lightly touched, and that a table may easily be turned or tilted in this way if several people rest their fingers lightly on it. This explanation, however, could not apply to those cases where, as it was asserted, the table was not touched by anyone and yet moved.

In order to silence the hostile " naturalistic " critic, on the one hand, and also because of the instinctive rationalism of many of the adherents of Spiritualism, on the other hand, it became more and more obviously desirable to encourage impartial and scientific investigation into the alleged physical phenomena of which the three most important were, (a) the production of raps, knocks and similar noises ; (b) the movement of an untouched object ; (c) the production of material forms, whether hands, faces, or complete human figures.

It was alleged by Spiritualists that each of these three phenomena occurred in the presence of suitable mediums, usually during a trance state, and that they were inexplicable by any known mechanical or physical laws. On the other hand, sceptics asserted that phenomena of class (a) and (b) were either fraudulently produced or were due to unconscious muscular actions, while those in class (c) were always gross and deliberate frauds. Confining ourselves, for the present, to classes (a) and (b) we may divide the problem for investigation into two parts. The first task is to establish the reality of *Telekinesis* (=movement at a distance) as a fact. This is a matter of making exact observations under conditions which exclude every known method of moving a given object by normal means, and (by far the harder task) of recording these observations in such a way that outsiders, who simply read the report, can realize that every possible method of fraud has been eliminated. The second task, which is properly speaking the more specifically scientific one (the first being more akin to that of a detective), is to elucidate the physical processes involved in Telekinesis ; for even if we assume that a spirit lifts a table we are not thereby absolved from the intellectual obligation to find out how he does it.

As early as 1854 and 1855 fairly good studies of

Telekinesis had been made by the Comte de Gasparin and by Professor Hare, but we may take Crookes' researches in 1870 as the real starting point of all modern scientific inquiry. His papers on the subject are few, and a considerable portion of them is polemical and taken up with silencing his critics, but they are invaluable nevertheless : " A block of granite," said Richet, " that no criticism has been able to touch." Crookes had the good fortune to study the very remarkable and powerful medium D. D. Home, but his success resulted at least as much from the fact that he himself was peculiarly fitted for the task. He combined scientific acumen and intellectual integrity with a rare tact and sympathy, so that he won, and retained, the complete confidence of the medium. This is an exceedingly important factor, which, unhappily, many researchers neglect to take into account. The majority of mediums are justly timid and suspicious of the scientist who wishes to investigate their phenomena and put them to tests, for he has so often misjudged and calumniated them, so often roughly handled them while they were in trance, so often submitted them to nervous shocks by shining a sudden light or by grasping at a materialized spirit form. The first and most important factor in any scientific research in this field is that of the medium's faith in the investigator. When Crookes, Crawford, Geley, and a few others said they would not do a thing their mediums knew that it would not be done, and, as a consequence, these investigators were rewarded tenfold by the phenomena they obtained.

D. D. Home was an earnest religiously-minded spiritualist, of nervous sensitive temperament, easily depressed or moved by his environment, and physically rather fragile. He seems to have been the most remarkable all-round medium on record, and a very good account of his mediumship will be found in Lord Dunraven's *Experiences in Spiritualism*, which is a record of séances held by the author and his father. From the

point of view of the scientific establishment of Telekinesis the book is of small value, since this was not the
object of the writer, but it records several highly
interesting phenomena, of which the most striking is
certainly the passing out of Home's body horizontally
through an open window, its floating unsupported over
the street below, and its entry through the open window
of another room (see p. 156).

The first experiments which Crookes made with
Home were concerned with his ability to make objects
move without touching them. Having put an accordion
into one of Home's hands, and then isolated this by
inserting it in a cage which was open at the top and
which could just be passed under a table, Crookes
observed that the accordion moved up and down and
emitted various notes, although held by the end opposite
the keys, and further, when Home's hand was removed,
the accordion hung unsupported in the air, waving up
and down, and emitting sounds.

Next Crookes fitted up a board so that one end
rested on the end of a table, while the other end hung
from a spring balance, which then, with the board
horizontal, gave a reading of 3 lb. When D. D. Home
rested his fingers lightly on the fulcrum, the far end
of the board was depressed until the balance recorded
9 lb. Later the apparatus was improved by having a
knife-edge fulcrum, and above this, on top of the board,
a bowl of water was placed. A second bowl, smaller
and perforated at the bottom, was supported from an
outside stand so that it dripped into the water in the
first bowl, and Home placed his fingers in this. Thus
he could exert no muscular action except on the knife-
edge fulcrum, and this could only be of the slightest,
being due to the displacement of water by his finger-tips.
Moreover a clockwork recording drum was attached to
the spring-balance, so that a continuous graph of the
readings of the latter was obtained. Experiments
were tried with Home's fingers in the bowl of water,

with them resting on the stand, and also when he stood three feet away from the apparatus and his hands and feet were firmly held. Under all these conditions the balance was depressed, and the fact thereby established that he could exert a mechanical force capable of moving material objects although these were not in contact with him.

Using a more delicate instrument, constructed on a similar principle, Crookes demonstrated that a lady medium could produce the same effects, though the force she exerted was perhaps a matter of grains where that of Home was measured in pounds. He also testified positively to having witnessed the levitation of objects and of persons, in a full light, under conditions which rendered fraud unthinkable. The few salient passages here quoted refer to occurrences taking place at his own house, with only his private friends present besides the medium, and in ordinary full light. On page 97 of his *Researches in the Phenomena of Spiritualism*, he says :

" I have had several repetitions of the experiment considered by the committee of the Dialectical Society to be conclusive, viz. : the movement of a heavy table in full light, the chairs turned with their backs to the table, about a foot off, and each person kneeling on his chair with hands resting over the backs of the chair but not touching the table. On one occasion this took place when I was moving about so as to see how every one was placed." Again, on page 99 of the same book, he refers specifically to the levitation of persons.

" On one occasion I witnessed a chair with a lady sitting on it rise several inches from the ground. On another occasion, to avoid the suspicion of this being in some way performed by herself, the lady knelt on the chair in such a manner that its four feet were visible to us. It then rose about three inches, remained suspended for about ten seconds, and then slowly descended."

And again :

" The most striking cases of levitation which I have

witnessed have been with Mr. Home. On three separate occasions have I seen him raised completely from the floor of the room. Once sitting in an easy-chair, once kneeling on his chair, and once standing up. On each occasion I had full opportunity of watching the occurrence as it was taking place."

Crookes naturally expected that his competence as an observer, his veracity and his ability to distinguish between hallucination and a real phenomenon would not be questioned; but he unfortunately under-estimated the prejudices and the meanness of spirit of some of his reputed peers. The only error of judgment with which we may fairly charge him, as a scientist who wished to settle the question as to the fact of telekinesis, is that he did not sufficiently realize the importance of making a full and precise record of every occurrence, every spoken word, the time of each event, and the dispositions of all the objects of the room, etc. But against this we must put the fact that in 1870 no one realized the extent to which destructive criticism of such observations would be pushed by people who in other departments passed as reasonable and judiciously-minded. Since Crookes' day the task of recording observations of this sort in such a way that no one could find a loophole by which to escape from the duty of admitting the reality of telekinesis has been undertaken and carried out by several scientists, whose observations, owing to the limitations thus imposed on them, are far less interesting in themselves than Crookes' were. Moreover, it has been well argued by Dr. F. C. S. Schiller that the pursuit of the crucial experiment which shall finally silence all criticism is largely chimerical, because the evidence must always rest on testimony, and thus become weaker as time goes on. The aim of the investigator, he says, should rather be to study the phenomena experimentally, varying conditions and amassing observations until the phenomena become to some extent controllable, repeatable at will, and ultimately capable of some explanation. On this path Crookes is the great pioneer, and it would seem that the fruitful results obtained by Crawford, Geley and Osty, who all acted in the same spirit, would justify Schiller's point of view.

Our aim, however, in this place is to go over some of the best evidence for the fact of telekinesis first, before we study its explanation. We must therefore turn to the next important series of investigations, centring round the famous medium Eusapia Palladino, who had the honour of being studied by, and of convincing, more scientists than any other physical medium. Eusapia began her career as a medium when she was about fourteen years old, but it was not until 1888, when she was thirty-four, that she came into prominence through a letter in which Professor Chiaia, of Naples, invited the great alienist Lombroso to verify the genuineness of her mediumship. Professor Lombroso was a convinced sceptic and opponent of Spiritualism, and a man whose scientific reputation was of the highest. Like so many more convinced materialists he began by deriding the suggestion that there was anything to investigate, and refusing to look into the matter; but eventually, in 1891, he held two sittings with Eusapia during which supernormal movements, etc., occurred, so that he courageously published his testimony to the reality of telekinesis, though carefully withholding his assent to the spiritistic explanation of it. From that day, Eusapia's fame as a medium grew until it quickly equalled, in the domain of physical mediumship, that attained by Mrs. Piper in the sister-domain of mental mediumship. During the ensuing quarter of a century she was studied, under all the test conditions that they could invent and apply, by such men as Lombroso, Morselli, de Rochas, Ochorowicz, Flammarion, Richet, the Curies, Bergson, Myers and Sir O. Lodge—to mention only names which are likely to be familiar. In addition she was particularly well studied, from the point of view of those who look for crucial evidence recorded in such a way that all the relevant circumstances of lighting, control of hands and feet, etc., are minutely given, by a commission of the S.P.R., composed of three men who were experienced in conjuring and well informed about the fraudulent procedures adopted by mediums— namely, H. Carrington, W. Baggally, and the Hon. E. Fielding. All these investigators agree that, although Eusapia was known to be liable to simulate phenomena, particularly by freeing one of her hands unobserved, yet genuine phenomena of telekinesis did occur when the control was such that fraud was physically impossible under the conditions.

On one occasion, for example, at Genoa, she was lifted with her chair on to the table. Carrington (page 136) quotes an account of this event thus :

" Suddenly Professors Morselli and Porro perceived that Eusapia had been raised, along with her chair, and carried up to a level above that of the surface of the table, upon which she redescended in such a way that her feet and the two front legs of the chair rested on the surface of the table, which was partially broken. Meanwhile, the medium moaned as if intensely frightened, and asked to be put back with her chair on the floor. But almost instantly she was carried up again with the chair, and this levitation lasted some seconds, so that M. de Albertis and Professor Porro, without preconcerted arrangement and with completely simultaneous thought, succeeded in passing their hands under the feet of the medium and of the chair. Shortly afterwards Eusapia, still seated, redescended on to the table ; she was held by those to right and left of her, the chair was pushed or thrown down backward on to the floor ; and the medium, seized by several of those present, while still moaning was carried back to the floor and seated again in her place."

A very good series of seances was held during 1905-6-7 at Paris, at the Institute of Psychology, under the direction of MM. d'Arsonval, Ballet, Bergson, Courtier, Curie, and Richet. Many special precautions were taken ; for example, Eusapia was seated on a weighing machine and the table to be levitated had its legs surrounded by conical sheaths which prevented her gripping the legs with her knees. We will quote one entry from the detailed record by Courtier (1905, séance 7) :

" Eusapia requests everyone to stand up, and asks M. de Gramont to come and hold her legs. Eusapia is standing on the Marey balance. M. de Gramont holds her legs. The others present, d'Arsonval, Courtier, Favre, Vaugeois and Yourievitch, form a chain standing up. d'Arsonval controls Eusapia's left hand and Yourievitch her right hand.

" The table then rises so high that two legs come almost out of the surrounding sheaths. At 10.53, with the same control of hands and legs the table rises again. ' Higher still ! Out of the sheaths ! ' some one says. The table rises very high, and falls outside the sheaths."

The majority of the séances with Eusapia seem to have been conducted mainly with the object of obtaining levitations (and also materializations) under conditions which excluded fraud—i.e., in the pursuit of crucial evidence for the conviction of outsiders, rather than in the hope of gaining insight into the nature of the phenomena and control over their production. Nevertheless, some important observations were made, at one time and another, which were capable of leading to a rational interpretation of the physical phenomena. For example, on several occasions, when an object was moved, one saw what appeared to be an extra limb protruding from some part of Eusapia's body. An instance quoted by Carrington (page 117) is given by Prof. Bottazzi, and relates to a séance held in 1907.

" While Galeotti was controlling Eusapia's right hand he distinctly saw the doubling of the left arm of the medium. ' Look ! ' he exclaimed, ' I see two left arms—identical in appearance ; one is on the little table, and it is that which M. Bottazzi touches, and the other seems to come out of her shoulder—to approach her, and touch her, and then return and melt into her body again.' " (In this last sentence, it seems that the middle two *hers* refer, not to Eusapia, but to Mme. Bottazzi, who was touched by this third limb, and felt the contact while Galeotti observed the mechanism by which the psychic touch was produced.)

On another occasion, when Eusapia depressed the pan of a letter balance by drawing her two hands downwards on either side of it, but without touching it, she was accused of fraud because the observer thought he saw a fine thread joining her fingers. But this thread was not an ordinary one, being, in fact, like the additional left arm, a temporary extrusion from her flesh. Ochorowicz confirmed this interpretation in Eusapia's case, and also did a striking series of experiments with a Polish medium, Stanislawa Tomczyk, in which he obtained good photographs showing the levitation of small objects of various forms—sphere, cylinder, bell, pin, etc.—and succeeded in photographing the ray-like threads which supported these objects. Later Schrenck-Notzing repeated and confirmed this work, and showed that the structure of the threads, "rays," or "efflorescences," as they have been variously called, was not like that of silk, cotton, hair, etc. etc., but was distinctive, being heterogeneous, almost discontinuous at some places, where it seems to become vaporous or nebulous. The most important property of these projections, however, is certainly their power of adapting their form and distribution to suit the requirements of the work to be done.

We may mention here Schrenck-Notzing's later demonstrations of Telekinesis with the medium Willy Schneider, during the course of which he convinced nearly 100 notable members of learned professions of its reality, and of the total exclusion of fraud as a possible factor. The séance room was first carefully examined, the medium was stripped and examined, then dressed in a special garment, on to which were sewn luminous tapes, to reveal his every movement. During the séance, which was conducted in red light, two people held the medium's two wrists, while a third held his legs ; moreover, the objects to be moved were enclosed in a cage of gauze. Under these conditions it was seen that a sort of extra limb or rod came from the medium, penetrated the gauze, and displaced the things inside the cage. From an evidential point of view these experiments are probably the best yet done.

Two other observations made with Eusapia have, in the sequel, been of great theoretical interest and importance ; namely, the fact that she could decrease her weight at will, as if she were able temporarily to get rid of some of the matter composing her body, and the significant fact that when an object, say a table, was levitated, its weight was added to her own weight. This last demonstrates that there is a mechanical connection like, for example, a rod, even if it be invisible, between the object raised and the medium—a fact which weakens considerably the case for interpreting physical phenomena as due to the agency of spirits.

It has been left to a British scientist, Dr. W. J. Crawford, to realize the importance of facts such as the above, and to undertake a series of really experimental séances with the object of unravelling the mechanical process which underlies Telekinesis. In their simplicity and fertile diversity his experiments reveal their author's genius to be akin to that of a Fabre or a Faraday, and his method and spirit form a model on which future research, if it is to be fruitful, should largely be based.

Dr. Crawford worked during the years 1914 to 1920 with a small family circle of Spiritualists, several of whom appear to have been mediumistic in a minor degree, while one, Miss Kathleen Goligher, was a powerful telekinetic medium. His experiments, re-

corded in three published volumes, were directed in the
main with a view, not to establish and demonstrate the
fact of levitation, etc., but to elucidate its physical
mechanism; for although he himself believed in the
agency of spirits, he nevertheless saw that for a table
to be raised in the air some physical process must be
used, force must be applied, and there must be a
mechanical reaction somewhere, even if only on the
molecules of the air. As a matter of fact, he found, as
the conclusion to be drawn from a large number of
experiments made with spring balances and weighing
machines, that in the levitation of a comparatively light
object 97 per cent of the weight of the object was taken
by the medium, the remainder being distributed among
the sitters; when, however, a heavy table was lifted,
there was a reaction upon the floor. He interpreted
these results, and also those of some experiments showing that when a compression balance was placed at
varying heights above the ground under the levitated
table the vertical pressure on the balance pan increased
rapidly with the height of the latter, by propounding
the theory that the medium extruded from her lower
limbs a species of rod, which acted as a cantilever, and
that this rod was capable of having a curved form, of
supporting itself on the ground if necessary, and of
having variable rigidity. The rod was able to move to
a limited extent, could vary its cross section and its
flexibility, and could alter its free end both as to shape
and hardness. On page 62 of *Psychic Structures* he sums
up the description of these levers as follows :

" In the first place, each psychic rod in the neigh-
bourhood of its extremity was solid, i.e. built up of
matter solid to the touch, and therefore presumably of
matter with which we are ordinarily familiar. At a few
inches or less from its extremity this appearance of
solidity vanished and nothing could be felt but a flow
of what appeared to be material particles, if the line of
the structure were intercepted by the hand of the

experimenter. That is to say, from a distance only a few inches from its extremity right up to the body of the medium all appearance of solidity vanished, and nothing could be felt but a flow of cold, spore-like particles. In other words the solidity seemed to change to something resembling a gaseous state. Nevertheless—and let this be well marked and digested—the whole rod, apparently made up of a solid end and a gaseous body, operated exactly as if it were wholly solid from the body of the medium outwards. It resisted pull, push, and sheer stress of large magnitude. And in this sort of thing resides the chief mystery connected with the physical phenomena of Spiritualism."

By numerous ingenious experiments with moist clay, methylene blue, carmine, etc., he conclusively proved both the fact that these rods came out from the medium's body, and that they returned into it. In a note dated June 7th, 1920 (given in D'Albe's book), we read : " I have been making some observations on the movements of the plasma, and have succeeded in watching it wriggling up her legs on three occasions under her skirt. It appears to wriggle up with the sinuous movement of a serpent."

By other experiments he showed that the medium's weight and the volume of her thighs diminished when the *ectoplasm*, as the substance extruded is called, was projected, and in many instances he was able to feel the structures (a cold, heavy, damp feel, or as hard and rigid as a metal, according to circumstances) and ultimately, after much experimenting, to see them. He found that, while generally invisible in red light, and decomposed by ordinary white light, they could be seen by phosphorescent light. Accordingly, he placed a luminous card just in front of the medium's feet, and watched the structures just over its surface.

" The medium had her feet and ankles locked in the box. It was absolutely impossible for her to get her feet out. The operators (i.e. the Spirits) were asked to bring out the structure from the box and to hold it over the phosphorescent sheet. I stood at the side of the medium looking down on the cardboard sheet. In a short time a curved body somewhat like the toe of a boot advanced over the inner edge of the cardboard and then retired. . . . The operators made the structure end into many shapes for my edification, and I watched these changes occurring. The toe part could lengthen out until the whole thing resembled a thin pointed straight rod. I watched the end portion contract and then gradually lengthen until the pointed shape was reached. After the pointed stage was reached the pointed end would sometimes curl round into a hook. This hook-like end could evidently grip things such as a table leg. It twisted and untwisted before my eyes. Or the structure could contract and spread out sideways until it resembled a mushroom or a cabbage leaf."

Thus by a remarkable and intensely interesting series of patient experiments, conducted in a manner which won the confidence and friendship of the medium and the regular circle, Crawford was able to achieve results which, as he says, speak for themselves and carry the proof of their genuineness in themselves, independently of all test appliances and tyings-up of the medium. The numerical consistency of the various weighing experiments excludes fraud, as does also the convergence of evidence drawn from mechanical effects, from the senses of touch and sight, and from the detective experiments in which the path of the rods was traced by dyes or their end-form was revealed by clay impressions. We have now the outline of an intelligible explanation of telekinesis and of rappings, resting on the capacity of a medium to extrude a substance (called ectoplasm for the sake of a name), which substance can be modified at will and can be moved at will within limits, and which returns back to the medium's body. The chief mechanical problem which is now left to solve, and it will probably prove insoluble, is as to the manner in which energy is transmitted from the medium to the solid working-end of a structure, via the gaseous main body of it, and how the whole is rendered rigid or flexible at will : that is to say, the problem which every living being presents, of the action of mind on the body, is here presented in a rather unusual and striking form by these unusual and temporary ectoplasmic structures.

An important and ingenious research on telekinesis, conducted at the Institut Métapsychique International (Paris) by Dr. Osty, with Rudi Schneider (brother to Willy S.) as medium, is reported in the *Revue Métapsychique* for 1931, No. 6, and 1932, No. 1. The object of the experimental arrangements was to obtain *automatically, instantaneously,* and *without the medium's knowledge,* photographs of telekinetic movements at the actual moment of their occurrence.

An expensive ultra-violet apparatus was installed, and an ingenious system devised for taking photographs with it automatically the moment a given object placed on a table should move. To this end a beam of infra-red rays (which, like the ultra-violet ones, are invisible) was projected over the table and reflected to and fro so as to enclose the object, and finally made to fall on a Thallium Sulphide cell, where it generated an electric current whose strength varied with the intensity of the beam of infra-red rays.

Now if any object were to move so as to intercept the beam (or, if transparent, to diminish its intensity by 30 per cent) the current would fall sufficiently to open up the ultra-violet lamp, to release shutters of cameras suitably placed, and thus to take several photographs of everything near the table, medium, and sitters.

The idea in using the ultra-violet light was that the medium should not know that photographs had been taken ; but in practice the fluorescence it produced on objects in the room, and also the noise of the shutters opening and closing, invalidated this. In an alternative arrangement the interception of the infra-red beam was made to ignite a magnesium flash, so that photographs were obtained in the ordinary manner.

As regards actual telekinetic movements the results were not very good, but they were interesting in that they demonstrated the presence of ectoplasm near the object which Rudi endeavoured to move. For example, on November 10, 1930, he failed to move a handkerchief on the table ; nevertheless, *something* intercepted the beam of infra-red, for the magnesium was lighted on two occasions, directly after Rudi had told the sitters to hold his hands tightly, as he did when he felt that " the force " was ready for an effort at telekinesis. The photographs, however, showed that the handkerchief was in its original position, nothing else was out of its place, the medium and sitters were in their seats at some distance from the table, and there was no visible material object to explain the interception of the beam. Numerous other séances, with different electrical and optical devices, lead all to the same conclusion ; namely, that when Rudi tries to move the given object he projects something which is invisible, but is dense enough (or, *becomes* dense enough) to absorb at least 30 per cent of the beam of infra-red which was used.

The serious student should study the reports, as they mark an advance in the technique of research, and the method used makes the detection of any fraud which depends on the use of the medium's (or anybody's) limbs, or indeed any material object whatsoever, a certainty ; since the photographs follow automatically and immediately upon the motion of the given object.

BIBLIOGRAPHY

CROOKES. Researches in the Phenomena of Spiritualism.
DUNRAVEN. Experiences in Spiritualism with D. D. Home.
H. CARRINGTON. Eusapia Palladino.
RICHET. Thirty Years of Psychic Research.
CRAWFORD. Reality of Psychic Phenomena.
  Experiments in Psychic Science.
  Psychic Structures at the Goligher Circle.
FOURNIER D'ALBE. The Goligher Circle.
SCHRENCK-NOTZING. Physikalische Phänomena des Medium-
  ismus.
  Experimente der Fernbewegung.

CHAPTER FIVE

MATERIALIZATIONS

1

FOR countless centuries people have believed more or less firmly in ghosts and phantoms, although the rarity of such apparitions and their peculiarly evanescent character have prevented the accumulation of any very convincing evidence for their objective reality, and have enabled more sceptical minds to deny it altogether, as a superstitious fancy supported only by manifestly unreliable third-hand testimony. With the development of eighteenth and nineteenth century rationalism, indeed, scepticism obtained a temporary ascendency among the educated, mainly because the spread of science had raised the standard of evidence required to bring conviction, and evidence of a high quality is, naturally enough, exceedingly difficult to obtain in this region of nature. Nevertheless, we have now reached a point where the reality of phantoms can be demonstrated under certain conditions and their possible occurrence under other conditions inferred ; and further, we can go so far as to see in part how they are generated, and to watch the actual process.

Before considering the more recent work of psychic researchers which will provide us with some grounds for an explanation of the genesis of phantoms, we will mention briefly the classical case of " Katie King," as it is unique in many important respects. Although Richet, as we shall shortly see, has observed and described a fully materialized and apparently living phantom, and Dr. Gibier has witnessed the production of several such while the medium, Mme. Salmon, was locked in a closed cage, no one besides Crookes has yet been granted such a perfect and relatively stable manifestation. Probably, indeed, no other investigator has deserved it, for it demanded on his part a very high development of patience, tact, fineness of feeling, as well as self-efface-ment and transparent honesty—for example, although he took some forty-four photographs of the spirit form, he never published them, in spite of their immense value to him as confirmation of his word and of the consequent credit he would have reaped from them. He denied himself this because he had promised Katie, when she allowed him to photograph her, that he would not publish the prints.

The extraordinary story of Katie King's appearance, her recurrent existence for about three years, and her final departure, is given in Crookes' *Researches*, and ought to be read in full. It will be seen that this marvel-lous spirit-form appeared frequently at séances for a period of about three years, and on these occasions was practically indistinguishable from a real living person, except for her power of vanishing instantaneously. We read, for example, that at a séance at Hackney Katie appeared for about two hours, walking about the room and conversing with those present. Crookes asked and obtained permission to clasp her in his arms, and thus verify the fact that she was as material a being as Miss Cook (the medium) herself.

Katie, moreover, and this is a point in which she differed most from the majority of materialized forms, had her own quite personal character. She made friends with the whole Crookes' household, and was especially fond of playing with the children, telling them stories of her earth-life, so that no one could help treating her as a real living person, and a singularly charming and lovable one.

The general procedure of a séance was that Miss Cook, the medium, lay down on a couch or on the floor in the library, which opened out through folding doors (of which one was taken off its hinges and replaced by a curtain) into Crookes' laboratory, where those taking part in the séance were assembled. " I prepare and arrange my Library myself as the dark cabinet," says Crookes (p. 124), " and usually, after Miss Cook has been dining and conversing with us, and scarcely out of our sight for a minute, she walks direct into the cabinet, and I, at her request, lock its second door and keep possession of the key through the séance ; the gas is then turned out and Miss Cook is left in darkness. On entering the cabinet Miss Cook lies down upon the floor, with her head on a pillow, and is soon entranced."

It will occur to the reader of the above paragraph that a possible mode of fraud open to Miss Cook was that of securing a second key to the far door of the library, and having an accomplice who came into the cabinet and laboratory in this way and enacted the part of Katie ; all other modes of fraud are excluded by the facts that (a) Katie King was a perfect model of a living human being, who possessed a heart (pulse normally 75), and breathed, moved, talked, and apparently had her own recognizable character and personality ; and (b) the medium and Katie King were often seen, and were also photographed, together at one and the same moment.[1] Moreover, there were many physical differences between the two. Crookes says : " Katie's height varies ; in my house I have seen her six inches taller than Miss Cook. . . . Katie's neck was bare last night ; the skin was perfectly smooth both to touch and sight, while on Miss Cook's neck is a large blister which, under similar circumstances, is distinctly visible and rough to the touch. Katie's ears are unpierced, whilst Miss Cook

---

[1] On one occasion Crookes, together with C. Varley, F.R.S., made Miss Cook's body part of a weak electric circuit, fastening the wires to her so that if she were to move much the current would cease. When the materialized form appeared outside the cabinet the current (as indicated by a galvanometer) did not cease, although it varied slightly owing to small movements of the medium. This proved that the medium was inside the cabinet during the period that the spirit-form was outside.

habitually wears ear-rings. . . . Katie's lungs were
found to be sounder than her medium's, for at the time
I tried the experiment Miss Cook was under medical
treatment for a cough."

The sole normal explanation of Katie would be that she
was some third person, acting the part, and introduced
by Miss Cook via the back door of the library. But this
suggestion is put out of court partly by the wholly
abnormal variation of Katie's height, partly by the
accounts of her instantaneous disappearances,[2] and
partly because the circumstances of Miss Cook's visits
to the Crookes' household, and her perfectly easy and
open behaviour there, preclude this idea of complicity,
which would necessitate many secret meetings and
elaborate arrangements. On this point we may quote
two passages from Crookes : " During the last six
months Miss Cook has been a frequent visitor at my
house, remaining sometimes a week at a time. She
brings nothing with her but a little handbag, not locked ;
during the day she is constantly in the presence of Mrs.
Crookes, myself or some other member of my family,
and, not sleeping by herself, there is absolutely no
opportunity for any preparation even of a less elaborate
character than would be required to enact Katie King "
(page 124). And on page 128 he says : " To imagine
that an innocent schoolgirl of fifteen should be able to
conceive and then successfully carry out for three years
so gigantic an imposture as this, and in that time should
submit to any test that might be imposed upon her,
should bear the strictest scrutiny, should be willing to
be searched at any time, either before or after a séance,
and should meet with even better success in my own

[2] Miss Florence Marryat describes graphically how Katie melted
under a full light on one occasion : " I can compare the dematerialization of her form to nothing but a wax doll melting before a hot fire.
First the features became blurred and indistinct ; they seemed to run
into each other. The eyes sunk in the sockets, the nose disappeared,
the frontal bone fell in. Next the limbs appeared to give way under
her, and she sank lower and lower on the carpet like a crumbling
edifice. . . ." See *There is no Death*, by Florence Marryat (Rider).

house than at that of her parents, knowing that she
visited me with the express object of submitting to
strict scientific tests—to imagine, I say, the Katie
King of the last three years to be the result of imposture does more violence to one's reason and
common sense than to believe her to be what she
herself affirms."

I do not know whether Crookes ever committed himself definitely to the belief that Katie was, as she said,
a spirit who had formerly lived on earth and was now
incarnated again at the expense of the medium, or
whether he would admit as a possible alternative the
idea that Katie was a material projection of a secondary
personality of Miss Cook.

In the light of later work this latter would appear the
most probable and rational interpretation, and it is
supported also by those cases where some hostile person
has suddenly seized a phantom and found that it was
the medium herself ; for in such cases (once Miss Cook,
and once Mme. D'Espérance were treated in this way)
the garments, veils, etc., which transformed the medium
into the pseudo-spirit have instantaneously disappeared !
In such cases we see the medium, in a trance, acting the
part of a spirit, not by actually incarnating the secondary
personality in a separate temporary body (which is
presumably as difficult a feat as it is rare), but by
creating *ad hoc* veils, garments, etc., or even more
organic features, with which to clothe her own body and
enact the spirit part. Of course this idea of "transfiguration," as it is called, would not apply to the case
of Katie in any of the instances where she was seen
together with Miss Cook, but it is a phenomenon which
has been observed with later mediums, and it is a lower
and less developed form of the same process which
produces a fully independent phantom. I have mentioned it here, somewhat out of its logical position,
because it not only explains some of the famous
so-called " exposures " of mediums but also indicates

that the psychological source of the spirit is to be sought in the medium, not amongst the souls of the departed.

2

The solution of the chief mystery of materialization has already been given in our study of telekinesis. It was there described how a medium, in order to move a given object without normal contact, will project from her body a material substance which has the power of self-movement and of self-organization into the form of a limb, rod, lever, etc. This being granted, the power of building up a hand, a face, or a full human body, is only an extension which, though it might be too difficult in practice for any given medium, is theoretically possible. Dr. Crawford's description of the manner in which an impalpable and invisible gaseous emanation coming from the medium condenses and hardens at the free end, and organizes itself into the shape of a pointed rod, a hook, or the toe-end of a foot, etc., suggests to us that with a little more substance and more skill almost anything might be formed.

In the light of the ectoplasm theory the following account by Richet (p. 521) of an experience at the Villa Carmen is at once intelligible :

" The most extraordinary of all the experiments is certainly the fourth (October 20th)—

" Fairly good light. The curtain remains closed for about an hour. I open it ; a white spot on the floor grows rapidly, and two horns protrude from the mass, from which other horns appear, very mobile, pointing in every direction. The mass, then much larger, disaggregates into particles, taking on the semblance of a hand ; it does not look like the cast of the previous day, it is a greyish hand with ill-defined outlines. This hand moves, looking like the hand of a mummy emerging from some stuff ; it raises and lowers itself like a hand. Marthe's hands are held by me and are quite motionless.

The fingers of the ectoplasm, thin and spindly, seem to end in cloudy masses. I can examine them very closely. I touch one of these spindles ; it feels like a cold liquid. I can press it, and it seems like the bone of a finger, covered with skin. The hand rests on my knee, and I feel the slight friction of a body of little resistance. The hand then rises of itself, swaying on a long stem that connects it with the floor ; it falls back on to the floor with a slight noise ; it remains there, and I *think* I see the two bones of the fore-arm as though wrapped in cloudy muslin.

" The hand then rises, bends, and moves towards me. The wrist is lowered and the fingers pendant ; they move, and there seems a tortional movement of this strange fore-arm. I still think I see the carpal bones in the muslin-like cloud.

" The hand rests on my knee again. I feel its weight, very light ; it makes little movements at my request that I can feel quite well. Then Marthe says to me : ' That is the muscles beginning to form,' and I see, or I think I see, something dark in the space between the two bones. The hand rises, and moves very close to me, having no connection with the ground but a slight white trail. It then falls to the ground with a slight noise, rises from it, and suddenly disappears at the moment that Marthe gets up."

In spite of one or two odd observations of this nature made with Eusapia and Marthe Béraud by Richet and others, the development of the ectoplasm theory did not progress satisfactorily until Schrenck-Notzing, continuing and complementing the work of Mme. Bisson, pursued his investigations with the same medium, Marthe Béraud, who was now known as Eva C. This research was undertaken before Crawford's work with the Goligher circle, but the two investigations are quite independent, Crawford having set out to unravel the mechanical mysteries of telekinesis, while Schrenck-Notzing set out to study the genesis of materializations.

The conditions under which Schrenck-Notzing experimented were designed to eliminate all possible modes of fraud, whether due to accomplices or to the surreptitious concealment or use of objects to represent phantom forms. For this purpose, séances were held at various places, with and without outside persons, and the séance room was carefully inspected before and after each séance. Eva C. had no access to the séance room, except during the séance, while she was under observation. She herself was carefully examined all over her person, including all the natural orifices, before and after séances; and she was dressed in a single special black garment, which was then sewed down the back, before entering the séance room. In this way the possibility of the concealment of materials was reduced so that the only place unaccounted for was her stomach. As a theory of regurgitation was advanced, by which she was accused of swallowing muslin and other materials and then bringing them up in the séance and using them to simulate faces, etc., this last refuge had to be eliminated. Schrenck-Notzing had no difficulty in showing that Eva C. had not the physical formation characteristic of regurgitators; that she never brought up the contents of the stomach, gastric juices, etc., when the ectoplasm emerged from her mouth; that when given an emetic after a séance at which materializations had been produced the contents of the stomach were perfectly normal; and that when he made her eat fruit which would stain anything in the stomach the materializations were nevertheless uncoloured. Of course, the regurgitation hypothesis was in any case quite absurd and inadequate, for no one could bring up selectively a chosen portion of what is in the stomach, nor could they prevent the gastric juices from attacking a material like paper or fabric, nor could they cause it to evolve and form itself under observation, nor could they make it disappear instantaneously. Moreover, even when Eva's head was enclosed in a veil, the materialization came through the veil and disappeared back again through it, and was successfully photographed on the outside of the veil.

The only other source of fraud was the possibility of an accomplice. Mme. Bisson, who had adopted and trained Eva, is the only person who can be suspected in this connection, because she was always present during the séances. But at any rate on one occasion she herself was searched as thoroughly as the medium, and yet the phenomena occurred as usual.

Schrenck-Notzing worked always in good red light, which enabled him to observe well, and which he gradually increased until the medium could stand 100 candle-power. Moreover, he gradually educated Eva during his four years' research, training her to do without the customary spiritualistic rituals, such as the formation of a chain, singing of hymns, talking to the phantoms, etc., all of which ritual is conducive to mal-observation, and consequently renders fraud more easy. Finally, in view of the importance of exact records of the progress of a séance and of the necessity for exact observation, he dictated notes of the course of events during the séance, and continually checked his visual impressions by photography, using several cameras, including a stereoscopic one, simultaneously.

As a result of this laborious and ingeniously conducted research Schrenck-Notzing demonstrated conclusively that Eva was able, during her trance, to disengage from her body a substance, known as ectoplasm, which was able spontaneously to move, grow, assume various forms, and retreat back into the medium's body. The extreme rapidity of this recession into the medium, especially when some shock, such as an unexpected magnesium flash is given, is remarkable and accounts for the peculiar and repellent nature of some of the photographs; for many of these reveal faces or heads in which various distortions and disintegrations have occurred, so that they resemble closely the effects obtained by warming a photograph until some of the gelatine melts.

Dr. G. Geley continued the work of Schrenck-Notzing with the same medium, and his observations entirely confirm the main points of the German investigator's work. Summarizing these results, we may say that the place of origin of the ectoplasm may be almost any point on the medium's body; although in particular the mouth and other mucous surfaces are the most usual with Eva C. Dr. Crawford, on the other hand, traced the " psychic rods " which emerged from the medium's ankles, back to the thighs and loins. Geley also observed the ectoplasm appearing as luminous patches on the left side of the medium, from the top of her head, and from her finger-tips.

According to Crawford, the psychic rods were mainly gaseous, and only the free end appeared hard and capable of organization. Geley notes that the ectoplasm is very variable in appearance, being sometimes vaporous, sometimes a plastic paste, sometimes a bundle of fine threads, or a membrane with swellings or fringes, or a fine fabric-like tissue. It may be white (the most frequently observed colour, probably because it is naturally the most visible), grey or black in colour ; and it may even be luminous, as if phosphorescent. Its visibility may wax or wane, and to the touch it may feel soft, elastic, fibrous or hard. It has the power of self-locomotion, and moves generally with a slow reptilian movement, though it is capable of moving with extreme rapidity. It is capable of both evolution and involution, and is thus a living substance. It is extremely doubtful whether it ever, even in its most perfect formations, actually loses contact with the medium and pursues an independent life, even momentarily, though such a supposition must be borne in mind as being a possibility. The attempts made by Schrenck-Notzing to obtain a separate portion of ectoplasm and analyse it did not lead to much, the only substances obtained being fragments of human skin, saliva, fat globules, mucous and food residues, all of which are probably extraneous matter picked up by the structure in its passage from the body. Nevertheless, he reports that another experimenter, L. (Lebiedezinsky?), succeeded in 1916 in obtaining a small fragment of ectoplasm (from Stanislawa P.) in a sterilized porcelain receptacle. This fragment had a diameter 1 cm. and thickness $\frac{1}{2}$ cm., and weighed 0·101 grams. Divided into two portions, one being analysed at a bacteriological laboratory in Warsaw, the other at a bio-chemical institute in Munich, it was found to be albuminous, to contain a large number of leucocytes, and to resemble lymph and chyle without being identical with them. It seems hardly likely that in the end the ectoplasm will turn out to be anything more than a slight modification of the substances composing the human body; that is to say, any chemically-analysable material associated with the materialized forms is probably material with which we are already familiar, such as protoplasm, for example. The peculiar properties of the ectoplasm, like the peculiar properties of protoplasm, are seemingly due to the vital force which directs it, and this escapes analysis.

The following account by Geley (p. 205) gives a good idea of the development of a materialization :

Séance : January 11, 1918 ; 5 p.m.

Present : Mme. Bisson, Dr. Geley, Mme. de Vesme, M. le Cour.

Control : Dr. Geley, left hand ; Mme. Bisson, right hand. Strong, red light.

" Put to sleep, she rapidly falls into a trance, and the phenomenon occurs almost at once. It develops entirely under my eyes.

" Eva's two hands were well in sight on her knees. Between the right and left thumbs, which were touching, a membrane forms, joining them. . . . Eva slowly and regularly draws her two hands apart.

" The membrane stretches and elongates, just as a
rubber skin joining the thumbs would do. But an
important point, and the reverse of what a rubber
membrane would do—this ectoplasmic membrane
thickens and broadens at the same time that it lengthens.
As far as I know, there is no means of fraudulently
imitating such a phenomenon. . . . (Later) I see, in the
middle of the ectoplasmic mass, two fingers appearing.
These two fingers, an index and middle finger, are well
formed and have nails. Anatomically they are perfect ;
their colour is rather dark. I touch them curiously.
They are colder than normal. They are living fingers,
and make movements of bending and stretching out.
While I observe them, and without any apparent reason,
I see them suddenly, in a space of a moment, melt and
vanish. Total duration of this phenomenon—15 minutes."

We have already seen, when studying telekinesis, that
a medium could extrude temporarily some of the
material of the body, as, for example, when Eusapia or
Miss Goligher diminished their weight on request.
Crawford found experimentally that when the " structures " were out the volume of the medium's thighs
diminished, returning to normal when the ectoplasm
returned. It thus appears that the ectoplasm is largely,
if not wholly, composed of matter which is in normal
flesh, though this matter appears to be temporarily
disaggregated and reorganized in new ways. We ought
then to find that a partial dematerialization of the
medium always occurs when a materialized phantom is
formed. No doubt the quantity of matter required to
build up an ectoplasmic figure is usually small, as only
parts of the latter need be at all solidly built—but
Katie King must have taken an enormous proportion
of Miss Cook, and yet there is no hint that the latter was
observed to diminish in bulk.

M. Aksakoff[3] declared on one occasion that Mme.

---

[3] I have not yet been able to read his account of this case, which
was published in 1896.

D'Espérance was dematerialized while the spirit form was produced. Richet does not seem to credit this instance, but he nevertheless calls attention to one of his own photographs of Bien Boa and Marthe Béraud, which shows that the medium's left sleeve seems to be quite empty (page 508).

In spite of the value of the photographs of materializations obtained by Schrenck-Notzing and others, it is obviously desirable to have other records and objective proofs of the reality of such things. Accordingly, much trouble has been expended in the direction of obtaining direct moulds of ectoplasmic hands, and indeed in getting moulds which are objective proofs in themselves, apart from any testimony as to the circumstances in which they were made. This latter is rather an exacting ideal, but it has practically been obtained by Richet and Geley. The séances for these experiments were held at the " Institut Métapsychique " in Paris, the medium being F. Kluski, and the controllers Geley and Richet, who held the medium's hands during the proceedings. A bath of melted paraffin was placed nearby, and the room was only dimly lighted with a red lamp. After a certain time had elapsed a hand was materialized, dipped itself in the paraffin, allowed the wax to set, disengaged itself by dematerializing, and the glove was thus left as a permanent record. The actual operation, from start to finish, only took a minute or so, and during the whole process the medium was passive and had his hands securely held.

Geley devotes considerable space to a description of the moulds, and gives photographs of them, and I will summarize his chief points :

(a) The wax gloves themselves are exceedingly thin, being no more than one millimetre in thickness. This is important, because it is impossible to produce such a glove by dipping one's hand in the wax, removing it, cutting the glove and carefully disengaging the hand, and then melting the cut edges together. Such a process requires a much thicker layer of wax, or else it will break.

(*b*) The model hands were often produced of some demanded shape or size, so as to eliminate the production of previously-prepared gloves (although this was also prevented by the control).

(*c*) The gloves were often adult in form and in the detail of the lines of the skin, and yet so reduced in size as to seem to be moulds of an infant's hand.

(*d*) The gloves were frequently made with the fingers bent down, to demonstrate that no solid object, such as a real hand or a model, could have been used, since such a rigid object could not be withdrawn.

(*e*) Moreover, when submitted to expert moulders, the gloves were certified to be first impressions of a living hand, the fineness of detail in the markings being beyond that obtainable in any other way.

(*f*) Dr. Geley obtained expert opinion from M. Bayle, chief of the Finger-print Department of the Préfecture de Police that some of the moulds were not made by the medium's hands.

(*g*) Richet and Geley demonstrated that the moulds were actually made during the séance and with the paraffin provided, by the device of introducing surreptitiously various colouring matters, the most convenient being Cholesterin, which gives a violet colour when sulphuric acid is added.

(*h*) The process of making a model hand in some fusible material, and then, having dipped it in wax, dissolving away the contents of the glove so formed is a mode of fraud excluded for a variety of reasons :

(1) It requires a very lengthy period of time to dissolve the substance.

(2) A pail of water for the purpose is necessary.

Now Geley had no pail of water there, and the mould was produced in a minute or so ; yet it was made with his own identifiable wax, and therefore this process could not apply, even had Kluski been free to move his hands. Moreover,

(3) Kluski's gloves were demonstrably direct moulds, not made from an intermediary cast, because the markings of veins, lines, etc., were extremely fine.

From a survey of the main points of this investigation, we are able to realize how nearly the ideal has been approached of producing by psychic means some permanent effect which cannot be imitated, under any conditions, by normal means. These Kluski gloves are almost of this ideal character.

BIBLIOGRAPHY

CROOKES. Researches into the Phenomena of Spiritualism (Cheap Reprint—" The Two Worlds Publishing Co.," 1926).

RICHET. Thirty Years of Psychic Research.

SCHRENCK-NOTZING. Phenomena of Materialization.

G. GELEY. Ectoplasmie et Clairvoyance.

SCHRENCK-NOTZING. Phénomènes Physiques de la Médiumnité.

CHAPTER SIX

IDEOPLASTICITY[1]

THE forms of the ectoplasmic structures vary greatly, and provide the materials for an interesting study. Sometimes a simple cloud appears, and condenses till gradually a face or hand is seen evolving in it ; at other times, the head or hand appears suddenly, fully developed. Often, and apparently generally with Eva, the product resembled a two-dimensional picture rather than a solid model. The simultaneous photographs taken from various angles frequently showed that the materialized head, though beautifully formed and modelled on the side facing the observer, was practically blank at the back, and indeed often almost lacked any thickness at all ; and when the images were fairly solid they were only modelled in parts, and those portions which were concealed remained amorphous. The frequent draperies, veils, turbans, etc., worn by materialized spirits would thus appear, as Geley suggests, to be simply rough easy devices for concealing gaps and defects in the phantom forms, and for enabling mediums to economize their sculptural efforts.

A highly interesting point about the séances with Eva is that the evolution and growth of the structures could often be seen, so that the phenomenon carried its own proof of genuineness—since the concealment of dummy hands or pictured heads, either by the medium or by an accomplice, would be quite inadequate to simulate a

[1] The substance of this chapter appeared in *The Occult Review* for January 1929.

progressively evolving form. Not only did the form evolve in complexity of structure, but it also often grew or diminished in size, while remaining of the same proportions, and this sometimes at the request of the investigators.

The apparently two-dimensional and picture-like faces produced by Eva were an unexpected, and at first disconcerting result, and certain features of them soon seemed to point conclusively to fraud. Some of the photographs, for example, showed recognizable likenesses to pictures of President Wilson, Poincaré, the King of Bulgaria and other personages, which had previously appeared in the French illustrated press. Most damning was one which shewed a piece of paper, with creases, and the printed inscription *LE MIRO*. It was obvious to sceptics that Eva had simply cut out a piece of *Le Miroire*, concealed it, and then produced it as a piece of ectoplasm during the séance. The crudity of such a fraud is certainly staggering, but the critics of psychic research will always seize any loophole that is offered and make their assertions of fraud without investigating facts to see whether the supposed procedure conforms to them. Schrenck-Notzing knew that Eva could neither conceal such cuttings, nor rig them up unobserved, nor, had she done so, succeed in making such things at all convincing under the conditions of the séance. Moreover, he knew that these photographs only showed an instantaneous phase of a materialization which actually evolved and grew. In order to confute his critics, however, he set up various photographs and pictures from illustrated papers, draped them suitably with muslin, etc., to imitate the materializations, and photographed them under exactly the same séance conditions ; the results were not in the least comparable with his photographs of Eva's productions, and they shewed none of the shadows which even the flattest of Eva's materialized heads shewed.

The picture-like materializations, however, are highly

instructive and give one the clue to a general theory
which applies to the whole field of psychic science :
they must be interpreted as being thought-images in the
mind (not necessarily the consciousness) of the medium
which have been temporarily objectified and incarnated.
Given that the medium extrudes ectoplasm, it is obvious
that she wishes to do or make something with it, and that
it will thus be organized and moulded by some idea in
her mind.　Miss Goligher, influenced doubtless by the
mechanical interests of Dr. Crawford, evolved rods and
levers, but most mediums, who are, as a rule, pious
spiritualists with no particular scientific interests and
theories, wish to materialize spirits, or at least hands
and faces which they and their friends may take to be
genuine incarnations of some departed soul.　Probably,
indeed, the ectoplasm itself is inherently disposed to take
on a definitely human shape, although two powerful
mediums, Guzig and Kluski, have frequently produced
materializations of animals—an eagle, a squirrel and a
dog, for example.　With Eva C. in her early spiritualistic days (when she was Marthe Béraud) the most
important form was an Arab known as Bien Boa.　His
appearance has been well described by Richet, who
managed to prove that the materialization was complete
enough to have normal respiration.　He says (p. 505) :

" The materializations produced were very complete.
The phantom of Bien Boa appeared five or six times
under satisfactory conditions in the sense that he could
not be Marthe masquerading in a helmet and sheet.
Marthe would have had not only to bring but also to
conceal afterwards the helmet, the sheet and the bur-
nous.　Also Marthe and the phantom were both seen at
the same time.　To pretend that Bien Boa was a doll is
more absurd still ; he walked and moved, his eyes could
be seen looking round, and when he tried to speak his
lips moved.

" He seemed so much alive that, as we could hear his
breathing, I took a flask of baryta water to see if his

breath would show carbon dioxide. The experiment succeeded. I did not lose sight of the flask from the moment I put it into the hands of Bien Boa, who seemed to float in the air on the left of the curtain at a height greater than Marthe could have been if standing up. While he blew into the tube the bubbling could be heard, and then I asked Delanne, ' Do you see Marthe ?' He said, ' I can see Marthe completely.' Aischa was far off, and could be seen clearly, asleep in the other corner of the cabinet. I could see myself the form of Marthe sitting in her chair, though I could not see her head and her right shoulder."

" However striking this was, another experiment seems to me even more evidential : Everything being arranged as usual (except that Mlle. X., being indisposed, was absent), after a long wait I saw close to me, in front of the curtain which had not moved, a white vapour, hardly sixteen inches distant. It was like a white veil or handkerchief on the floor. This rose and became spherical. Soon it was a head just above the floor ; it rose up still more, enlarged, and grew into a human form, a short bearded man dressed in a turban and white mantle, who moved, limping slightly, from right to left in front of the curtain. On coming close to General Noel, he sank down abruptly to the floor with a clicking noise like a falling skeleton, flattening out in front of the curtain. Three or four minutes later, close to the General, not to me, he reappeared, rising in a straight line from the floor, born from the floor, so to speak, and falling back to it with the same clicking noise.

"The only un-metapsychic explanation possible seemed to be a trap-door opening and shutting, but there was no trap-door, as I verified next morning, and as was attested by the architect."

Generally speaking, spiritualistic mediums will endeavour to produce materializations of particular deceased persons in whom their clients are interested ; for their clients visit them with the hope of speaking to or seeing some departed dear one. But as this feat is usually not at all easy (unless the client is satisfied with a very rough likeness) it is perhaps more common for them to materialize one or two stock figures who are supposed to be " guides " of the medium, and who act as intermediaries between him and the various spirits invoked by the client ; this practice of having a guide or " control " obviously saving the medium a vast deal of trouble, and serving to cover up deficiencies in his formation.

Sometimes we are able to see clearly the influence of suggestion on the form of the materialization ; for example, on December 6th, 1919, a long conversation had been held in front of the young medium Willy Schneider, the subject of which was the idea of psychic threads, lines of force, etc. The same evening a séance was held, and for the first time the ectoplasm was observed in a thread-like form. Similarly, on January 17th, 1913, Schrenck-Notzing showed Stanislawa P. a photograph of Eva C. in which two ectoplasmic fingers were placed on her hair ; the same evening Stanislawa copied the effect, materializing two fingers on her hair during the séance.

Under the influence of her protectress, Mme. Bisson, Eva later produced a simulacrum of the late M. Bisson, but when she came in contact with the more scientific and anti-spiritistic mind of Schrenck-Notzing, she produced simulacra of a less spiritualistic genre ; for example, heads which she did not claim to represent anybody in particular, or fairly close imitations of published photographs of celebrities.

We thus reach the important conclusion that all the materializations of the séance room are objective expressions or representations of ideas in the mind of the medium, who works with ectoplasm as a sculptor does with clay. This is the phenomenon of *ideoplasticity*, the physical counterpart of the mental phenomena of dissociation and the assumption of fictitious or new personalities. One might expect much light to be thrown on the subject by the methodical psycho-analysis of a good materializing medium, though I do not know that this has yet been done. One could expect interesting connections to be established between the forms and actions of the phantoms and the unconscious desires and complexes of the medium, for physical mediumship involves a marked degree of mental dissociation and a hypnoidal trance state, as well as a certain physical dissociation and the creation of a partially independent organism. It is, so to speak, a form of wish-fulfilment one stage nearer to reality than is reached in phantasy and dream.

Dr. Geley has developed the theory of Ideoplasticity at some length in his book *From the Unconscious to the Conscious*, and has shown its importance in relation to the field of normal biology. It would take us too far to go into all the aspects of this theme, that the essential feature of all living organisms is not any mere synthesis of parts, but the operation of a central directing mind force, or *Psycho-Dynamism* (to use Geley's technical term, which is rather more general than the word *Idea*). But it is very germane to our subject to mention the more numerous cases where an idea (involving probably volition, emotional feeling, and intellectual representation) has a notable effect on the body, actually modifying its structure and functions. Of course, we all are familiar with some simple cases, as, for example, the temporary flow of blood to the cheeks, or of tears, which accompany the feelings of shame or sorrow, or the obvious physical symptoms of anger, fear, etc. Much more striking are the examples drawn from psychiatric literature—for instance, the mechanism of symptom formation in hysteria, and the almost magical curative power of hypnotic suggestion. The physical action of an idea is neatly illustrated in an experiment by Delboeuf.[2] He hypnotized a subject, suggested to her

[2] See M. Bramwell, *Hypnotism*, p. 84.

that her right arm was insensible to pain, and then burnt each arm with a red-hot iron, making identical burns. She felt the pain in her left arm only. Both burns were dressed similarly, and during the ensuing twenty-four hours the burn on the left arm was painful, and developed a large blister ; in the right arm there was no pain, and no inflammation, but only the plain scar, the exact size of the iron as applied. Clearly then, the pain, the inflammation, and blistering in the one arm were secondary results of the initial burning process, produced through the mediate operation of the mind of the patient ; being unaware of any initial pain in the right arm, however, the mind did not interfere with the normal routine of cell-life on that side.

More striking still, perhaps, though also more complicated, are the cases of stigmatization. A devout nun, practising austerities and meditating intently on the Passion of Christ, will sometimes experience a trance, almost always accompanied by visual hallucinations in which Jesus is seen, which results in the appearance of the crucifixion marks in their appropriate places. As a rule these wounds seem to bleed every Friday, for some time, and to heal up in the week. Such cases are fairly numerous,[3] and indubitably illustrate the power of a strongly visualized idea to realize itself by modification of the living tissue. In all these cases we find, according to H. Thurston, a bad medical history, together with a strong concentration on the wounds of the Passion, often continued over a long period before the actual vision with stigmatization occurs.

As an illustration of what is typical in these cases of stigmatization I will briefly summarize the story of Therese Neumann of Konnersreuth, Bavaria. I take the facts from Herr Jaschke's account, given in *Psychic Science* for July 1929.

Therese Neumann was born in 1898, the child of a

---

[3] See a paper by Rev. H. Thurston (P.S.P.R., Part 83), who says he has studied the accounts of sixty cases.

tailor who owned a small farm. Up to the age of twenty she was strong and healthy, doing heavy work at home on the farm, and later as a servant. At that age, however, a fire occurred, and she apparently strained herself assisting to put it out, and collapsed with a stabbing pain in the back. Spinal paralysis set in, and she was soon sent back from hospital as incurable. Severe attacks followed, then partial and finally complete blindness. Contraction of the muscles forced her left foot up under her right thigh, and sores appeared on her back. At the end of 1922 she practically ceased to take nourishment, owing to ulceration in the throat. In this almost hopeless condition of invalidism she suddenly, in April 1923, recovered her sight, and in May 1925, after a vision, she managed to raise herself and walk with assistance. In September the vision recurred and she was completely cured.

Now in November 1925 she fell ill, of acute appendicitis, according to the doctor. However, praying to St. Theresa, she again saw the vision and was immediately cured. In February 1926 she again fell ill, with influenza. During this illness she had a vision of Christ on the Mount of Olives and received a stabbing pain in the left side, from which flowed blood. Again, next week, on Thursday night, another vision of Christ crucified, accompanied by blood from the wound, which healed next day. This was repeated on the three next Thursdays, and the wound and bleeding grew more severe on the Good Friday which followed. At the same time blood came from the eyes, and wounds appeared in the hands and feet. Since May 1926 these latter have ceased to bleed, but have deepened through the hands and feet. Every Friday the wounds of the side and head bleed, and visions of the Passion of Jesus are seen. It is stated that from 1923 to 1926 Therese only took liquid nourishment, and that from Christmas 1926 even that ceased, and that she has existed since then (i.e. to July 1929) on literally nothing, except her daily Holy Communion. Nevertheless, every Friday she loses a quantity of blood, and her weight remains approximately constant at 110 lb. [4]

In the above case of Therese Neumann we may note that although the child was apparently quite robust until the age of twenty, yet as a result of shock and strain produced by the fire she suddenly developed an altogether abnormally bad pathological state of spinal paralysis, blindness, temporary deafness, ulceration, etc. Secondly, she was a devout Roman Catholic, and at the age of sixteen had developed a great reverence for St. Theresa, her patron saint. We have therefore the typical conditions of a bad medical history and intense religious preoccupation prior to the stigmatization.

These two examples show us that even a highly stable organism like the physical body is yet, in spite of the inertia of its heredity and its habits, amenable under somewhat exceptional circumstances to quite drastic modifications at the instance of a pure idea; it is, in fact, essentially *ideoplastic*. And when we come to the semi-material amorphous living ectoplasm it is obvious that this ideoplasticity is far more complete. The ectoplasm may be said to have an inherent tendency to organization, but it is of no mechanical kind; its propensity is to take any form which may be dictated or imagined by the medium. Probably, in fact, the extrusion of ectoplasm and its " materialization " into phantom forms such as Bien Boa, or Katie King, represent a physical realization of desires, phantasies, day-dreams which are in the medium's subconscious mind. The analogy with psychological dissociation and with wish-fulfilment, day-dreams, and the accompanying pseudo-personalities and spirit-controls, enable us to interpret the whole in terms of Life rather than in terms of Death. That the phantasy which finds temporary physical expression, the wish which is dramatically or symbolic-

[4] See also *The Story of Therese Neumann*, by Father Pacificus (Burns and Oates).

ally fulfilled with all the reality of a dream, is sometimes not specifically the medium's, but may be primarily the sitter's, does not in the least invalidate the interpretation. There is reason to believe that the sitter often contributes not only some of the psychological material of the drama, but also some of the ectoplasmic material which builds up the actors.

It may perhaps be objected against the theory of Ideoplasticity in its widest applications that it implies the existence of mind, or of a subconscious psychical entity, apart from any cerebral basis. Those who hold that thought is secreted by the brain, and those who adopt the theory of Psycho-physical parallelism, will argue that the development of conscious intelligence goes *pari passu* with the development of the brain, and declines with the decline of the body ; that all thought is invariably accompanied by corresponding activity in the brain cells and nerves ; and that an injury to the brain damages the psychic processes correspondingly. In short, they say that no psychological activity can occur without an antecedent or a simultaneous activity of the brain.

Against this view, however, we have the facts relating to subconscious thought in general. In the first place, subconscious thinking proceeds apparently without effort ; that is to say, it is not noticeably fatiguing, whereas conscious thought produces fatigue quite obviously. In the second place, subconscious thought bears no kind of qualitative relationship with cerebral development ; the examples of the calculating boy and the musical prodigy make this clear.

Finally, however, there are certain medical cases which show that conscious psychic life may proceed normally even when portions of the brain which are usually considered essential have been removed, or are completely septic. Bergson's studies of Aphasia led him to deny that memories were stored in the brain, as physical traces or " neurograms " ; and if the materialistic view does not hold for memory it certainly does not apply to other psychological processes. Moreover, some interesting cases are quoted by Flammarion (*Before Death*, p. 38) which undermine any physiological theory of thought. " My learned friend, E. Perrier, presented to the Academy of Sciences, in his lecture of December 22nd, 1913, an observation of Dr. Robinson's concerning a man who had lived for nearly a year with almost no suffering and with no apparent mental trouble, with a brain that was nearly reduced to a pulp, and was no longer anything but a vast purulent abscess. On March 24th, 1917, at the Academy of Sciences, Dr. Guépin showed, through an operation on a wounded soldier, that the partial ablation of the brain does not prevent manifestations of intelligence. Other examples might be cited. At times there remain only very slight portions ; the mind makes use of what it can."

The last sentence expresses the correct attitude for us to adopt towards this problem. The body is the instrument of the soul ; in particular the brain is the instrument which is used by the mind. It is not the machine which creates mental phenomena, but the machine which is driven by psychological forces.

BIBLIOGRAPHY

GELEY. From the Unconscious to the Conscious.
SCHRENCK-NOTZING. Phénomènes Physiques de la Médiumnité.
RICHET. Thirty Years of Psychical Research.
FLAMMARION. Before Death.
Psychic Science Quarterly. July 1929.
REV. THURSTON. Paper on Stigmatization, P.S.P.R., Part 83.

CHAPTER SEVEN

MEDIUMSHIP AND ITS INVESTIGATION

1

IT is to be remarked that one essential feature of Mediumship appears to consist of a mental, and sometimes also a physical, dissociation. Every instance of Cryptæsthesia[1] involves the activity of a subconscious part of the mind, which seems to escape, momentarily at any rate, from that subservience to the " Here-Now " which characterizes a well-knit waking personality. In the majority of cases when any considerable degree of cryptæsthesia is shown, the normal personality of the medium is definitely obliterated, and either a manifestly secondary personality takes its place, or else a " control " or " communicator " claiming to be a genuine spirit, but which in our opinion is again really a secondary personality. So also every act of telekinesis, materialization, or other physical phenomenon involves the extrusion of ectoplasm from the medium's body, often, if not always, with the purpose of giving material form and body to the secondary personality or to ideas which it wishes to realize.

It is a natural consequence of this fundamental fact that the best phenomena of mediumship should take place when the medium is entranced, and that minor effects should require at least a state of sleep, or " absence," in which the medium's attention is not fully held by the distractions of the outside world. Taking it by and large we may say that the strength of the phenomena is proportional to the degree of abstraction from the external world. Hence the universal

[1] i.e. acquirement of knowledge by supernormal means.

practice amongst mediums of either putting themselves into a state of trance, or having themselves hypnotized by someone else, or again of achieving a suitable state of semi-trance or " absence " by rituals such as crystal-gazing, which, by helping them to become lost to the outside world, tend to set free the subconscious faculties.

Since the disposition towards mental dissociation, as shown for example in hysteria and insanity, is hereditary we find that mediumship itself often appears in several members of one family. As examples we may mention that D. D. Home's mother was clairvoyant ; that Helen Smith's mother and grandmother both had mediumistic faculties ; that all the members of the Goligher family seem to be mediums in lesser degree, while Kathleen acts as the primary medium. Again, Ossowiecki's grand-mother was noted for her clairvoyance, and his mother and one brother are lesser mediums. The father of the well-known French medium, Madame Fraya, gave Dr. Geley one of his best cases of auto-premonition of death ; Kluski's father and paternal uncle were definitely medium-istic ; and two of the best-known modern ectoplasmic mediums, Willy and Rudi Schneider, are brothers.

A further illustration of the connection between psychic effects and dissociation is given by the many instances when a mental trauma or shock produces or greatly augments mediumistic powers. No doubt many of the phenomena often alleged to accompany death, particularly a violent death, are instances of this sort ; but we see the connection more certainly in the life histories of several well-known mediums. The wonderful clairvoyant powers of Mrs. Piper developed after a sudden fright and two surgical operations ; Eusapia Palladino was dropped in her infancy, with the result that a hole was made in her skull, and from this hole cold breezes were observed to come during her séances —presumably the ectoplasm issuing thence. More-over she lost both her parents in early childhood, under terrifying circumstances, her father being murdered

by brigands. In the case of the famous Ossowiecki
mediumistic powers of a lesser sort showed themselves
in early childhood, but they were vastly augmented by
a terrible experience when, after six months' confine-
ment in a Bolshevik prison under the worst conditions,
he was condemned to death and led out to the scaffold,
only to be reprieved at the last minute. His experience
is exactly parallel to that of Dostoevsky (described by
him in *The Idiot*), only that the latter suffered as a
result from epilepsy, an obscure disease dependent on
mental dissociation, of which he had previously shown
signs, but which now was very considerably augmented.
Finally we may condense an account of the early history
of Stanislawa Tomczyk, given by Schrenck-Notzing.

At the age of twenty Stanislawa was mixed up in a
crowd of rioters, surrounded by soldiers, and (unjustly)
arrested and put in prison for ten days. The shock of
all this produced symptoms of hysteria, and at the same
time various telekinetic phenomena occurred in her
presence—the doctor's inkpot, for example, moved itself
about when he wrote out a prescription for her. After
her release these things attracted the notice of local
spiritualists, who initiated her into séances and thus
directed and developed her mediumship. After a while,
as she appeared to have remarkable powers, she was
carefully studied first by Ochorowicz and later by
Schrenck-Notzing. Hers is a clear instance of the
appearance of psychic powers, together with hysterical
symptoms, as a consequence of mental dissociation.
Moreover her personality is definitely split into three
recurrent sections : namely, the ordinary waking Stanislawa ; the " Stasia " of the trance state, who is herself
at the age of ten years, and simply represents a regression to an earlier time which is entirely characteristic
of some forms of hysteria ; and finally the " Little
Stasia " which she believes to be the double of " Stasia,"
and to which is attributed all the phenomena of the
séances. " Little Stasia " is an invention, a spirit

invoked to account for the happenings, or a name given
to a centre of personality of which Stanislawa is unconscious. " Stasia " on the other hand is more than a
figment of imagination ; for Stanislawa when entranced
acts and speaks like a little child of ten. " Stasia,"
then, is a more substantial secondary personality,
analogous to Miss Beauchamp's " Sally," with the
difference that whereas Sally was adult, Stasia is
definitely a regression to a juvenile stage.

2

The general personal character of mediums, neglecting
the inevitable exceptions (many of which, however, are
more apparent than real), is one of instability, as indeed
might be deduced from the considerations given above.
The average medium has not a fixed and well-knit
personality, such as one expects in a capable business
man or a naval officer, but is apt to be sensitive,
capricious, unaccountable, moody, irrational, and often
sentimental. Most mediums are gifted with more
sympathy and altruism than are usual in more stable
types, and they are often generous of their time and
energy (*vital* energy, be it observed) to an extent that
would amaze the public if it were generally known.
There are of course mercenary souls among them,
though probably few among those with any considerable
gifts, but in general they really believe that they receive
their gifts from God, and that they are in the service of
a higher power and have a mission in life to help others ;
just as priests, nurses, and doctors do, not entirely
without material reward, but certainly not in the spirit
of commercial enterprise which makes money the
primary and service the secondary consideration.
Although I do not believe in the validity of their intellectual doctrines, I must wholeheartedly admit that
spiritualists have an ethical code which tends to promote various human virtues among its adherents. The

best mediums have been admired and loved for their
moral character and their personal charm by a wide and
very varied circle of friends, and though it is of course
obvious that in any walk of life there are outstanding
personalities who are morally superior to the average, I
think we may recognize certain desirable qualities
amongst mediums which are characteristic of them,
and also of some imaginative artists and some religious
types, but not specially characteristic of others ; sympathy and unselfishness being prominent.

As an example of a quite typical mediumistic disposition we may take Willy Schneider, who has been studied
carefully by Schrenck-Notzing. We are thus dealing with
a critical and competent account, instead of the usual
biographical eulogy written by admiring friends or relatives. Schrenck-Notzing states that Willy shows no
important physical anomaly or signs of degeneration,
no motor or sensory troubles, and has a mental development normal for his age and social status. His memory
is good, his character gentle, docile, and modest, but
his will-power is rather feeble and he is easily influenced.
His moods are unstable, changing quickly from gaiety
and carelessness to pessimism and despondency. He
has a fondness for masquerades and dancing as well as
a love of Nature. His imagination is vivid, but he has
little capacity for abstract thought. He shows marked
sympathies and antipathies towards certain people, and
is capricious in temper. Without much power of self-
discipline he is yet obstinate, and is extravagant and
fond of an easy life. At times he is self-willed, and also
given to inexact statements and trivial falsehoods which
he seems at the time to believe to be true ; but if one
corrects him and convicts him of error a regular sentimental " scene " with tears and repentance will follow.

Schrenck-Notzing states that if there is a prolonged
gap of say four to six days between the séances, Willy
gets into a depressed, morose mood and is evidently in
a state of mental tension. The séances appear to relieve

this tension and put him again into a cheerful and friendly mood. As with Eusapia Palladino and Eva C., there appears to be an organic need for ectoplasmic extrusion, an internal force which, if inhibited for long, causes crises and mental disturbances. Finally, Willy is artistically inclined, having a natural aptitude for music, and also for comic acting and mimicry. He has also an acute moral and religious sense. The disposition to hysteria is, as Schrenck-Notzing points out, quite noticeable in all the above traits, but as Willy has fortunately not suffered any particular shocks, but has led a quite comfortable and sheltered life, it has remained merely a disposition and has not developed into an actual malady.

3

It is characteristic of unstable persons that they are very suggestible, and in dissociated states, such as hypnosis or trance, this suggestibility is very greatly enhanced. Hence arises one of the chief difficulties which complicate the study of metapsychic phenomena, a difficulty always present in ordinary experimental psychology, but raised to the nth power when we deal with the supernormal. The results of any experiment of this sort are apt to be determined very largely by the ideas, whether subconscious or conscious, of the medium and of the sitters, be they ordinary consultants or scientific inquirers ; and it is extraordinarily hard to disentangle the essentials which properly belong to the phenomenon from the accretions which are supplied by conscious or unconscious suggestion. It is a truism that if an investigator has any kind of a theory the medium will produce phenomena which tend to confirm it. The mechanical mind of Crawford conceived of an explanation of telekinesis in terms of levers, and the Goligher circle produced levers ; under the influence of a biologist they would probably have materialized hands instead. De Rochas, and many early researchers, strongly believed in the hypothesis of an astral body, and they found good evidence for their theory because the mediums accepted the suggestion. In the same way the popular belief in ghosts, spirits, and so on is a strong enough suggestion to create the habit, almost universal amongst mediums, of producing hands, faces, forms, and voices of spirits. All this is consequent upon the essentially ideoplastic nature of ectoplasm and the extreme suggestibility of the medium.

In the realm of mental phenomena we find the same thing, and it is often even more difficult to detect and discount every suggestion. To begin with, the mediums have accepted a whole network of suggestions which forms the mental environment in which they work and which limits seriously their range and versatility. The demand for darkness made by physical mediums is perhaps an instance, for some have been educated to work in the light ; but the various rituals adopted are certainly examples of suggestion. One medium will only become clairvoyant when gazing into a crystal, another when inspecting your palm, a third on telling the cards, a fourth if music is played, a fifth when computing mystic numbers, and so on. All the various rituals belonging to the old witches and magicians or the modern mediums are a tangle of suggestions derived from various superstitions or preconceptions which have crystallized into formulæ. In view of this great suggestibility it is very difficult to analyse any given communication in such a way as to expose what, if any, parts of it show supernormal action or knowledge. The art of psychic research is very largely the art of excluding, or at least of exposing, errors due to suggestion, which, be it remembered, may be telepathic as well as normal.

A second important consequence of the suggestibility of an entranced medium is the fact that any suspicion of fraud, particularly when narrowed to a definite mode of fraud, tends to create it. When Eusapia Palladino was " exposed " at Cambridge for practising various tricks (such as the substitution of her hands) Ochorowicz and others rightly blamed the experimenters, firstly for permitting it and not controlling her rigidly (which was tantamount to a suggestion that she could deceive them), and secondly for their whole attitude, which was one of suspicion that she would try to trick them and of hope that they would detect her in the act. And in the same way a hostile and sceptical attitude tends to inhibit the medium's faculty while friendly encouragement and faith will enhance it ; the medium, like the musician, responding to the suggestions coming from the audience.

The most important rule for the investigator to remember is that, while retaining complete independence of thought and, if possible, indifference to the nature of the phenomena to be produced, he should treat the medium fairly and sympathetically and maintain his faith in his ability to produce results. It is essential that the medium should be able to trust the investigator absolutely, and have no fear that the latter will go back on his word and seize an ectoplasmic structure, or make use of his trance-state to test for anæsthesia by digging a needle under his nails or by blistering his skin (as Stanley Hall did to Mrs. Piper), for without this sense of security and confidence the medium will not achieve a deep and stable state of trance, but will necessarily be disturbed and unable to produce much, if anything. In the past, scientists have subjected mediums to much brutal and callous treatment in their zeal for physiology, forgetting that their subjects were unusually sensitive human beings. Moreover it is possible to be just as callous in a purely psychological study, without any resort to physical experiments, and many clever researchers have thought to get the better of a medium by suggesting falsities, asking for news of fictitious persons, etc., and generally behaving more like a police inquisitor than a genuine inquirer after knowledge. However much this sort of thing may appeal to the detective mind it is really unscientific, and it is a procedure which is singularly futile in psychic research for the simple reason that it creates the very frauds and fabrications that it is designed to discover. A clever lawyer may make a simple witness say almost anything ; but to make a child, or a half-wit, or an hysterical patient, or a hypnotized subject, or finally, an entranced medium, say anything one need not even be clever. It would probably not be an exaggeration to say that quite half the responsibility for the frauds and misstatements committed by mediums should be borne by their investigators.

The scientist generally works on material which either is not alive or, if alive, does not demand much human response from him. Of course, a doctor is the obvious exception to this rule, and doctors are often remarkably good practical psychologists, able to handle irresponsible and impressionable people tactfully, firmly, and yet sympathetically. Now a medium almost always requires, as a fundamental condition for efficient functioning, an atmosphere of good-will, sympathy, and confidence. He is easily affected adversely by any hardness of outlook, materialism, or the rather inhuman abstractness of many great intellects. For this reason he hardly ever can produce good results under the control of a committee of investigators composed of strangers, chosen because they are celebrated as scientists, lawyers, conjurers, business men, etc. ; i.e. selected precisely for the qualities which are most antipathetic to the medium. It is therefore entirely fallacious to argue that because the results found by some such independent committee are meagre in comparison with those reported by more sympathetic observers, therefore the latter are untrustworthy and should be attributed to fraud or malobservation. The empirical fact is that the committee itself constitutes an adverse condition for the medium, in just the same manner as an audience picked from professedly unmusical people, and assembled for the set purpose of detecting errors and resisting æsthetic impressions, would constitute an adverse condition for a musician. One has only to imagine a Pachmann recital before a select committee of Philistines, one of whom times all his rests with a stop-watch, while another introduces resonators surreptitiously to entrap an unsuspected overtone, and a third stops him and insists on beginning again with the music stool two inches lower, and so forth ! How would the poor artist convince them of his ability to express anything in music ? The atmosphere of his audience would rob him of his technique of expression ; his touch and his pedalling would become clumsy and uncertain, for he depends, and the medium depends no less, on mental and spiritual conditions, and these have been tampered with.

4

Once an investigator has created the proper mental conditions which conduce to good results his next task, in experiments dealing with physical phenomena, is to achieve physical control of the medium and sitters adequate to prevent or reveal all possible modes of fraud. The procedure must necessarily differ in different cases, but in general the following precautions should be taken for rigorous work.

(1) The medium should, if possible, be without any friends who might be deemed accomplices. This means in effect that the investigator and his companions who form the circle must previously have so gained the medium's confidence that they have become in fact friends.

(2) Neither the medium nor any unauthorized person should be able to have access to the séance room in between the séances. This is best achieved in the investigator's house, or in special institutions.

(3) The medium should be stripped, examined, and

re-clothed in specially provided garments before the séance, and again examined directly after it.

(4) In telekinetic experiments the objects to be displaced may be put inside a cage of wire gauze ; or some equivalent device used to exclude normal action.

(5) In materialization experiments the cinematograph can give the most valuable confirmatory evidence.

(6) The light should be the best that the medium can stand, and it should be gradually improved until the medium has been trained to work in a full and strong illumination. On this point there is much that might be said, for the whole subject of lighting is full of uncertainties.

Apparently the action of light may be harmful to the success of a séance in two distinct ways :

(*a*) by disturbing the trance state, and so making for timid and abortive efforts to achieve phenomena which in a more secure and deeper trance would be produced with more ease and certainty ;

(*b*) by actually disintegrating the ectoplasm, which is apparently unstable in strong light, unless it has previously organized a kind of outer skin to protect it.

Mediums always believe firmly in this latter disintegrating effect, and there is really a good deal of evidence that it is a true physical effect, and not merely based upon suggestion and fear. We know of normal biological effects of light, and we know that it does in fact hurt the lowest and most primitive forms of living substance. The embryos of all animals spend an initial period developing rapidly in darkness ; seeds germinate best in the dark ; growth generally takes place most quickly at night ; so that the idea that ectoplasm is adversely affected by strong light seems *a priori* probable. On the other hand, just as the human skin can be trained by gradual exposure to bear stronger and stronger radiation without blistering, so can the ectoplastic medium be trained to bear considerably more light than that in which he first began to work.

An empirical observation which may be of general application is that, in at any rate some cases, the ectoplasm seems less affected by what are termed " cold " lights, such as moonlight, or the phosphorescence of a Zinc Sulphide screen. I do not know if any physicist has yet made an investigation to determine precisely which wave-lengths are noxious and which are not ; one would expect the shorter ones to do more damage than the longer ones, but it has been alleged that red light is just as noxious as blue light, if of the same intensity ; its common usage being due to the fact that it enables the shutter of a camera to be left open ready for a flash-light photograph, and not due to its lack of action on the ectoplasm. [2]

Another observation bearing on the practical conduct of experiments is that the ectoplasm always emerges from a dark place ; either its initial extrusion and building up into a form takes place while the lighting is still very dim, or else it is extruded from a part of the body which is in deep shadow—commonly the back, as the medium is often seated with a cabinet or curtained space directly behind. Nevertheless, once the ectoplasm has been built up into an organized form and has got partially free from the medium's body, it can then stand a greater intensity of light, apparently because it has protected itself with an outer layer of firmer texture.

(7) A useful general principle to be applied in every kind of experimentation is the following : that if an experiment is attempted whose value depends upon the unpreparedness of the medium and circle, and it does not succeed, then it should be repeated with the addition each time of some fresh but essentially irrelevant feature (preferably quantitative) so that, while the essentials of the experiment remain unaltered, any fraudulent preparation is circumvented.

As an illustration of the need for carrying out this principle let us consider an experiment done by D'Albe

[2] See note at end of chapter.

when studying the Goligher Circle.   He put a button, a piece of rubber, and a drop of mercury into a decanter and asked the medium to remove the button by means of a psychic rod without inverting the bottle.   The drop of mercury was there in order to prevent anyone from inverting the decanter and replacing the rubber.   The experiment did not succeed.   At the next séance it was repeated with complete success ;   but D'Albe discounts this because he hints that a sitter, knowing the contents this time, might have brought with him a drop of mercury, emptied the decanter, and replaced the rubber plus his own mercury instead of the spilled drop.   Now clearly experimentation of this nature is valueless, and so are D'Albe's conclusions from it ;   for what notice can be taken of an experimenter who devises a test and when the medium passes it rules it out of court ?   The drop of mercury was only a check as long as the others did not know of its presence beforehand—although incidentally D'Albe never looked to see whether it *had* been spilled on the floor, as he did not at first think of the possibility of a sitter being clever enough to bring a drop with him. But had he realized, in all his experiments, the import- ance of this principle of varying the unessential details, he would, as a matter of normal habit, either have used oil, say, the second time, or better still, have used a weighed amount of mercury, different from the quantity first used.   The essence of this sort of experimentation is to present the fundamental and necessary features of an experiment as simply as possible to the medium and circle, and to attach one, always different, accidental but identificatory feature which is known only to the investigator ;   and if this private and unessential detail is measurable, so much the better.

(8) Finally, another golden rule for the investigator : always remember that accusations and imputations of fraud must be supported by evidence which is as strong as that demanded in support of allegations of super- normal actions.   If, for example, the light is so dim that

an investigator cannot be sure that what he sees is an ectoplasmic structure, then it is *ipso facto* not good enough for him to be sure that what he sees is the medium's leg lifting a stool. Testimony resting on eyesight is not worth much either way if the visibility is poor, and one must remember that it is just as easy to mistake a real ectoplasmic structure for a limb as vice versa—assuming of course that the former exists and does simulate the latter ; but unless you admit that as a possibility, why investigate at all ? Practically all the past " exposures " of fraud and adverse reports are seen to be extremely vulnerable when examined critically ; quite slap-dash methods of argument and crude testimony as to facts seem to suffice here, because, after all, the average man finds that fraud is the most comfortable and convenient hypothesis. If there were no supernormal actions we should not be brought up against some knotty intellectual problems ; common-sense would be reassured, and extravagant and hysterical people like these mediums would be shown their right place, presumably a hospital. No, it is not surprising that most of the best mediums have been exposed as frauds from time to time ; but what does cause us a little annoyance is that so many men of keen and critical intellect should have accepted these exposures so uncritically.

NOTE TO CHAPTER VII

In his recent researches with Rudi Schneider (see *Revue Métapsychique*, 1932, no. 1) Dr. Osty has found certain effects for different wave-lengths, which may have a general validity ; although of course other people, using different mediums, will have to corroborate his observations before we can take them as of universal application.

He finds that *red* light, if *strong*, hinders the *production* of ectoplasm. If the ectoplasm has been produced in the dark, however, and then condensed to a more solid form, it can stand a strongish red light. Consequently it is best to protect the medium from the light by a screen, or provide a dark cabinet near him in which the ectoplasm may be condensed, and to confine the strong red light to the region in which the already condensed ectoplasm is to operate.

Ultra-violet light does not destroy the condensed form of ectoplasm, neither does it render it fluorescent.

Infra-red light is more easily absorbed when of long wavelength.

Ordinary bright light, if of very brief duration (for example the magnesium flash), stops the action of the ectoplasm. This is probably not by disintegrating it (as is popularly thought), but because the condensed ectoplasm simply *runs away* from the bright light, with exceeding rapidity ; for often its activity is immediately resumed undiminished directly the flash is over, which would not be the case if the condensation had to begin all over again.

The bright light, if brief, does not affect the medium himself. On the other hand a weaker light, when prolonged, causes uneasiness and muscular spasms—and this also applies to the Red and the Ultra-violet light. Thus, when we consider the effect of light on the *medium,* its duration is much more important than its intensity.

BIBLIOGRAPHY

GELEY.   Ectoplasmie et Clairvoyance. (Eng. Trans. as Clairvoyance and Materialization.)

SCHRENCK-NOTZING.   Les Phénomènes Physiques de la Médiumnité.

D'ALBE.   The Goligher Circle.

CHAPTER EIGHT

FOUR-DIMENSIONAL PHYSICS

1

FOR many years past there has been a small group of thinkers who have turned to the hypothesis of a fourth dimension as a mode of explaining supernormal phenomena. In general they have also accepted the spirit hypothesis, and vaguely imagined the spirits as four-dimensional beings capable of making objects in this world move at will along a fourth dimension. Owing to the arbitrary element in this sort of view it has not become popular, for we feel that if only we allow the existence of a few more dimensions and of beings capable of action in them we can go on to explain everything ; it is too childish and *ad hoc* to be intellectually satisfying. Nevertheless the speculations of modern physicists have made the doctrine of a four-dimensional universe a commonplace and indeed an apparently necessary axiom, although the chief spokesmen are always careful to emphasize the fact that they only use the words in the Pickwickian sense ; mathematically, they say, we need four (or more) dimensions, but of course that doesn't mean anything physical ! However, there are signs in the most recent physical theories that more dimensions are necessary, physically as well as mathematically, to explain the vagaries of photons and electrons. Sir James Jeans, for example, uses an analogy which may be found illuminating. " Imagine," he writes, " for instance, a race of blind worms, whose perceptions were limited to the two-dimensional surface of the earth. Now and then spots of the earth would sporadically become wet. We, whose faculties range through three dimensions of space, call the phenomenon a rain-shower, and know that events in the third dimension of space determine, absolutely and uniquely, which spots shall become wet and which shall remain dry. But if the worms, unconscious even of the existence of the third dimension of space, tried to thrust all nature into their two-dimensional framework, they would be unable to discover any determinism in the distribution of wet and dry spots ; the worm-scientists would only be able to discuss the wetness and dryness of minute areas in terms of probabilities, which they would be tempted to treat as ultimate truth. Although the time is not yet ripe for a decision, this seems to me, personally, the most promising interpretation of the situation . . . the phenomena of the space-time continuum are four-dimensional projections of realities which occupy more than four dimensions."

We are not concerned in this place with the difficulties of radiation and the physics of the electron, although we are interested to see that the physicists are requiring a multi-dimensional universe ; what concerns us, however, is to discuss the psychic phenomena which seem to demand an explanation in terms of four dimensions. Some of these are dealt with in the chapter on Precognition, as they seem to require the interpretation that Time is a fourth dimension. Others, to be considered in this chapter, require us to regard the fourth dimension as spatial, and assume that things can move along it. The reader will probably get confused and exclaim, " But in one chapter your fourth dimension is spatial, and in another temporal; do you then really mean five dimensions altogether ? " To which I reply : " Not unless I am forced to have five." It seems to me that it is possible that one extra dimension, the fourth, will suffice once we have thoroughly got rid of our ingrained assumption about the nature of time, and have habituated ourselves to a new, as yet unformulated, interpretation of the words involving time ; words like *motion*, etc. At any rate since we reduce Time to a fourth spatial dimension we are philosophically justified in considering it, during this chapter, purely in its spatial aspect.

2

Of the writers who have attempted to explain metapsychic facts by this hypothesis we may mention three in particular. C. H. Hinton, a brilliant young mathematician, set himself the task of training his mind to visualize (if we may call it visualizing) the simplest four-dimensional solid—a tessaract. He gave detailed instructions for others to follow, but few will have the patience to carry them out ; though I think it is probable that he did actually succeed in his object and acquired the power to represent mentally to himself a four-dimensional body.

After Hinton, a Russian mathematician, Ouspensky, speculated on the implications of this theory and his book *Tertium Organum* is certainly a remarkable work, although it wanders away from the main point. Perhaps its greatest value lies in his attempt to formulate what might be called a philosophy of A-rationalism ; a parallel in Logic to the mathematics of the fourth dimension.

Finally there is Professor Zollner, who set out to investigate the matter experimentally and, to this end, held séances with the medium Slade, to whom he suggested various suitable displacements of material bodies along the fourth dimension. It is in his experiences that we find the most convincing demonstration of the fourth dimension, and his book *Transcendental Physics* should be studied by every serious inquirer. The fact that the séances took place in 1877 does not make them the less genuine ; nor should Slade's conviction under the Vagrancy Act, at the instance of Professor Ray Lankester, prejudice the reader who studies the facts.

Mr. Massy (who translates Zollner's book) states that the magistrate himself described the evidence for the defence as " overwhelming " ; " but in giving judgment he expressly excluded it from consideration, confining himself to the evidence of the complainant, Professor Lankester, and of Dr. Donkin, and basing his decision upon *inferences to be drawn from the known course of nature*—a main question in the case being whether there are not some operations in nature *not* generally known."

Of course as long as the law of the land assumes that all alleged metapsychic phenomena are fraudulent, and excludes the *possibility* of, say telekinesis or prevision, then any medium is bound to be convicted of using subtle devices to defraud any client who likes to prosecute him ; the finding of the court follows automatically from the definition of the crime, as in the parallel case of obscenity which is " anything calculated to corrupt those whose minds are capable of being corrupted by it." Of course the legal question in both these instances is complex ; the law endeavours to protect the ignorant from exploitation, and that is a difficult thing to achieve without sacrificing impartiality. But surely the united brains of the legal profession might achieve definitions which were not complete examples of arguing in a circle !

Zollner begins his theoretical discussion of the Fourth Dimension by pointing out that our present sense of a three-dimensioned world is not innate but acquired. Our sense-perceptions, he says, take place at the surface of the body, and are thus strictly two-dimensional. A child contemplating its hand would see a number of two-dimensional retinal images, as it turned its hand round, which would be unrecognizable as images of one and the same object. But the child has a sense of touch and knows about the hand and its motion in this way also, so that gradually the child's mind " learns to reconcile the variableness of the image of the hand with the invariableness of the object itself by the idea of three-dimensional solidity."

Professor Schubert (in his *Mathematical Essays*) refutes this argument by saying that, since perception takes place in material nerve-endings which are always three-dimensional objects, we never perceive two-dimensionally at all, but arrive at the idea of a surface by intellectual abstraction. This does not seem to me a proper refutation. While it is true that the retina is a three-dimensioned object, and that the retinal impression is made on material particles, yet the *mental* fact, or "appearance," may be two-dimensional. A picture, though the paint is indubitably material, is seen by the mind as a surface. Schubert does not seem to allow for the psychological half of perception, which is just what Zollner was talking about. As the latter continues : "So likewise in the stereoscope the representation of the corporeality—i.e. of the third dimension—springs up in the mind when the task is presented to our intellect to refer at once two different plane pictures, without contradiction, to one single object." In this example the two appearances are simultaneous, whereas in the example of the child's hand they were successive ; but in the former two real objects were present, while only one was there in the latter. In both cases what are actually perceived are two-dimensional images, but the mind integrates them into a three-dimensional object. "We have come to the idea of the third dimension in order to overcome the apparent inconsistency of facts, of the existence of which experience daily convinces us," says Zollner. Whether we may agree or not with this as a statement of historical fact, the important point which his remarks illustrate must not be obscured. Let us suppose a being who had a mind, a strictly two-dimensional vision, and the sense of touch, and then we may say that he would come to the idea of a third dimension (and eventually would incorporate it so thoroughly in his general mentality as to attach it

automatically to his perceptions) in order to reconcile
in his mind the general invariableness of objects with the
continuous variations of their appearances.   Indeed,
Maeterlinck (*The Life of Space*, p. 71) asserts that
experiments have been made on a person who
was born blind but who acquired the sense of sight
at the age of seventeen, and that they confirm this
view.

" To him all objects appeared flat, even the human
face, in spite of the prominence of the nose and the
concavity of the orbits.   And for several days he lived
in a world which had only two dimensions."

Now how would such a being interpret the world,
before he had arrived at the conception of the third
dimension ?   Imagine him confronted with a cube which
someone rotates slowly in front of him.   He sees first a
square surface, then this changes gradually to a rect-
angle, then contracts to a square again, and this is
repeated.   He arrives at the conception of a plane
object which is continuously changing its shape, i.e.
growing smaller or larger in *time*.   He is unable to
conceive of the various square surfaces of the cube as
existing all at once, arranged in three-dimensional space,
but interprets the whole as a temporal sequence of plane
surfaces, or as the life history of a flat object.   In other
words, what for us lies in his third dimension, for him
seems to lie in time and not to exist in space at all except
at successive instants.   If we should succeed in making
him apprehend space as we conceive it, he would say,
" But *Time* is the third dimension."   May we not extend
the analogy, and say that *our* Time is really a fourth
dimension of space ?   that the physical life history of a
plant or a man is a four-dimensioned " thing " which
exists as a whole always, and that our minds merely
perceive successive three-dimensional sections of it ?
This, at any rate, is the conception to which a study of
the facts of Precognition leads us.

But we now have to consider the matter from a

different angle, and discuss the cases in which ordinary material objects suffer displacements in our space which seem for their interpretation to involve motion along a fourth dimension.

The phenomena of *Apports*, or the sudden appearance of objects apparently from nowhere, of the passage of one object through another, of the tying of knots in sealed cords, and others of like nature involve one of two possibilities ; either the motion of a material object along a fourth dimension, or else its disintegration into minute particles and the passage of these through the pores in an obstacle, with the final reassemblage of the parts back into their original arrangement so as to reconstitute the object as it was before.

This second hypothesis of molecular disintegration and reintegration appears to be on the whole the fashionable theory of apports ; and yet I cannot but feel that it is gigantically improbable. No doubt it is just conceivable that a mind should be able to disintegrate and even reconstruct a simple piece of dead matter, like a stone ; and it is certainly easy to imagine an ectoplasmic structure passing through a solid object in this sort of manner, because the ectoplasm is eminently amenable to de-materialization as well as to materialization. But the list of observed apports is so complex and varied, and is by no means limited to objects of simple structure ; besides jewellery and watches, it includes fresh flowers and living birds. I do not think we can assume that a bird can be disintegrated into its component molecules and reassembled again alive ; at any rate such an assumption is unwarranted when we can explain the apport by means of a theory which is already supported by quite different facts drawn from physics.

In order to make the idea plain and simple we may resort to the old device of the analogy drawn from an imaginary plane world. Let us suppose that there exists a community of Plane Beings situated on a surface, and that they have no conception of the direction perpendicular to their plane. In their plane world a room or a box will consist of a closed plane figure, for example a square. Let us suppose this room is closed, and its linear door is shut. The Plane Being will say that it is inconceivable that an object should come from the outside into the interior of the room unless either the door is opened or else the object breaks through the wall. But we, who are aware of the third dimension, can imagine the object lifted off the plane and put back inside the square room. This action, which is quite unimaginable for the Plane Being, would constitute for him a miraculous " apport." During the time that the object was outside his plane he would consider that it had gone clean out of existence ; it would certainly have gone clean out of *his* surface-world. Moreover, if we told him that his room was not entirely closed, but that we could see into it from the top, he would attach no meaning at all to our words, since he could have no conception of viewing a plane surface from the perpendicular direction.

The analogy leads us to imagine that an apport, or any case of sudden and total disappearance of an object, may be due to a displacement of the object, along a fourth dimension which is perpendicular to each of the three of which we are aware ; and that a closed solid, like a room, is open when viewed along this fourth dimension. Zollner assumed that when objects were displaced in this way the active agent must necessarily be a four-dimensioned Being, and was in fact one of the Spirits. But we may now consider ourselves as four-dimensional beings, and moreover as the sole authors of all metapsychic phenomena, and it is once again clear that the spirit hypothesis is an unnecessary addition which does nothing to help us to explain the observed physical facts.

3

The recorded instances of apports are less abundant, and also less evidentially satisfactory, than those of other physical phenomena. There appear to be two reasons why this should be so. In the first place we seem to be dealing with a feat of great intrinsic difficulty ; which, after all, is to be expected since an apport involves telekinesis with the added complication of a fourth-dimensional motion. Secondly the nature of the phenomenon makes it difficult to observe and record with the detail, and in the circumstances, which are required to make the evidence completely convincing. An apport is always sudden and usually quite unexpected ; almost invariably the actual object apported is unexpected even though the séance is held for the purpose of obtaining apports. Again, it seems less under the control of the medium than other phenomena ; while it is even more easily imitated fraudulently. Nevertheless instances have been observed under conditions which excluded the fraudulent production of the particular apports produced. For example, the April 1927 number of *Psychic Science* contains accounts of séances held with an apport medium, Herr Melzer, at the British College of Psychic Science. On one occasion Herr Melzer was detected preparing for a fraud, by having two small stones affixed behind his ears with flesh-coloured sticking paper. This was unfortunate, but forgivable when we remember that a medium practises the most uncertain of all professions (or arts ?), is peculiarly liable to this particular temptation, and has to live up to his reputation and produce results even when the virtue has gone from him. A medium depends for his living and his prestige on the production of phenomena, over which he has really hardly any control, and which may fail completely time after time when they are wanted and yet occur in prodigal extravagance in the privacy of his home when they are valueless to him. Is it not natural that, unless his probity is much above that of the average business man, he will almost necessarily learn to have a reserve of trickery on which to draw in case of need ?

But Herr Melzer's reputation was not built up from tricks with concealed stones. In his visit to the British College in 1926 he produced several apports of fresh flowers, whose condition and bulk precluded all possibility of previous concealment. The séances took place in good light, and the medium was entranced during their course, and apparently was " controlled " by various spirits. As a rule the apported object appeared suddenly, from " nowhere," in the medium's outstretched hands ; or it was seen by the sitters for a fraction of a second falling *towards* the medium from out of the air. We read that, " Twenty-five anemones—or a dozen roots of lilies of the valley with soil attached, pure bells, and delicate leaves—or violets appearing fresh and fragrant after a two and a half hours' sitting—have all been received, when the medium's hands had been empty a second before, when no friends of his were present at the sittings, and when no opportunity could have presented itself to conceal them that would not have resulted in broken stems and blossoms."

In face of the apports of fresh flowers, in a condition and quantity which exclude the possibility of previous concealment and production by a conjurer's sleight of hand, it is entirely irrelevant to talk about his peccadilloes with small stones behind his ears. One might just as well refuse to recognize the genuineness and beauty of *Tristan and Isolde* because Wagner's own life was full of infidelities. Moreover we may note a curious psychological fact which has some bearing on the subject. Herr Melzer, when normal, is inordinately fond of flowers ; and when, in his trance state, they arrive as apports he sometimes attempts, as if driven by an uncontrollable pathological impulse, to devour them, roots and earth and all, lacerating himself thereby with the thorns of roses, and presenting a rather disgusting spectacle to the onlookers. In this manner several good apports of flowers, on whose perfect condition depended much of the prestige that the medium deserved for their production, were quickly spoiled and crushed by his irrational behaviour. We may legitimately argue that a medium who took the trouble to conceal the flowers first (although in the circumstances the thing is incredible) and to produce them by sleight of hand, would take pains to avoid damaging them and would exhibit them in as perfect a condition as possible.

Certain mediums, like Herr Melzer, specialize in the production of apports ; but the phenomenon occurs also in odd instances with a great variety of mediums. For example, Crookes records that during one séance with Miss Fox, a small handbell, which he had seen shortly before in his library, and which his sons, who were in the library, averred was in fact there, was brought into the dining-room, whose door was locked during the séance. Again, when Schrenck-Notzing was studying Stanislawa P. (Feb. 11, 1913) he saw and photographed an apport of a piece of mimosa, 20 cm. long, and found that the cross-section of the stalk fitted a branch of mimosa in another part of the house, where Stanislawa had never been. And Morselli also observed apports with Eusapia Palladino. A striking example of the sudden disappearance of a large object, such as could not be manipulated by prestidigitation, is given by Zollner. During a séance with Slade, in bright daylight at about midday, a small round table (measuring about 2 ft. 6 in. high and 18 in. diameter and weighing nearly 10 lb.) laid itself on the floor underneath the card table at which Zollner and Slade were seated with their hands joined. Wishing to look at the round table Zollner bent down and found it had totally disappeared !

" To my and Slade's great astonishment we found the space beneath the card table completely empty, nor were we able to find in all the rest of the room that table which only a minute before was present to our senses."

After sitting down again for a few minutes Slade said that he saw lights, which Zollner did not see, . . . " but as I turned my head following Slade's gaze up to the ceiling of the room behind my back, I suddenly observed at a height of about five feet the hitherto invisible table, with its legs turned upwards, very quickly floating down in the air upon the top of the card table. Although we involuntarily drew back our heads sideways—yet we were both so violently struck on the head that I felt the pain on the left of mine fully four hours after the occurrence."

This astonishing event took place in the best daylight, and is in any case of a nature that does not lend itself to imitation by conjuring. It is one thing to produce a rabbit out of one's hat on the stage, and quite another casually to annihilate a small table in the room of a scientist who is holding your hands, and then make it appear again in the air.

4

The above instance of the apported table was a spontaneous unexpected occurrence; but Zollner's claim to fame rests upon his ingenious attempts to provoke phenomena which necessitated fourth-dimensional operations. He was a true experimentalist, fertile in imagining possible consequences of his theory, and yet quite ready to accept what happened and to observe unexpected phenomena. So it came about that although the majority of his proposed experiments were not carried out in the way he first wished, yet his unlooked-for results were often just as convincing. An example of his method, successful this time, is described on page 59 of his book.

" I took a book-slate bought by myself; that is, two slates connected at one side by cross hinges, like a book for folding up. In the absence of Slade I lined both slates within with a half sheet of my letter paper which, immediately before the sitting, was evenly spread with soot. This slate I closed, and remarked to Mr. Slade that, if my theory of the existence of four-dimensional beings in nature was well founded, it must be an easy thing for them to place on the interior of the closed slate the impression of feet hitherto produced only on the open slates. . . . To my great surprise Slade consented to my laying the closed book-slate (which I had never let out of my hands after applying the soot) on my lap during the sitting, so that I could continuously observe it to the middle. We might have sat at the table in the brightly lighted room for about five minutes, our hands linked with those of Slade in the usual manner above the table, when I suddenly felt on two occasions, the one shortly after the other, the slate pressed down on my lap, without my having perceived anything in the least visible. Three raps on the table announced that all was completed, and when I opened the slate there was within it on the one side the impression of a right foot, on the other side that of a left foot."

As will be seen from the above account Zollner, quite naturally, worked on the spirit hypothesis and formulated his deductions in terms of it ; but we are more justified to-day in assuming that the feet were not those of a spirit, but ectoplasmic projections from Slade. In either case the geometrical difficulty of making impressions on two adjacent inside surfaces of the book-slate is insuperable without the fourth dimension, but disappears when that is conceded.

Zollner's fertile imagination suggested various different phenomena which he proposed to Slade. For instance, the tying of knots in an endless cord ; the interlocking of two wooden rings, cut in one piece each from different kinds of wood ; the transference of small objects into and out of closed boxes ; and the reversal of the direction of twist in snail shells. Not all of these succeeded in the form proposed, but they all led to valuable results of one kind or another.

The experiment of tying knots in an endless cord is perhaps the neatest as well as the most famous experiment. Consider the analogy from our Plane Beings again. Imagine a line drawn in a closed oval. This constitutes an endless cord, and the Plane Being cannot imagine a method of converting it into a genuine figure of eight (8), in which one part crosses the other, although he could imagine it distorted into a spurious eight in which two points are brought into contact thus :—8. The real figure 8 constitutes a knot in an endless cord for him ; but we can imagine it produced by twisting in the third dimension so that one part of the oval is made to cross over the opposite part. Zollner, following Riemann and other mathematicians, saw that to produce a true knot in an endless material cord it would be necessary to twist the cord in the fourth dimension. He therefore took two soft leather bands and fastened the ends of each together, sealing the joins. He proposed that Slade should produce a knot in each. Seated at the table with Slade, with the two separate leather loops on the table, but covered with his own hands, Zollner felt them moving, and on looking at them found that they had been knotted together. The fact that the leather bands were also very much twisted Zollner regarded as an indication that it was not a case of simple penetration of matter, involving disaggregation, but of four-dimensional torsion.

In the same way the ends of a new hempen cord, 148 cm. long and 1 mm. thick, were knotted together and the knot sealed on to a piece of paper, and (without Slade having touched it) placed on the table, the seal being covered by Zollner's two thumbs and the loop hanging down in his lap. Four knots were found tied in this endless cord at this séance, which was held in daylight at eleven o'clock in the morning.

The same phenomenon has been reported, though

infrequently, by other observers ; for example, Dr. Nichols obtained it with Eglington in 1878.

Other proposals of Zollner's are worth noting. For example, he had two wooden rings, one oak, the other alder, each turned from one piece, and requested Slade to get them interlinked ; his idea being that such rings interlinked would be incapable of fraudulent manufacture or imitation, since microscopic examination could always reveal if one had been cut to admit the other, so that their mere existence would constitute an objective and lasting proof of the supernormal, independently of all testimony as to their history. Actually Slade did not succeed in interlinking them, but instead they were slipped round the central leg of a circular table whose top and base, which were firmly fixed on, entirely prevented the rings coming on to the leg in any normal manner.

Another device for obtaining an independent objective proof was to find snail shells of a species with a characteristic direction of twist, either right- or left-handed, and ask Slade to reverse the spiral by a fourth-dimensional twist ; this would be a feat analogous to making two photographic portraits, one of which has been printed in reverse, coincide, both being kept face upwards. Again Slade did not accomplish what was asked, but instead of this he passed the snail shell through a solid ¡table ; Zollner noted that the shell immediately after passing through the table was extremely hot, a fact that has been observed in other instances.

Another interesting observation of his, which appears to be worth further investigation, was that the " spirit-lights " that appeared during the course of the séances cast sharp shadows which were approximately of the same size as the objects. A light which appeared to come from under the table cast shadows of the legs of the table which were both sharply defined and sensibly of the same size as the legs. From this he inferred that

the source of light was really a very great distance away
and had small apparent size ; in other words that the
rays were parallel.

Of course Zollner recognized that, however fertile he
might be in suggesting various experiments to prove the
fourth dimension, he had no sort of claim to demand
that they should be made to " work " in his way, and
that his main business was to observe what did in fact
happen, " remaining patient and in a passive receptive
disposition for the things which should come." This is
the true scientific spirit, and it is just what makes his
remarkable book, which would be interesting even if it
were considered as fiction, of prime importance to the
student of metapsychic science.

Zollner was by no means the only investigator to
obtain good evidence for " the passage of matter through
matter," or, alternatively, for fourth-dimensional displacements. I quote the following from Campbell
Holme's *The Facts of Psychic Science* (page 336).

" Dr. George Wyld, M.D., Edin., who was anxious
to witness the phenomenon of an iron ring being passed
on to the arm of a medium while he held his hand, had
a ring specially made of iron 5/16th inch diameter (i.e.
in thickness), oval in shape, and of such a size that it
could not be passed over the hand of the medium, J. C.
Husk. He took it during four years to every séance he
attended, . . . finally, . . . on December 18th, 1884
. . . while Dr. Wyld held Husk's left hand the ring was
placed on the latter's left arm. Just before the phenomenon occurred Wyld held the ring in his left hand.
It was taken from him in the dark, and immediately a
cry of pain from the medium announced the accomplish-
ment of the phenomenon. Dr. Wyld, of course, was
careful to hold continuously and tightly the medium's
left hand with his right, until the light was turned up.
The ring was then identified by secret marks, and an
hour later it fell on the floor. After this success Dr.
Wyld had a still smaller ring made and on January 28th,

1885, it was put on Husk's wrist while his hand was held
by a friend of Dr. Wyld, and next day identified by the
latter by microscopic markings made for the purpose.
It is said that Husk wore this ring until his death in
1920.   Maskelyne, the conjurer, examined the ring on
Husk's wrist, but he was unable to account for it, and
stated his opinion that it could not be removed intact
without great injury to the hand.   A committee of the
S.P.R., who examined the ring in place and tried vainly
to remove it after compressing the hand with metallic
tape, did not consider that its presence on Husk's wrist
could rank as a demonstration of the passage of matter
through matter, because they believed that if Husk were
chloroformed it might be forced off.   The statement that
Dr. Wyld [sic] held Husk's hand when the ring was put
on, being merely human testimony, was not considered
relevant.''

As a matter of fact, a case of this kind is always rather
unsatisfactory because of the doubt that must occur to
others, especially as time goes on, as to whether the
medium's hand was really held *continuously*.   For if, in
the excitement, Husk's left hand were freed one might
account for the phenomenon by supposing that Husk
actually contracted his hand to the required extent, and
slipped the ring on normally.   Such a contraction would
be in line with what is known about the partial de-
materialization of the medium (as in the cases of Mme.
D'Espérance and Marthe Béraud) or the diminution in
the volume of Miss Goligher's limbs, or the reverse
process of elongation of the medium noticed with
D. D. Home.   It is more reasonable to assume such a
temporary diminution of Husk's hand, so long as we are
not convinced that it was continuously held, than to
assume a fourth-dimensional movement.   In the same
way, if we are convinced that either the ring was dematerialized, or else the wrist, so that one passed through
the other, it would be easier to assume that the wrist
suffered dematerialization, because the matter compos-

ing the wrist is organically controlled by the medium, whereas external inert matter is not. A better case, perhaps, is one quoted by Campbell Holmes (p. 333) in which handcuffs were manipulated by Mr. Everett. Serjeant Cox, well known as an early investigator, borrowed two pairs of handcuffs from Clerkenwell Prison. Neither of them could be opened without its special key. Serjeant Cox fastened these handcuffs to a chair, and requested Everett to take them off. " In five minutes he had released both handcuffs and placed them on his own wrists ; one of each pair being round a wrist, and the other two linked together, and all securely locked. In this condition, in 16 seconds his coat was taken off. In 18 seconds the handcuffs were both taken off and thrown down on the floor, unlinked from each other, but still locked."

So far we have considered only cases in which an inert object is apparently made to move outside our space ; but as an example of the medium apparently moving bodily along the fourth dimension the famous case of Mme. Salmon may be cited (*Annales des Sciences Psychiques*, 1901). Dr. P. Gibier, director of the Bacteriological Institute of New York, studied Mme. Salmon in his own laboratory. On one occasion he locked her in a cage made of wire trellis of fine mesh, sealing the edges of the door and the padlock with gummed paper. A curtain covered the cage, to protect the medium from the light, which was dim. Various materialized forms came out of the cage, and finally Dr. Gibier was asked by one to attend to the medium. He was about to pull the curtain aside and unlock the door of the cage when the medium fell, unconscious, into his arms. On turning up the light, after placing Mme. Salmon in a chair, he found that the cage was just as he had left it, with the door padlocked and the gummed strips undisturbed. This phenomenon was repeated by Mme. Salmon on two other occasions. Here again an alternative explanation is to suppose that the medium dematerialized herself sufficiently to pass through the wire mesh ; but it does not seem to me that this alternative is a simplification.[1]

BIBLIOGRAPHY

C. H. HINTON.   A New Era of Thought.
  The Fourth Dimension.
OUSPENSKY.   Tertium Organum.
Psychic Science Quarterly.   April 1927.
CAMPBELL HOLMES.   The Facts of Psychic Science.
ZOLLNER.   Transcendental Psychics.
MAETERLINCK.   The Life of Space.
SIR J. JEANS.   The Mysterious Universe.

[1] Another case of the transportation of a medium which may be mentioned, although the testimony as to the precise attendant circumstances and relevant details is inadequate from the point of view of rigorous proof, is as follows : On July 28, 1929, the Marquis Centuriano Scotto (an Italian nobleman, and private medium) vanished from a locked séance-room and was found two and a half hours later in a locked granary sixty yards away.   The account by Bozzano, who was present, is given in Mrs. Hack's *Modern Psychic Mysteries*.   Unfortunately it omits many important points, such as the state of the window of the room, also whether the granary had a window, etc. ; in a word, it is an inadequate report.

PART III

CHAPTER NINE

CRYPTÆSTHESIA

THE mental phenomena of psychic science all relate to the gaining of knowledge otherwise than through the recognized channels of sense perception ; hence the general term *cryptæsthesia*, used by Professor Richet, is a suitable one to cover the field, meaning as it does a hidden mode of perception. We may divide most of the phenomena of cryptæsthesia into three main groups, according as the thing which is known exists located somewhere in space without the range of the knower's senses, or is placed in Time differently from the knower, or, finally, exists solely in the Mind of some other person, as an idea or an emotion. Thus we have, in the first place, *clairvoyance*, covering all those cases in which a material object is perceived (otherwise than through the five senses) ; in the second place, *prevision* and *retrocognition* of events which are to come or are already past ; and in the third place, *telepathy*, the perception of ideas, etc., in another's mind, or the transmission of ideas from one mind to another. We shall find that in many, if not in most, cases of cryptæsthesia it is not easy to determine which mode is operative, and that in many cases there may be a combination of two or even all three modes. Moreover, when we have studied Clairvoyance and Precognition in the chapters devoted to them, we shall, I think, begin to feel that they are only apparently different, in that

139

their content is in the one case a present material object, and in the other case objects existent in the future; but that, considered as modes of perception, they are identical. Moreover, the trend of modern physics, as expressed for example in Jeans' *Mysterious Universe*, is to regard all material objects as essentially mental phenomena, although their substantiality is not in any way negatived by this conception. " The old dualism of mind and matter . . . seems likely to disappear not through matter becoming in any way more shadowy or insubstantial than heretofore, or through mind becoming resolved into a function of the working of matter, but through substantial matter resolving itself into a creation and manifestation of the mind." Now if this is a tenable view in physics it suggests that pure telepathy, or the perception of ideas in another's mind, is not radically different in kind from ordinary perception of material objects. In other words it becomes quite reasonable to say that Clairvoyance, Precognition, Telepathy, and normal perception of the material world round us, are so many forms of one and the same thing, namely, perception in general, and differ, not in themselves as attributes of the percipient's mind, but merely in their application to things perceived. We thus differentiate between them merely for our own convenience in describing and classifying their effects, just as we make arbitrary classifications in other sciences, such as physics or botany, and study under separate headings things which really are but different forms or actions of something identical in each.

Cryptæsthesia, then, is probably at bottom one thing, a generalized Perceptivity. But in order to discuss its modes we must separate them, and study the evidence for each one by itself. This means that we must exclude all but one mode at a time, which is a very hard task to accomplish. For example, consider the Queen Draga case, given by Richet, which is one of the most interesting examples of cryptæsthesia recorded; though whether the mode operative is one of Clairvoyance in space, or Precognition in time, or of Telepathy in pure mind, seems impossible to determine.   Richet says (p. 166) :

" The third fact, which on thinking it over appears to me one of the most striking examples of cryptæsthesia yet obtained, is the following : I give the details, for it shows astonishing lucidity acting at a distance of 1200 miles, and exact notes were taken.   In June 1906, at 10.30 p.m., in the presence of my friend Octave Houd- aille, Mme. S., Mme. R., and her twelve-year-old daughter, after some incoherent phrases, we got the following sentence by raps, more distinct than ever before. (In the whole course of my experiments with Mme. R. the raps were unintelligible only twice or three times.)   ' BANCALAMO.'   I could not refrain from saying, ' O, it is Latin ! Calamo.' But the dictation continued imperturbably, ' BANCA LA MORT GUETTE FAMILLE.'   Thence onwards the answers were inco- herent.   I thought at first that the first word must be Italian—Bianca-Blanche ; but no one present could interpret the words.

" The next day, Thursday, at 2 p.m., the news of the assassination of Queen Draga of Serbia was received at Paris.   Some Serbian officers, having bought over the palace servants, entered at midnight and assassinated King Alexander, his wife, and her two brothers ; her two sisters escaped by a miracle.   Not for a moment did I connect this tragedy with the previous evening's séance.

" On Friday, reading in the paper some details relative to the crime, I learned that Draga's father was named Panka, and this came as a ray of light.

1. The word BANCA is very near PANKA. (I will return to this later.)
2. The time at which the message was given, 10.30 p.m., is, to the minute, the time at which the assassins left the Hotel de la Couronne de Serbie ;

correcting for Belgrade time which is one and a
half hours in advance of Paris time.

3. The words apply with startling exactitude to the
    peril menacing the whole family of Panka; the
    words ' Death lies in wait family ' could hardly
    be more appositely chosen in view of the situation
    at midnight in Belgrade."

In the first place we might suppose that Mme. R.
had clairvoyantly perceived for an instant some of the
assassins' preparations; but then we should not understand how she knew what these imported, unless perhaps
she saw some written plan or heard the discussions.
This would seem to involve either the hypothesis of the
projection of an ectoplasmic body, or of the fourth
dimension, and in view of the distance involved the
latter seems more probable.

Secondly, however, we might consider the time at
which the message was given, namely, when the assassins
left the hotel in order to go out and commit the murder.
Mme. R. did not say, " Death *has* overtaken the family,"
but, in view of other cases of undoubted prevision, it is
quite reasonable to suppose that she saw the event
before it occurred, and, realizing its still futural character,
expressed herself in prophetic form.

Finally, and no doubt most readers will instinctively
tend to prefer the hypothesis, the message may be
wholly telepathic in origin; the thoughts of the assassins, highly charged as they must have been, with
emotion and concentrated purpose, may have impressed
the sensitive medium in Paris. But for none of these
explanations have we any shred of definite evidence;
we only have evidence for the fact of the occurrence of
a supernormal event of the kind we call cryptæsthetic.

There is a special class of phenomenon, the so-called
psychometry, in which the medium is enabled to acquire
a great deal of miscellaneous knowledge apparently
through mere contact with an object, which is probably
due to an admixture of clairvoyance, retrocognition, and

telepathy ; but it is quite impossible to disentangle the factors which may be at work, so that our best course is to consider psychometry as a form of general crypt-æsthesia, and not try to pigeon-hole it. Examples of psychometry are quite numerous, as it is a common mode of mediumship, but in comparatively few cases do we have the attendant circumstances so arranged as to preclude fraud (through previous study of a person's history) or telepathy.

Nevertheless, although fraud can conceivably be postulated for any one single case taken out of a large number, it cannot possibly be postulated for a whole batch of cases with a fertile medium (e.g. Mrs. Piper) ; because no medium could spend the time or money required for elaborate and clandestine researches into the history and relatives of all the possible or likely sitters who may come to consult the psychometrist.

A good case of psychometry, involving the possibility of telepathy and one definite instance of clairvoyance, is that given by Drs. Dufay and Azam. I will summarize it briefly here. Dr. Dufay of Blois was interested in a clairvoyant named Marie, with whom he did several experiments. On one occasion Marie spent the night in prison (she was acquitted) and in the morning Dr. Dufay was sent for on account of a suicide which had occurred in the prison. The prisoner, who was accused of murder, had strangled himself with his neckerchief. Dr. Dufay obtained the magistrate's permission to question Marie about this man, of whom she was not supposed to know anything, and of whose suicide she also can be presumed to have been entirely ignorant, since prisoners are naturally not told these things, and Dr. Dufay says that even the sister of the women's department had not yet been told of it. Accordingly Dr. Dufay wrapped a piece of the kerchief up in paper, had Marie fetched, hypnotized her, and put the packet containing the piece of kerchief in her hands, without having spoken to her at all up to this point.

Marie started up and threw the packet away, declaring that it was something that had killed a man. On being questioned, she said that it was a neckerchief, that a man had hanged himself with it, and that he was a prisoner who had assassinated someone with a cooper's *gouet*, or kind of hatchet.

This much information might conceivably have been acquired normally (though this seems unlikely) or else telepathically during the hypnotic state. But the magistrate then whispered to Dr. Dufay that the *gouet* had never been found, so the latter asked Marie where the instrument was. She quickly " saw " it, at the bottom of a pool, which she described sufficiently for the police to recover the *gouet* there that day.

The question arises whether she actually saw the *gouet* in the pool (clairvoyance), or whether the spirit or mind of the recently deceased murderer informed her of it (telepathy from the dead), or whether in some way the past history of the murderer was carried by the necker-chief ! In any case, what sort of stimulus or action is it that a material object is capable of giving to a psychometrizing medium ?

Dr. Rudolph Tischner did a series of psychometric experiments during the War. Out of about a hundred experiments with two mediums, about forty gave good positive evidence of supernormal knowledge—probably involving an indeterminate mixture of clairvoyance, telepathy, and retrocognition. One interesting case is that in which the medium, H., described the picture on a hundred rouble note inside a box (expt. 157). In another, when H. was given a spectacle case containing a rosary which had been blessed by the Pope, he said at once :

" I think I am worried by the spectacle case—I see the Pope—they call to me ' You must say, I see the Pope ' —I saw a brilliant white form " (expt. 110). The former experiment reads like direct clairvoyance, but in this case H. did not see or describe the rosary—

instead, he got the one important idea connected with
it, namely, the Pope. Probably, then, since Dr. Tischner
knew all about the object, telepathy is the most reasonable hypothesis here. But experiment 155 is more
interesting and more convincing still. In this case, an
unknown object, securely wrapped up in a box, tied,
and sealed, had been sent by Mr. Dingwall to Dr.
Tischner, to be presented to H. Mr. Dingwall and his
immediate friends were the only ones who knew what
the box contained, and no one at the séance knew what
it was. (Dr. Tischner was in Germany, it must be
remembered, while Mr. Dingwall lives in England, and
is a prominent member of the S.P.R.)

Amongst other remarks, having no very great relevance, H. said of this object : " *The object must come from
a foreign land—I can feel the cold—Siberia—primitive—
it points to a primitive country—something made in a
foreign country—the East—the Stone Age—something
' versteint ' (stoned)—came in a ship across the sea.*"

Much of this might be random, vague guessing,
applicable to many objects, but the definite associations
with cold, the Stone Age, a primitive country, and
something " stoned," are not likely ideas for an object
that might well be a tie-pin or ring or pencil or other
personal belonging. As a matter of fact, the box contained a flint axe-head, dating from the Achulean period,
which Mr. Dingwall had found in the New Forest. The
associations with cold, Siberia and the East, are explained by the observation that the axe-head dates back
from a period when the climate of England was probably
much like that of the colder parts of Siberia to-day.
Altogether, then, the experiment is highly evidential of
cryptæsthesia, and exclusive of probable telepathy,
unless one is prepared to admit that H. had access to
Mr. Dingwall's memory. Ordinary telepathy is excluded
by the fact that, of the people present during the
experiment, none knew what the box contained, while of
the people who knew its contents, none knew when the

experiment was taking place, and therefore (unless they thought of nothing else for days !) may be presumed not to have been thinking of it at the time.

An exceedingly interesting case is given by Dr. Osty (*Supernormal Faculties in Man*, pp. 34–38) which apparently involves psychometric retrocognition of an unusual power. Briefly, an engineer, M. Galloy, gave Dr. Osty a photograph representing an ill-defined egg-shaped object, saying that the contents of the object were unknown to anyone. Dr. Osty gave the photograph to Mme. Morel when she was in an hypnotic trance, and thereupon Mme. Morel gave a long description of a man dying a violent death, a strange funeral scene, in which uniforms and brightly coloured garments were conspicuous, and a tomb like a small underground house. She saw that the object was shut up with the body in the tomb. She described how the object was filled with blood, and then hermetically sealed.

As a matter of fact, the photograph represented an ancient Ampulla, found in a necropolis near Baalbec, which is probably unique of its kind. It is conjectured by the owner to contain some very rare and precious liquid, and to have belonged to some important person, dating from the Roman occupation of Egypt, shortly before the Christian era. But, as the owner asked £5000 for it, Dr. Osty could not buy it and ascertain whether the contents really were blood. It is interesting, however, to see what a circumstantial story, all of it quite probable, Mme. Morel at once delivered on being given a very poor photograph of an object at whose nature she certainly could not guess.

Dr. Osty, whose researches in psychometric clairvoyance are as valuable as those of Schrenck-Notzing on ectoplasm, does not satisfactorily solve the mystery which attaches to the use of an object. He establishes the fact that it materially assists a medium at the start to be given, though but for a moment, some object which has recently been touched by, or has often been in the presence of, the person who is to be the subject of the medium's clairvoyance. But if the object is removed after the medium has got in touch with the personality, the flow of information is not inhibited. Moreover, as one of his best cases, that of M. Lerasle, proves, the medium can give information about a person, relating to events which have happened *since* that person has touched the psychometric object. M. Lerasle disappeared from home one day, and did not return. The family eventually gave Dr. Osty a neck-tie from his wardrobe, and with this to establish contact, Mme. Morel found the man, tracing his path from the house through a wood, and indicating where the corpse was— for M. Lerasle had gone out to die alone, as old men sometimes do.

It cannot be supposed that the object used for psychometry really carries with it the memory-traces of all the persons who have touched it ; but what is the exact nature of the link which such an object establishes ? For there can be no doubt that to touch some personal object, such as a neck-tie or pencil or anything else, does facilitate or promote clairvoyance on that person for some mediums, just as the process of telling the cards, or gazing into a crystal will stimulate and provoke clairvoyance in other mediums. The only attempt at an explanation of this interesting fact which I can offer is based upon the hypothesis of a fourth dimension, and will be dealt with when we discuss Precognition. (See p. 171.)

Amongst all the cases of psychometric clairvoyance we find, of course, more error than truth, as well as much that is more or less probable guesswork rather than supernormal information. Many people conclude from this that the successes of mediumship are due to chance, and that the errors show that no supernormal faculty exists. This, of course, is childish, since we are dealing with a faculty which is highly fugitive and frail, not under conscious control, sporadic and untrained—

indeed, at present untrainable, although we may perhaps be able to train suitable persons to inhibit conscious thought and so allow any supernormal faculties which are there to emerge and discover themselves. But the question of error is very important, since unless we appreciate its prevalence and find some means of discriminating between the information which is probably true and that which is probably false, we may be led astray with disastrous consequences.

It appears from the whole weight of evidence, though crucial proof is lacking, that a medium is even more sensitive to telepathic impressions from the mind of a consultant than he is to supernormal impressions from actuality. Moreover, whether the impression comes from one source or the other, it is rarely received integrally and definitely, but comes as a sort of " feeling of thusness " which must be interpreted and expressed by the medium. At first the medium may be conscious of a visual or other sensorial image, which symbolizes the idea, and which he has to translate. For example, Osty's medium, M. Fleurière, says : " The vision of a dead man, instead of presenting itself under the natural form of a corpse in a coffin, may appear under twenty different forms. Sometimes I have the impression of a branch which cracks, breaks and falls . . . occasionally I have this vision of death under the form of a black line cleaving a grey crystal, or extending into a cloudy sky. Or it may be a light which is slowly extinguished, or a meteor vanishing on the horizon."

In fact, M. Fleurière sees a great diversity of symbolic visions corresponding to the circumstances or states of the person whose life he delineates, and these visual symbols are the forms under which his supernormal information presents itself to his mind. But the interpretation of symbols is notoriously an unsure process, and lends itself to much fabulation. Incidentally, this symbolism raises interesting questions. It is curious how the religious and other mystics, the poets, and the subconscious minds of us all, require symbolism to convey their thoughts ; curious that a mode of mentation which is conspicuous in savages should also be found necessary whenever we deal with the transcendental. All the more curious because it seems psychologically to involve a previous rational idea, of which it is a picturesque translation. Thus we can understand that a man who harbours a repressed wish for his father's death might dream that he saw the king depart from the station in the royal train. His unconscious mind says, " I wish my father would die," and then, in order to pass the Freudian Censor, translates this into the conventional symbols : father =king, and dying =going away on a journey. But this symbolism, understandable enough if we start with the ideas of father and death as original thought-contents, would be inexplicable without them. So M. Fleurière's symbolism necessitates the conclusion that he first of all (unconsciously) has the idea " this man will die," and then symbolizes this, and sees a visual image of a branch cracking, and lastly translates this symbol with his conscious mind. But why should there be this intermediate stage of symbolism at all ? Or is it only a secondary accompaniment, an hallucinatory overflow, as it were, of the idea ?

Be this as it may, the interpretation of symbols is by no means the only source of error. Telepathic impressions of conjectures and hopes in the sitter's mind seem even more numerous and serious. A medium may simply act as an unwitting mirror to his consultant. A painful, but instructive, example of this is given by Osty (p. 215). In March 1916, Louis M. received a letter from the front, telling him that his son Jean was seen to be wounded in the head during an attack, but, as the Germans occupied the ground, the body had not been recovered, though death was certain. In his sorrow and anxiety M. went to a medium (M. Fleurière), to whom he was unknown, and, without revealing anything, had his life delineated. The medium said, *inter alia*, " *I see one of your two sons seriously wounded in the war, in the forehead, on the right and across—perhaps also in the left shoulder—I do not see death, perhaps he may be a prisoner.*"

This, be it observed, gives an example of definite cryptæsthesia, probably telepathic. But M. now began to think that, since the letter had only inferred death because his son was seen to fall wounded in the head, perhaps the medium was correct in his suggestion that Jean was a prisoner. Accordingly, he went to another medium, giving her a letter written by Jean, to establish contact. She promptly saw him, wounded and bandaged in the head, and predicted his recovery and return. This strengthened M's. hope, and, when he heard later that all the other dead had been recovered but Jean's body had not been found, he may naturally be held to have more than half believed his hope. After this he, or his friends, obtained psychometric clair-voyance about Jean on sixteen occasions and each time got some piece of information showing that he was alive, a prisoner, well cared for, suffering from loss of memory, would write soon, would return eventually cured, etc. Only one medium, to whom Osty had given one of Jean's letters, said " There is no future for this person ; he is dead."

And yet the truth was that Jean was dead ; or, at any rate, that no trace of him has been found, and no record of his treatment in the hospitals of Germany or Switzerland ; nor has any news ever come of him. Undoubtedly he was killed outright at Verdun, and probably buried by a shell.

All these mediums, in fact, had simply echoed back the hopes and convictions which existed unexpressed in M's. mind ; so that their very sensitiveness to telepathic impressions destroyed their value in this case as in-formants. This, indeed, is an example which should be studied, because it reveals the extent to which an honest medium may unconsciously dupe us, or, perhaps we should say, to which we can dupe ourselves. And it makes us realize the almost insuperable difficulty of proving any one mode of cryptæsthesia to the complete exclusion of the other modes ; which is the task to which we must address ourselves in the next three chapters.

BIBLIOGRAPHY

RICHET. Thirty Years of Psychical Research.
TISCHNER. Telepathy and Clairvoyance.
OSTY. Supernormal Faculties in Man.
DUFAY AND AZAM. Paper in P.S.P.R., Part 16.

CHAPTER TEN

TELEPATHY

1

IT is one of the curiosities of the workings of the popular mind that the less an alleged supernormal phenomenon corresponds with the previously known course of nature, the more readily it is credited. Thus the belief in prevision has always been widespread, in spite of the concurrently accepted doctrine that nothing exists except the present. Again telepathy, or the direct and immediate interchange between two minds without any corresponding mediate physical communication, has been widely accepted by people who also insist that all knowledge is gained through the five senses, and that the mind can only express itself and make contact with other minds by means of physical signs and movements. And on the other hand there is general disbelief in the theory that a human being can project an ectoplasmic structure with which to move objects or manifest itself materially, although such a theory in no way contradicts, but only extends, previously established biological knowledge. The popular belief which is preferred to this comparatively normal theory is that of a miraculous and completely unintelligible action of disembodied spirits on inert matter.

The popular acceptance of telepathy as a short and easy explanation of all supernormal observations is not really justified; for although telepathy undoubtedly is a provable phenomenon, it is by no means the only, or even the correct, explanation of many of them.

The early members of the S.P.R. showed a distinct lack of scientific rigour when they endeavoured to label all cases of supernormal phenomena as telepathic. The famous work, *Phantasms of the Living*, which embodied several hundreds of instances of so-called spontaneous telepathy collected by Gurney in answer to his *questionnaire*, does not demonstrate the operation of pure telepathy in any single instance with any certainty. The many examples given there, interesting as they are in themselves, and valuable as showing the prevalence of spontaneous and sporadic Cryptæsthesia amongst quite normal everyday people, do not exclude the possible operation of either prevision or clairvoyance. Of course, spontaneous cases, recorded often after a considerable interval, are not likely to indicate decisively one mode rather than another ; in any given case it is impossible to exclude two of the three possible causes.

The same thing is true of the very large majority of instances commonly cited as demonstrating telepathy ; they do not exclude the alternative theory of clairvoyance. I do not say that clairvoyance is, in fact, the proper explanation of them ; on the contrary, I think that telepathy is a more usual factor, but that it is not by any means proven in these cases.

The popular idea of telepathy is that it consists in a transmission of thoughts from the mind of an agent (A) to the mind of a percipient (P) and their reception by the latter. This is supposed to be a voluntary conscious act on A's part, and an involuntary passive rôle is assigned to P. Moreover, the transmission is compared vaguely with the analogy of wireless waves. There are thought-waves, or thought-rays, which the brain of A emits and which, after travelling through space, fall on the brain of P, which resonates sympathetically, there to evoke the corresponding thoughts.

Now all this talk of thought-waves is childishly loose, and the analogy is absolutely false.

In the first place a wave-theory is valueless unless it expresses the observed facts. In the science of Radiation it is useful to have a wave-theory because radiation is emitted by vibrating sources, can be reflected and refracted, can produce interference and diffraction effects, can be polarized, and finally travels through space with a measurable velocity and diminishes in intensity according to the square of the distance travelled. If any single experiment were devised which demonstrated that telepathy shewed any one of these phenomena there might be some sense in propounding a wave-theory as a guess ; but it would not become at all likely unless at least several of these effects were demonstrated. And in point of fact there is not a single particle of evidence that thought-transmission shows any analogy at all to the behaviour of a wave—nor, for that matter, to the behaviour of a stream of corpuscles either.

The whole theory (if it can be called a theory) depends on the entirely discredited hypothesis that every thought or idea corresponds with a definite vibration of particles in the brain. When I think of the idea " chair " it may well be that my brain particles arrange themselves in a given manner and vibrate in a certain way. Indeed, at any given instant, they must be doing so. But there is not, in the whole of psychology or physiology, one shred of evidence that the next time I think of a chair the arrangement and vibrations of the particles are the same as they were last time ; or that a corresponding idea in another person's brain involves a similar arrangement or vibration. Indeed, in the nature of things, such evidence would seem to be inherently unobtainable.

Finally the analogy with wireless transmission is fundamentally false, because telepathy involves the communication of an idea, or a mental state, *directly* as such ; whereas speech, writing, telegraphy, and all other modes of communication involve the *indirect* communication of ideas by means of the *direct* transmission of a code of arbitrary signals which have been

previously assigned a conventional interpretation. If I
go to China and say a sentence in English to an unedu-
cated peasant my ideas are not transmitted, for although
he receives the sound-waves he has not previously
agreed that they shall have a certain arbitrary meaning.
Even gesture will be useless unless it corresponds with
something we all have in common, like the motions of
eating or drinking. Thus we see that telepathy is really
a unique phenomenon having none of the analogies
which loose thinkers have so frequently assigned to it.

2

In dealing with the question of experimental telepathy
it is well to consider two general points. Firstly, telepathy almost inevitably implies a sympathetic *rapport*
between the sender and the receiver ; and secondly, it
is vastly improbable that indifferent ideas, unassociated
with emotional tone, should be sent out or received so
easily as ideas having some affective force. Thus we
find, for example, that a greatly preponderating proportion of the apparent cases of spontaneous telepathy
either occur during some emotional crisis, or at least
involve the transmission of feeling as well as a bare idea.
For example, there is a typical case quoted by Hyslop
(*Enigmas of Psychical Research*, p. 164). Briefly, a
young man in Australia dreamed, at 1 a.m. on the
night of December 22–23, 1881, that the kitchen in his
father's house (in London) was on fire. He woke up
greatly impressed with the reality of his dream, and
wrote it in his diary, noting the hour. Six or seven
weeks afterwards he received a letter, dated December
22, 1881, from his father, telling him that there had
been a fire on Sunday last without any serious consequences.

The important point about the case, which Hyslop
calls " one of the best substantiated instances on
record," concerns the times of the various events. The

fire actually took place on the evening of Sunday, December 18. The man dreamed of the fire at 1 a.m, on December 23. But 1 a.m. in Australia was about 3.30 p.m., December 22, in London, since Australian time is $9\frac{1}{2}$ hours ahead of English time, and at this hour the father was writing his letter to catch the five-o'clock post. So that the only reasonable explanation of the event is to suppose that the father's thought, telepathically transmitted, was received by the son while asleep, and induced an hallucinatory dream in which the main fact was the fire. (Details of the dream show some correspondence with, and also divergencies from, the actual event. For example, the fire actually broke out in the servants' room in the attic, not in the kitchen.)

It is thus not to be expected that striking results will be obtained by unsympathetic experimenters trying to transmit numbers, triangles, etc. As an example of " how not to do it," we may cite Milne Bramwell (*Hypnotism*, p. 142). " For several years a committee of the S.P.R., of which I was a member, devoted itself mainly to telepathetic experiments. Our methods were simple and effective, and yet placed no unnecessary barrier in the way of the appearance of the phenomenon. The subject, generally hypnotized, was placed in an arm-chair and told that the operator would select different cards from a pack, and that the subject was to try to guess the cards in turn. The operator, who was so placed that the subject could not see what he was doing, drew the cards from the pack at random, told the subject that he had selected one, that he was looking hard at it, and that the subject would see or know what it was. Meanwhile the operator stared fixedly at the card for several minutes and concentrated his attention entirely on it. In these experiments, as well as in a long series of private ones, the percentage of correct guesses fell below the number which ought to have been reached according to the laws of chance."

As a result of this kind of experimenting Bramwell disbelieves in telepathy ; but one might fairly infer that his disbelief was prior to his experimentation, and conditioned its form ; since his whole book betrays antagonism to the supernormal, and people who investigate a subject of this nature in a spirit of hostility are ensuring negative results at the outset. Nothing is more important than to remember that one is dealing with a living personality, and that the psychological state of the various persons concerned must of necessity influence the phenomena produced.

Probably one of the most effective methods of collecting personal evidence for telepathy is that adopted by Miss Ramsden and Miss Miles and reported in the Proc. S.P.R., Parts 54 and 69. Of course, as scientific evidence to produce before strangers, their results are hardly of much use, for there is obviously the possibility of collusion ; but for those who trust the common honesty of the experimenters it seems likely to be a more fruitful method than the usual card-guessing, because it gives more scope to such telepathic action as may genuinely be there.

Briefly, their method was for Miss Miles to write on a postcard each day (often at a fixed hour) what her chief impressions had been, and anything she particularly wished to transmit. Miss Ramsden, the recipient, also wrote at the same time on a postcard what impression she had received. These postcards, bearing their postmarks, were preserved. In addition, a journal was kept in which facts omitted from Miss Miles' card, but nevertheless among her impressions in the day, were noted down if they were found to correspond with the recipient's impressions, and also, when necessary or possible, corroboration by friends was written. Many concordances between the agents' and the recipients' impressions are very striking, but unfortunately numerous instances are hardly evidential to the reader, because the postmarks are illegible or the card was not posted in good time. Of course, the whole postmark business is not in itself of very great value, as telegrams or pre-arrangement are perfectly possible, but it does, I suppose, give one a certain degree of confidence, since there are many amiable people who, without dreaming of deliberate falsification or fraud, might convince themselves that they had really seen a certain detail, after they knew it had been present in the agent's mind. What is really useful, however, in this method is its simplicity and its applicability to all sorts of private occasions. If two people wish to investigate telepathy for their own personal and private satisfaction, and not for the sake of scientific demonstration to the outside world, here is an obviously easy and convenient method. And in the end, when a sufficient number of intelligent people have had unequivocal personal evidence of the phenomenon, it will be accepted as part of normal experience.

The bulk of the work of the S.P.R., of Professor Richet, and very many others, in experimental telepathy, though valuable as demonstrating the existence of Cryptæsthesia, is not of a nature to demonstrate the particular mode of telepathy with any certainty. Almost all of it consists of experiments like those of Milne Bramwell, in which material objects, such as a playing card or a design drawn on paper, or a word written down, or small object held in the agent's hand, are guessed or " seen " by the percipient. It was formerly assumed by most investigators that when, in a series of trials, the number of correct replies was far in excess of that which could be accounted for by the laws of probability, then it must be a case of telepathy, in which the thought of the object was transmitted from the agent's to the percipient's mind. But obviously now that we have independent evidence that a sensitive person can " see " material objects themselves clairvoyantly, when such objects are unknown to any agent's mind, it becomes an open question whether in all these experiments it was not rather on clairvoyance than on telepathy that the percipient relied.

In the case given above of the Australian's dream clairvoyance is an improbable explanation, because the fire was not seen in his dream at the time when it occurred, but some days later at a time when, in all probability, the father's thoughts were occupied with it. If, therefore, telepathy is proven elsewhere it supplies the probable explanation in this case. But in all the cases of so-called " experimental telepathy," in which a material object is used, the result cannot prove telepathy rather than clairvoyance, although occasionally minor details in the result suggest one rather than the other mode of perception. For example, it sometimes happens in reading words that the percipient will give a word of totally different meaning, whose letters, in shape and number, give it a close resemblance to the word which was written. This suggests a visual misreading, though it may be due to bad visualization by the agent. On the other hand, the word given may be a synonym or a word of closely similar sound ; which suggests a mental perception rather than a visual one. In any case the evidence is not decisively in favour of either clairvoyance or telepathy in those cases, for there has not been an adequate isolation of possible causes.

The problem to be solved then is how to convey to the percipient an idea or a state of feeling which has no material representation and no symbolical or direct material expression at all. In other words it must simply exist in the agent's mind, and the only evidence which we can have for the success of the experiment must be the testimony of the agent himself. It is no use his writing down an idea beforehand and, say, depositing the document with a third person, and then getting a witness to testify to the correspondence between the result achieved and the original idea trans- mitted ; for this process would open the way to an explanation based on clairvoyant reading of the papers.

For direct and unequivocal proof of pure telepathy, i.e. the strictly psychological communication of mental states independently of all intermediate physical processes, we must ultimately rely on the unsupported testimony of the experimenter. This may seem highly unsatisfactory, but it is mitigated by a few further considerations.

In the first place, we may refuse to consider the testimony of any but men of acknowledged integrity and scientific disinterestedness ; men who as far as we can judge, have investigated in a purely impartial spirit of inquiry, ready and willing to find negative as well as positive results, and capable of carrying out their experiments in such a way as to avoid error and deception.

Secondly, we may note that in any case we cannot, in this sort of experimentation, do away with testimony ; and the mere multiplication of witnesses, though it undoubtedly makes deception and deliberate falsification harder, does not really improve the quality of the testimony ; one strictly honest man being no less honest than twelve like himself. Thirdly, the intrinsic nature of the phenomenon is such that it absolutely necessitates this procedure. To prove the intercommunication of minds unequivocally you must necessarily remove all intermediate material links, so that the mental content to be perceived remains purely mental and is not embodied in any physical symbol.

Finally if the conditions under which telepathy can be provoked experimentally are once ascertained it will be very easy for any particular individual to verify the facts himself, so that gradually they will be accepted because of common experience. On the other hand, if the original testimony is fallacious it will not be supported when a sufficient number of other people conduct experiments under similar conditions.

3

We are now in a position to turn to the crucial evidence for pure telepathy. In accordance with what we should expect from our knowledge of the connection between supernormal phenomena and the trance state we find this evidence in the behaviour of hypnotized patients. On *a priori* grounds we expect that telepathy will only take place readily when there is a state of sympathetic rapport between the two communicating minds, and that it will be helped by a strong affective tone. Now this is just the condition existing between the hypnotizer and his subject; the state of rapport being very strongly marked during the hypnotic trance, and still persisting during waking hours in cases where the operator frequently hypnotizes the same subject. Thus it is natural to find that in the accounts of the older mesmerists there are many instances of pure telepathy, though these are not considered here as evidence. We may, however, cite a case given by Ochorowicz, which I believe is to be found in his work, *De la suggestion mentale ;* but not having the book I quote it in translation from Flammarion's *Before Death.* Ochorowicz is one of the most important and reliable continental researchers, and we have already had several occasions to refer to him. I will quote Flammarion's extract of this case in full, noting, as he does, that Ochorowicz gives in addition forty-one other similar experiences, so that the phenomenon is not an isolated occurrence.

" It was my custom to put the patient to sleep every other day and to leave her in a deep sleep while I took notes. After an experience of two months, I could be certain that she would not stir before I approached her to induce the real state of somnambulism. But on this day, after having taken several notes and without changing my attitude (I was a few yards from her and outside her field of vision, my notebook on my knees and my head leaning on my left hand) I pretended to write, scratching my pen, but inwardly concentrating my will on an order which I gave mentally.

1. ' *Lift the right hand.*'

(I look at the patient through the fingers of the left hand pressed against my forehead.)

One minute : no action.

Two minutes : agitation of the right hand.

Three minutes : the agitation increases. The patient rubs her lids and lifts her right hand.

I confess that this experience stirs me more than anything ever has. I begin again.

2. ' *Rise and come to me.*'

She rubs her eyes, stirs, rises slowly, and comes to me with difficulty, her hand outstretched.

I lead her back to her place without speaking.

3. ' *Draw the bracelet off the left wrist and hand it to me.*'

No action. She stretches out her left hand, rises and goes towards Mademoiselle X——, then towards the piano.

I touch her right arm and probably push it a little in the direction of her left arm, while I concentrate my thought on the order given. She draws off her bracelet, seems to think, and hands it to me.

4. ' *Rise, approach the arm-chair by the table, and sit down beside us.*'

She rises, rubs her eyelids, and walks toward me. ' I must do something else,' she says. She searches—touches the table—moves a cup of tea. She draws back, takes hold of the arm-chair, pushes it towards the table with a smile of satisfaction, and sits down, limp with fatigue.

All these orders have been given mentally and without gestures, without pronouncing a single word.''

A single case of this sort, established with certainty, is sufficient to prove the existence of telepathy as a fact. But of course it depends for its certainty on one's belief in Ochorowicz. However, other experimenters, for example Gibier, Boirac, de Rochas, Janet, and Alrutz, have observed the same or closely similar phenomena. The following quotation from Gibier's *Analyse des Choses*, for example, confirms Ochorowicz.

" I have experimented with sensitive subjects in what has recently been called mental suggestion : for instance, a test which I have tried several times consisted in telling a sleeping subject : ' You will awaken when you feel that I wish you to wake up ' ; and I would then set myself to enter up my observations on the séance which I had just had with the hypnotized person. I hid myself behind a pile of books so that the subject (who *saw* in spite of having a bandage over his eyes) would see nothing on my face to warn him when I wished to awaken him.

" At some given moment, sometimes in the middle and sometimes at the end of my note-taking, I thought of *willing* the subject to waken ; if it was when I had finished writing I nevertheless continued to move my pen across the paper, tracing any words, such as, ' I wish you to awaken, wake up ! ' or other phrases having no connection with the situation, and the subject would wake up in not more than forty to sixty seconds."

Perhaps the most interesting cases are those in which a subject is hypnotized by telepathy, acting over a certain distance. The classical instance[1] is that reported on and observed by Myers (see P.S.P.R. Part 10) in which Dr. Gibert and Professor Pierre Janet experimented with Mme. B., a peasant woman. Dr. A. T. Myers, Ochorowicz, and some other physicians were also witnesses of these experiments ; and in a series of 25, tried at different hours on odd days between October 3, 1885, and May 6, 1886, under conditions that eliminated errors due to expectation or suggestion, there were 19 successes.

Mme. B. herself was middle aged and of stolid

[1] Other similar experiments were done by Boirac ; see his *Psychic Science*, Chap. X.

temperament and limited intelligence ; Myers says that
she did not make money, or seek to gain notice, as a
hypnotic " sensitive," and that she actually disliked
being put to sleep from a distance, and would try to
prevent it by putting her hands in cold water if she
could do so before falling into the trance. The peculi-
arity of these experiments is, of course, the fact that
Dr. Gibert and Professor Janet could hypnotize Mme.
B. by a mere act of concentrated will, at a considerable distance from her, and at any odd hour when she
was not expecting it. I will quote two short examples
from Myers' rather detailed paper.

" V. On April 23rd, M. Janet, who had woken her
up and left her awake, lunched in our company, and
retired to his own house at 4.30 (a time chosen by lot) to
try to put her to sleep from thence. At 5.5 we all entered
the *salon* of the Pavillon, and found her asleep with shut
eyes, but sewing vigorously (being in the stage in which
movements once suggested are automatically continued).

" VI. On April 24th the whole party chanced to
meet at M. Janet's house at 3 p.m. and he then, at my
suggestion, entered his study to will that Mme. B should
sleep. We waited in his garden, and at 3.20 proceeded
together to the Pavillon, which I entered first at 3.30
and found Mme. B profoundly sleeping over her sewing,
having ceased to sew."

In these experiments the operator was from a quarter
to one mile away from the patient. On the other hand,
in Myers' example No. IV, M. Gibert made to her a
mental suggestion, while pressing his forehead against
hers, but without any other gesture or speech. The
suggestion was that at 11 a.m. on the next day she should
look at a photographic album in the *salon*. In due
course next day she entered the *salon* at 11 a.m. in a
state of trance, and wandered round for twenty-five
minutes, finally taking up an album of photographs. At
11.30 she was seated on the sofa gazing fixedly at the
album and sinking into deep lethargy. The observers,

Myers, Janet, and the others, had stationed themselves in a room where she could not see them, but by looking through the partly opened door they could observe her.

What is perhaps the most satisfactory feature in these experiments is that they were originated not by a Spiritualist or an accredited spokesman of metapsychic science, who might be suspected of credulity by a layman, but by Pierre Janet, the greatest authority on hysteria with the possible exception of Freud. His attitude towards the supernormal may be judged from Sudré's comment : " Il s'est d'ailleurs toujours refusé à accorder le caractère métapsychique aux phénomènes qu'il constatait. S'il avait poussé ses sujets dans le sens de ce ' merveilleux ' dont il avait la sainte horreur, il aurait découvert tout ce que Richet, moins prévenu, fit entrer dans la science nouvelle." It is always more satisfying to draw one's evidence from opponents of the supernormal than from its partisans.

The sensibility of the hypnotized patient to telepathic impressions has been more recently confirmed by Dr. Alrutz, whose experiments we had occasion to mention when discussing hypnotism. Dr. Alrutz asserts, at the conclusion of his paper, that the power of the hypnotizer to wake the patient solely by thought and will has been proved indubitably.

" With my three chief subjects I practically never fail in this respect. A black cloth having or not having been thrown over the subject's head, he begins after a certain time, varying from 15 seconds to 2 minutes, to make movements, stretch himself, etc. He then throws away the cloth and opens his eyes, generally now nearly fully awake. The sittings generally last 2 hours, and I make the experiment when I like during this period of time. . . . At least 50 such experiments have been made by me, and all but one have been successful."

From these examples we may admit that telepathy has been demonstrated unequivocally (accepting the honesty of the experimenters of course) under certain restricted circumstances—namely (*a*) when the percipient is in a hypnotized condition, and (*b*) when the agent, being the hypnotizer, has concentrated all his conscious will and thought on the effect to be obtained. Thus it would appear, from just these cases alone, as if telepathy were an active transmission of thought from A to P, necessitating effort on A's part; and this view is certainly supported by the general character of Janet's experiences, and by details showing that Mme. B. faltered and paused on one occasion precisely at the moment when the operator gave up the experiment for a minute or two and relaxed himself by starting to play billiards.

4

We are now able to say that the rigorous demonstration of pure telepathy applies to the active, conscious, and intentional sending of a mental content by the hypnotizer, and its passive reception by the entranced patient.

From the logical scientific point of view we have no right to admit, as yet, that pure telepathy exists under other and less restricted conditions, although its existence under a certain condition opens up that possibility, as it shows that direct intermental communication, without any intermediate physical signs, is within the scope of nature.

But when we bring into consideration the whole bulk of psychic experience, and study the mass of detailed spiritualistic communications with the intention, not of excluding everything which is not unequivocally telepathic, but of judging probabilities and observing what seems to happen in these cases, we reach a different conclusion, and one which endows the factor of telepathy with a far wider practical significance. Few who read Osty's treatise carefully will refuse to agree that his general conclusions are, in the light of the great bulk of the evidence, reasonable and probable, if not wholly certain. He finds (and practically all other modern researchers would, I think, corroborate his general experience) that telepathy is primarily a function of the unconscious mind, and that not only does it occur most readily and to the largest extent when the recipient is in a state of mediumistic or hypnotic trance, or asleep, but that it also mainly, and most readily, concerns thoughts and ideas of which the agent is not actively conscious at the time. The examples of this sort of " transmission," which, at any rate in the common mediumistic instances, seems more analagous to an active reading of A's mind by the percipient, are innumerable, but as they are almost always trivial and always (necessarily) unexpected, it is difficult, if not impossible, to select any one that on analysis will by itself constitute an unequivocal proof of telepathic rather than clairvoyant action ; it is only the cumulative effect of hundreds of varied instances that makes one certain that this is the explanation.

According to the authors of *Phantasms of the Living,* their cases of spontaneous telepathy (a great many of which were at least as probably due either to clairvoyance or ectoplasmic projections, since they did not differentiate sufficiently rigidly between alternative causes) include a great proportion in which the presumptive agent was either asleep, or in a faint, or otherwise partially unconscious. Warcollier, in his recent work, states that about two-thirds of the instances of telepathy concern transmission during sleep. And in any case the great bulk of the information which is presumably acquired by telepathy is found in the automatic writings or trance sayings of mediums.

The fact that telepathy is mainly an activity of the unconscious mind introduces a further practical complication, due to the normal factors of symbolization, distortion, and elaboration. If an idea is received subconsciously and tends to rise into consciousness it may there become distorted to harmonize with the content of the percipient's conscious mind ; and if it conflicts

with his ideas, either of self-interest, or of reason, or
other strong tendency, it may be scouted and rejected,
and will probably only rise again to consciousness at a
later more propitious occasion, when some appropriate
external stimulus arises, or it will rise in a greatly
distorted and symbolical form. A particularly striking
instance of this sort of mechanism is the case of
Lord Dufferin's vision, recounted in the chapter of
Precognition.

Moreover, apart altogether from any question of
repression and avoidance of conflict in the recipient's
mind, it is *a priori* probable that many (if not most) of
the impressions telepathically received do not rise at
once to the conscious mind, either because they have no
particular interest at the moment, or because among a
multitude of impressions only a few will engage attention;
so that they lie latent, and only reveal themselves at
some subsequent occasion when, for some reason often
undiscoverable, they are stimulated. If, as seems almost
indisputable, this is normally the case, one can understand, in a general way, how it is that so many
" evidential " communications, containing details apparently unknown to the sitters present, but seemingly
derived from someone now deceased, can be produced
by a medium. The details may have been " read " by
the medium in the mind of the ostensible communicator
while he was alive, and only have emerged much later
on when provoked by the associations presented at the
séance. Again, it explains the often observed fact that
in a series of experiments an answer will often be given
which is incorrect with regard to the corresponding
question, but correct as a reply to a previous one which
had not been answered correctly at the time. Further
it explains all those cases where a presumably telepathic
vision or hallucination occurs, not at the moment of
the death or danger to which it refers, but some hours
or days afterwards. The Gurney and Myers group of
early researchers assumed arbitrarily that twelve hours

was to be taken as the working limit for this sort of thing, but modern experience goes to show that there is no justification for setting any time-limit to the period in which impressions may lie latent.

There is no shred of evidence that distance, as such, has any influence on the strength of telepathic impressions or on the speed or accuracy of their transmission, if indeed they are transmitted at all. In fact, the whole phenomenon is outside space, and very probably outside time too. But, just as contact with a relevant object, or better still the bodily presence of the person, enhances the accuracy and augments the wealth of information given in Psychometry, so here contact between the agent and percipient, either direct, or through an intervening object (and a few feet of air is to be included here as a connecting material), notably increases the ease and extent of telepathic action. By far the fullest and most accurate information is obtained when the person whose mind is read is actually present to the percipient ; this is obviously quite natural, and in line with the general experience as the state of *rapport*. But while this *rapport* is most complete between a hypnotized patient and his operator, it appears to be notable also as between the medium and his consultant ; and apparently it can arise between any two minds anywhere, in at least a minor degree.

In other words there are no observable or experimental limits to the action of telepathy, which seems to merge into a generalized, purely mental, percipience. It would seem that we all are subject all the time to impressions from other minds, and that it is only by virtue of their intensity and insistence, or because of certain appropriate conditions, that certain individual impressions stand out and force us to notice them, when we may recognize their telepathic origin.

The apparent universality of telepathy, and its lack of any discoverable limits, together with a study of the psychology of mysticism, have led some writers to suggest that our individual minds are not ultimately separate entities, but that they are all united, or at least that they interpenetrate, in what is called the unconscious. The individual self-conscious minds which seem so separate and isolated may, on this view, be compared to mountain peaks, whose lower slopes merge into the common level of the earth. The peaks are indeed separate, but the mountains may form a continuous whole, and a traveller may walk from one peak to another. The older philosophy of a universal mind, of which our minds are but fragments, each one very imperfect, is now being confirmed but modified. The universal mind exists, doubtless; it may even be the only thing that does exist, all else being but " appearance." But it is not quite like our ideal of a human conscious mind; it is rather more akin to Hardy's " Great Foresightless," at any rate when looked at from our human personal point of view.

BIBLIOGRAPHY

HYSLOP. Enigmas of Psychical Research.

MILNE BRAMWELL. Hypnotism : its History, Practice, and Theory.

MILES AND RAMSDEN. Experiments in Thought Transference, P.S.P.R., Parts 54 and 69.

FLAMMARION. Before Death (Chapter V).

OCHOROWICZ. De la Suggestion Mentale.

MYERS. Telepathic Hypnotism, P.S.P.R., Part 10.

BOIRAC. Psychic Science.

ALRUTZ. Problems of Hypnotism, P.S.P.R., Part 83.

OSTY. Supernormal Faculties in Man.

WARCOLLIER. La Télépathie.

CHAPTER ELEVEN

PRECOGNITION[1]

1

NOTHING is more fundamentally opposed to our instinctive habits of thought than an acceptance of the reality of precognition ; and yet the evidence in favour of this is conclusive. It is, in fact, the one outstanding " occult " phenomenon which is common to the magicians, soothsayers, prophets and inspired persons of every race and age. Yet common sense can accept tales of ghosts and telekinesis and hyperæsthetic sensibility with far less shock to its equilibrium than it can admit a true prevision of future events ; for our whole intellectual life is based upon the sense of time, and depends upon an apperception of the Now as real, and the Past and Future as non-existent.

We cannot function intellectually, we cannot *think*, except under the influence of our apprehension of space and time ; or, at least, very few can do so, and these but imperfectly. And yet, possibly in this very direction lies the path of twentieth-century science and philosophy. The Kantian doctrine that Space and Time are intellectual categories under which we apprehend Reality, that they are forms of perception, in fact, is a doctrine to which we shall be forced to return ; and Bergson's subtle treatment of the concept of duration places the question of the nature of Time in the forefront of modern philosophical problems.

By another path, that of mathematical physics,

[1] Portions of this chapter appeared in *The Quest* for April 1928.

Poincaré, Einstein, and Minkowski have brought the same problem to the attention of physical scientists, and demonstrated the necessity of a radical change in our instinctive intellectual assumptions. Our ideas of Time must alter ; though how that alteration is to take place remains a mystery. Can we conceive a four-dimensional space-time continuum ? We can certainly postulate it, argue about it, and use the idea in the solution of physical problems ; but can we really *think* it ? Can we, in actual fact, enlarge our consciousness so that it apprehends Time as a mode of space instead of as an entirely different concept having no relationship to space ?

This is, as it seems to me, the essential problem for twentieth-century psychology and scientific philosophy ; and it is a problem which, if it can be solved affirmatively, will be so solved largely by the help of psychical research and mysticism. For, to anyone who has read some of the mystics, it will appear evident that the goal of mysticism is an analogous enlargement of consciousness, in which the limitations of our present illusions of Space and Time disappear ; and we may perhaps usefully regard true clairvoyance and precognition as expressions, within the normal intellectual categories, of what has been experienced by a consciousness thus enlarged.

Let us now consider some of the instances of prevision, leaving aside all the traditional stories (many of which are striking) and confining ourselves at first to cases which have been recorded and verified by men of scientific repute. The earliest of the instances which I mention is an extremely interesting one, because it also shows the limitations of suggestion. It is a classical case, given by Dr. Liébault, the father of the modern Suggestionist school, and can be most conveniently found in Hyslop (p. 325). Briefly, the case is as follows :

A young man came to Dr. Liébault in a neurasthenic condition of great depression and fear. The cause of this anxiety was that some years back he had out of idle curiosity visited a sensitive named Mme. Lenormand to have his fortune told. Mme. Lenormand had predicted first of all that his father would die next year; then that he himself would be a soldier for a short time, would marry and have two children; and finally would die aged twenty-six. The man had regarded all this as humbug; but his father died suddenly, as foretold; he did become a soldier for a brief period, he married and had two children. Seeing these predictions exactly fulfilled, when his twenty-seventh birthday[2] drew near he became alarmed, and grew convinced that he would die on that day. In his distress he came to Dr. Liébault, whose fame as a hypnotist was then high, in the hope that something could be done for him. Recognizing that the man might easily die from sheer self-suggestion, Dr. Liébault determined to counteract this by making a second prediction. Accordingly, he presented the young man to another patient of his, an old man who had the reputation of a seer, and who, at the young man's question, promptly prophesied a much longer span of life for him. The man went away relieved, firmly believing the new prophecy, and happily survived the birthday he had formerly so dreaded. The definite self-suggestion of death on his birthday (which, be it observed, was more precise than Mme. Lenormand's prediction of death at the age of twenty-six) was thus given the lie and eradicated. Nevertheless, the patient suddenly fell ill of peritonitis and died the same year at the predicted age.

Another case of prevision which deserves attention is the Tardieu-Sonrel predictions of the Wars of 1870 and of 1914. It is given by Richet (p. 387) and by Osty (p. 38) and the reader should turn to one or other of these books for it. But it suffers from one serious defect, which deprives it of evidential value.

[2] i.e. the day on which he became twenty-six years old; counting the day of his birth as his first birthday.

M. Sonrel made the most remarkable predictions to Dr. Tardieu shortly before the Franco-Prussian War. As always happens, details of the near future were precise and striking, while the prophecy became very vague and general as it dealt with later years. We have Dr. Tardieu's word that these earlier precise predictions were exactly verified by the course of his life in 1870–71 ; and that finally, judging partly from internal and partly from external evidence that the time was near when Sonrel's further predictions, of war and France's trial and final victory with occupation of the Rhine, would be fulfilled, he went to Prof. Richet to reveal the whole prophecy to him. Prof. Richet thus learned of the prediction, and made Dr. Tardieu record it in April 1914 ; that is to say, a very long time after the precise and detailed predictions had become past history and a very short time before the vague and general prophecy was to be realized. The portion of this prophecy which relates to the Great War is not very striking ; it is the sort of thing which anybody might evolve for himself if he felt that a conflict was impending. But this is not to be wondered at, seeing that Sonrel's prediction was made forty-five years before the event.

With regard to predictions of the Great War, the Editor of *Psychic Science* (for July 1929) wrote the following paragraph, but I have not been able to verify the facts from the original papers.

" It is often asked why such world-shaking events as the Great War are not predicted. Well, they were predicted, and the whole of the predictions were printed in the Athens newspapers, *Asty* and *Ethnike*, in August 1914, including the history of the Entente, the dissolution of Austria, the German Republic, and the supremacy of England at the Peace Conference, together with eighteen other details. They were received with ridicule. The papers are on file at the Paris Institute and the full report is given in the Bulletin No. 6 of 1925. It was printed in *Light* of Feb. 27, 1927."

A very beautiful example of exact prevision of the immediate future, partly verified before the event, is the now classical example of the Casimir-Périer election,[3] given by Richet (p. 376) and by Geley (p. 177). Richet writes :

" M. Gallet, student of medicine at Lyons, was preparing some examination work in his room about 11 a.m. He was obsessed by a thought that distracted his work, and he wrote down in his note-book : ' M. Casimir-Périer has been elected President of the Republic by 451 votes.' Gallet cared nothing for politics, and the phrase dumbfounded him. He showed it to his comrade Varay, with whom he was working. After lunch Gallet went to his lectures, and meeting two fellow students, Boucher and Deborne, told them the premonition, at which they only laughed. After lecture the four students went to a café, and shortly after the Paris newspapers arrived, announcing the election of Casimir-Périer by 451 votes.

" Gallet is now a physician at Annecy, and a senator of Savoy ; Varay is a physician also, at Annecy ; Deborne is a pharmacist at Thonon ; Boucher a physician at Cruseilles. All four certify to the strict truth of the fact, which they remember quite clearly.

" The success of Casimir-Périer was very doubtful, and unlikely ; the betting was on Brisson or Dupuy. The probability of his election was very slight ; but even admitting an equal chance for the first three candidates, the probability that one of them would get 451 votes is 1 : 845. But the basis of calculation is very defective. Chance may always be invoked ; it is a convenient way of avoiding thought. What was the cause that compelled Gallet to write on the margin of his anatomical notes : ' Casimir-Périer has been elected by 451 votes ' ? This case is, to my thinking, one of the most decisive proofs of premonition on record."

[3] In this election there were six candidates, of whom Casimir-Périer was only third favourite, and 845 votes were cast

We have here three very good examples of precognition, two of which have been recorded and investigated by men of scientific repute, while the third, that of M. Sonrel's 1870 predictions, though recorded long after the events, nevertheless seems genuine enough.

Mme. Lenormand's prophecies were apparently provoked by the presence of her visitor; they concern his immediate personal future, and are quite analogous to the psychometric clairvoyance in which are revealed past incidents in the life of the sitter. It is as if everyone carried with him a record of his past and future, which the sensitive may apprehend.

M. Sonrel's predictions were much wider in scope, including not only details personal to his friend Dr. Tardieu, but also main outlines of national history. One can hardly say that Dr. Tardieu carried about with him the fact of France's victory and occupation of the Rhine.

But M. Gallet's prediction is the most curious, because it concerns a person and an event which had no connection with or interest for the prophet. M. Gallet, in the midst of his studies, was simply invaded by an idea which was foreign to his personal interests, and unknown by any living mind; for at 11 a.m. when he stated "M. Casimir-Périer has been elected by 451 votes," the election was in fact not over, and the votes had not been counted. The precision of the information is extraordinary, and is probably due to the fact that the event predicted was only a few hours distant. Always we find that precision and exactitude of detail are the greater the closer the events are at hand. This fact seems of considerable importance, and calls for some attention.

Let us now pass on to consider briefly a few more cases of precognition; for it would not be wise, in dealing with a phenomenon which is so little amenable to experiment and voluntary control, to rest satisfied with three instances only. I first simply refer the reader to Lodge's *Survival of Man*, or to page 365 of Richet's book, for an account of the *Marmontel* prediction by Mrs. Verrall, who by automatic writing described, some months before the event, a man reading *Marmontel* in bed by candle-light. I mention only briefly also the thrilling story of Lord Dufferin's premonitory hallucination, given by Flammarion (ii, 200). This involves symbolic elaboration and hallucinatory projection of a visual image, the whole being based on a precognition which evidently entered the subconscious mind of the percipient.

In this case, Lord Dufferin, staying in Ireland, saw at night a phantom man, of extreme and repulsive ugliness, carrying a coffin. This was an hallucination, and as such must have had a proximate mental cause, which must have been some idea in Lord Dufferin's subconscious mind. Some time after, Lord Dufferin was in Paris, as Ambassador, and was with a gathering of persons at an hotel. The others were deferentially waiting for him to enter the lift, when, with an exclamation, he muttered an excuse and withdrew. He had seen in the lift, acting as liftman, the very same repulsive figure of his vision. Others entered the lift to ascend, but on its way up the cord broke, and it dropped down the shaft, killing the occupants. On inquiry, it was found that the liftman was a stranger recently taken on at the hotel, and of unknown origin and history.

All this sounds, of course, like the most melodramatic ghost story, the details are true to fiction ! But suppose for a moment that Lord Dufferin's subconscious self perceived this accident somewhat indistinctly, getting a clear vision only of the liftman's features and of the fact of a fatal mishap. What then is more likely than that this precognition, on rising into consciousness, to be faced and dealt with there, should be at first scouted and dismissed by the percipient as silly and unreal ; and then, insisting on its right to be admitted, should partly clothe itself in a visual symbol and, in this guise of an ugly man carring a coffin, attain hallucinatory intensity ? Given the possibility of precognition as a fact, our knowledge of the workings of the subconscious mind enables us without much difficulty to account for the setting in which Lord Dufferin became conscious of the prevision. In fact we know, from the statements of many mediums, that supernormal knowledge often first clothes itself in symbolic imagery, and presents itself in disguise to the conscious mind of the percipient, who then must, in the light of his intuition and his experience, interpret the symbols.

The next case I quote is one given by Dr. J. Maxwell (p. 201). The importance of it lies mainly in the fact that Maxwell knew of the prediction and talked of it before it came to be fulfilled. He writes :

" The vision was related to me eight days before the event took place, and I myself had related it to several persons before its realization. A sensitive perceived in a crystal the following scene :

" A large steamer, flying a flag of three horizontal bands, black, white, and red, and bearing the name *Leutschland*, navigating in mid-ocean ; the boat surrounded in smoke ; a great number of sailors, passengers, and men in uniform rushed to the upper deck and the sensitive saw the vessel founder."

It is to be noted that eight days after Maxwell was told this vision the German boat *Deutschland* burst a boiler, and had to stand to. The vessel, however, did not sink, and there was no fire ; but doubtless there was a great deal of steam which the crystal gazer mistook for smoke. The sensitive misread the first letter of the name.

In the same book of Maxwell's, Richet incidentally contributes an excellent example of precognition. A certain Mme. X., being apparently in sympathetic *rapport* with the family of another lady, Mme. B., both foretold the death of Mme. B. and had a vaguer premonition prior to an accident which killed Mme. B.'s son.

I now come to some better examples of premonition, taken from Dr. Osty's excellent book. First, I take the case of Mme. Przybylska.[4] In 1920 this sensitive gave a series of séances in June, July, and August, during the course of the Russo-Polish War. The messages she received contained detailed information of the course of events in the war a few weeks ahead ; and these messages were recorded almost immediately by a committee of the Warsaw S.P.R. composed of people well known in Poland. These predictions, which gave names and dates, were practically fulfilled exactly in the course of the ensuing weeks ; and Osty considered it to be one of the very best cases of prevision on record. " By its precision in names, dates, and places," he writes, " and by the accuracy of the information given, it is perfect."

Osty has collected a considerable mass of evidence for prevision by going to a large number of mediums to have the events of his own life foretold, and recording in full all they say. Among them he has found a few who are specially gifted in this direction, and by going fairly regularly to these selected sensitives he has been able to obtain many details of his life in advance. Apparently he intended to continue his researches until 1931 (when the experiment would have lasted twenty years), and then to publish a monograph on the results. Meanwhile, the reader is given a few examples which are of great interest. For instance (p. 88) :

Mme Peyroutet, in whom he found a sensitive capable of foreseeing minute and accidental details of his near future, said to him on November 30, 1920 : " Your two sons who are at school will go for the holidays into the country near you. One of them will have no luck, he will pass his vacation lying down—it will not be serious."

Osty says that his two sons, both of whom were strong, healthy boys, came to Cher for the holidays. On December 26, the elder boy said his leg pained him. A boil developed, and was at once attended to, but on

---

[4] Geley (p. 182) gives a slightly fuller account of these predictions.

the 27th it became a large carbuncle, and on the 28th was surrounded by lymphangitis. On the 29th an incision had to be made, and the boy spent the rest of the holidays lying down.

Again, on December 2, Mme, Peyroutet said : " You will soon have a dog," and on March 31 repeated this. Dr. Osty, who was about to reside in Paris, had no intention of getting a dog ; moreover, had not possessed one for fifteen years. Nevertheless on April 11, during cold rain, a strange black dog was found shivering in the garden, and was taken into the house by the parlour-maid. As they could not restore it to the owner, the children begged to keep it, and eventually Dr. Osty allowed it to remain. Soon afterwards, however, it disappeared.

Owing to his method of procedure Osty naturally would tend to get predictions of the same event from various angles and at various time-distances. Thus we find (p. 175) :

" A simple and brief instance of precognition of the same event given at two different periods : Two years before its occurrence the percipient expressed it thus : ' Oh ! Peril of death after a while—perhaps an accident —but you will be saved—your life continues.' "

This sort of thing is, of course, open to the objection that everybody is in some sense in peril of death some-times (often quite without knowing it)—though perhaps this criticism is not entirely fair ; and that the vagueness of the peril robs the prediction of any value. This vagueness, however, is in harmony with what we know of " long shots " in prophecy.

The second prediction was given four months before the event (March 11, 1911) :

" Take care. You will soon have a serious accident. I hear a violent shock—a loud noise—You will be very near death—What luck ! you will take no hurt ! I see a man bleeding on the ground ; he is moaning, and all around him things are strewn ; I can't say what."

Osty notes that on August 15, 1911, he was driving his car, when a drunken baker, going furiously, pulled the wrong rein, and collided with him. Osty and a friend with him were unhurt; but " turning round he saw the horse galloping off, the cart in the ditch, wheels uppermost, and the baker stretched moaning and bleeding in the middle of the road with a number of loaves scattered round him."

A highly ingenious method of demonstrating clairvoyant precognition has been devised by Osty (*Revue Métapsychique*, Mai-Juin, 1926). The case is given as follows :

Before a public demonstration Osty, accompanied by others, went to the empty hall at the Institut in Paris, selected a chair at random from among the one hundred and fifty seats there, and gummed a label underneath it. Then he got a sensitive, M. Pascal Forthuny, to sit in the chair, and left him there with a stenographer. M. Forthuny then proceeded to dictate what he saw clairvoyantly of the unknown person who, some time later, would occupy this seat. Having done so, he withdrew. A considerable crowd had assembled outside, and when the doors were opened, a rush for seats ensued. During the demonstration M. Forthuny appeared and read out the description which he had previously dictated; and it was found to fit, with more or less exactitude, the person who was now occupying the selected chair.

The beauty of the experiment depends, of course, entirely on how far pure chance (as we call it) rules the disposition of seats amongst a crowd. In this case two hundred persons scrambled for one hundred and fifty seats, jostling each other into the hall. Moreover, the lady who was found in the labelled chair seemed to be there by pure chance ; indeed, she was apparently at the séance at all only by luck, since a series of small incidents had almost prevented her from attending it.

It has always been a popular belief that dreams could be premonitory, and that certain grave events, such as the sudden death of a parent or child, are sometimes foreseen in this way. But it has been left to Mr. Dunne to show, as I think satisfactorily, that the dream state is one in which the mind normally wanders about in the near future and past, making no distinction between the two, and merely registering details almost indiscriminately. In his *An Experiment with Time* he shows that the ordinary everyday dream contains images derived from *future* experiences, usually quite trivial and personal ones, to apparently the same degree as it contains images derived from memory. By recording all the images in one's dream immediately on awakening (a task which needs a little practice to do efficiently), and then analysing them all to sift out what is recognisably due to memory, and later rereading these notes after an interval of one or two days, one may trace the definite images which were derived from experiences one has had in the period which immediately followed the dream. Of course this method is valueless unless the analysis is really critical, unless all the probable coincidences are left out of the final reckoning of positive results, and unless the actual dream images, and not the subsequent rationalizations built up round them, are recorded in the first place ; but in good hands the method promises to be extremely valuable. I must recommend the reader to peruse the first half of Mr. Dunne's book in order to acquaint himself with the details, but cannot speak as favourably of the second half, which deals with the theory of Serial Time and a Serial Observer, as I think that this rests mainly on verbal confusions due to the retention of the ordinary ideas of time and motion, while the author is attempting to explain the nature of time as a fourth dimension.

From all these various examples—whether they concern extensive and impersonal predictions like those of the War, or whether they are of minute and personal details like Mme. Peyroutet's prophecy about the dog —the conclusion is forced upon us that the future can actually be seen, at least in part and " as through a glass, darkly." Is this a proof, we may ask, that the future is as fixed and unalterable as the past ? I do not know. But if it leads necessarily to the doctrine of Determinism, with the corollary that our sense of free will is an illusion, we must accept it with as good heart as we can. Let us not deny, or refuse to face facts simply because they are terrifying or unpalatable.

If the facts of the universe should be found to conflict with our religion, our morality, our æsthetics or our self-esteem, we must still face facts, and modify our philosophy accordingly, rather than live in a fool's paradise. People often object to the study of anatomy or physiology, because it conflicts with their delicacy or sense of beauty ; to the study of psychology, because it contradicts their moral or religious codes ; to the study of metapsychic facts, because they transcend the realm of reason and make the beginner feel that he is no longer at home in a familiar world. Such people truly live in a fool's paradise. They will not examine the universe to find out what its true nature is, and will not adapt themselves to it. But Science may not perjure itself thus by attempting to force the facts to conform to any system of religious, ethical, æsthetic or ego-centric belief whatsoever. The facts exist, and our beliefs must follow and conform to them. Precognition is such a fact ; and our doctrine of free will, if we wish to keep it at all, must be modified to accept and recognize this fact.

The prime question is, whether a future which can be foreseen is necessarily unalterable. That at any given moment there is a future state for each one of us already in existence, seems a necessary supposition ; but it is still open to us to conceive, if we like, of that future as essentially plastic and amenable to modification.

To take a concrete example : we may suppose that on December 2, Mme. Peyroutet saw Osty with the dog some months ahead. But this does not force us to conclude that, when the black dog arrived on April 11, the servant girl *could not* have denied it admission ; that the children *could not* have refrained from interesting themselves in it ; or that Osty was bound to agree to adopt it. Things happened as they did, because no one really worried about altering them ; so that what, on December 2, existed as the future four months ahead became in actuality the present. But had the servant, or the children, or Osty determined for any reason on another course of action, Mme Peyroutet's prophecy would thereby have been falsified.

We are, I say, entitled to take this view if we like ; and we are equally entitled to take the fatalistic view that everything is predetermined and unalterable. What we are not entitled to do, in the face of the evidence, is to deny the fact that certain persons can, under suitable conditions, exactly or approximately foresee the future, sometimes in isolated and minute details, and sometimes in broad outlines. And to this fact we must in some way or another make our philosophy of life conform.

2

When we attempt to visualize a processus for precognition we are met with considerable difficulties, many of which are purely verbal, and due to the fact that all our language and our ordinary concepts are derived from our sensible experience of the three-dimensional world which we feel as existing in time. Now we have to imagine a four-dimensional universe which is in a sense static, and in which every event, every phase of being exists " for all time " fixed somewhere, although obviously only a minute portion of it constitutes our present spatial world. This involves a radical change in our understanding of the word Time, and in the meaning of all words which involve the concept of Time ; words such as " move," " pass

through," " become," " grow," etc. It has always
seemed to me that writers land themselves and their
readers in hopeless confusion of thought through the
use of these words when discussing the fourth dimension ;
and yet, since the right words corresponding to the yet
unformulated concepts do not exist, this confusion
appears unavoidable, and I do not suppose for a moment
that I shall succeed any better than the rest. I would
have the reader remember, however, that when writers
like C. H. Hinton, H. G. Wells, or Mr. Dunne talk of
our consciousness " moving " along the Time dimension,
and argue that, since this motion itself takes time,
there must be another kind of Time which times our
motion through ordinary time, and so on, there is a
fallacy inherent in the use of the word " motion " in
this connection. We have to give a new meaning to
the word " motion " such that it harmonizes with the
new conception of Time as a fourth dimension, which
is qualitatively identical with the ordinary three space
dimensions, and we must avoid letting it connote in
our minds a spatial displacement which " takes time "
in the ordinary sense of the phrase. Let us consider
this matter a little in the light of modern conceptions,
with the hope of revealing at least where some common
errors of thought lie, even if we do not succeed in
attaining a satisfactory substitute of them as yet.

The theory of Relativity, which is at present un-
assailable in its general outline, postulates that the real
Universe is a four-dimensional continuum, and that any
given observer, by what is presumably a necessary
mental action consequent on his psychological nature,
perceives one of these dimensions as Time and the other
three as Space ; but that the particular directions
perceived as Time and Space vary according to the
relative motions of the observers concerned. Thus
Eddington, in his *Space, Time and Gravitation* (p. 48),
explains the matter :

" The observer's separation of this continuum into

Space and Time consists in slicing it in some direction, viz. that perpendicular to the path along which he himself is travelling. The section gives three-dimensional Space at some moment and the perpendicular direction is (imaginary) Time. Clearly the slice may be taken in any direction ; there is no question of a true separation and a fictitious separation."

The use of the word "travelling," which seems to carry with it our ordinary conception of Time, is likely to cause confusion. What is involved is clearly not a translation along any of the observer's three-space axes, for this path is perpendicular to them all, but something which happens in the fourth axis, and for which our nearest analogy and most obviously fitting poetic image is the word "motion." But it cannot *be* "motion," for that means a displacement in space, whereas this displacement is not in space. Neither can we really say that the observer's consciousness "moves," for consciousness is a mental state, not an object, and though it may seem to us to be associated with a definite spatial situation, it is not really located anywhere at all ; it is an abstract idea. The observer may be aware of a certain thing, but there is no definite entity called his " Awareness, " located anywhere, which can move in space, and to say that it " moves " in Time is simply to beg the question by a verbal confusion.

So Eddington's statement comes down to this, that the observer *is conscious*, or *lives, in a certain direction*, which direction he perceives as Time, while perceiving the three perpendicular directions as Space.

Thus we are led to replace certain familiar conceptions by others, more cumbrous and less easily imagined, but perhaps representing Reality more accurately. Instead of saying, " This solid object endures for a certain time at a given place, and then moves a given distance, its motion taking up a certain time," we have to say, " This thing has a certain four-dimensional shape, being very long in one direction ; but lo ! its shape is not now the same as before, since its long axis is now inclined to its former direction."

If on a diagram we represent the Time along one axis and the three-space dimensions all along the other axis (or, if you prefer, omit two of them and consider a point instead of a body) then the body at rest is represented on the diagram by a vertical line, and the body in motion by a line inclined to the vertical. Thus the portion A B

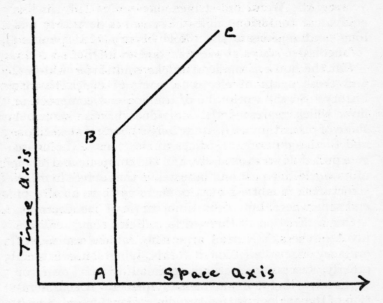

represents the four-dimensional shape of the stationary body enduring in Time, while the portion B C represents the shape of the same body moving in space as well as enduring for an equal length of time.

We are not able to visualize what the true shape of the body is in four dimensions at once, but by this device we assist our minds to realize that the idea of motion must eventually be replaced by an idea of four-dimensional shape. The ordinary three-dimensional shape of a stationary body is the same as its shape when the body moves,[5] but its real four-dimensional shape is not the same as it would have been had the body continued to remain stationary instead of moving. This four-dimensional Thing, A B C, is called a World-line.

If we consider an apparently stationary object like a house (its motion with the earth being negligible for our purposes) we see that it is so many feet long, broad, and high, and it endures in Time for say two hundred years. Its World-line (since one second of time is equivalent to 186,000 miles in space) is very thin and long, and represents the whole history of the house; its successive states at every instant in its life.

But the house is made of bricks, and these of atoms, and these again of electrons, each of which has its history. So the world-line of the house is composed of lines which represent the individual bricks, etc., and these of other thinner (but far longer) lines of the atoms, and these again of world-lines of electrons. The house gets pulled down eventually, and the component strands of its world-line part and interweave themselves in other structures; doubtless most of them come to an abrupt end somewhere, but perhaps not those of the electrons.

Our conception of the real four-dimensional universe involves the existence of a possibly infinite number of ordinary three-dimensional worlds, lying somewhere in orderly succession, perhaps parallel to our own, or perhaps cutting it in one or many planes. A consideration of the analogy with a two-dimensional world, which may have an infinite number of plane worlds superposed, parallel to itself, or of plane worlds all cutting it in one line or in many lines, makes this point clear. Let us then picture, as the simplest supposition, a number of ordinary " solid " worlds lying " parallel " to our own, stretching out in a series in a fourth dimension, which dimension is for practical purposes the same for all members of the human race (since they have practically

5 Apart from the " Fitzgerald contraction," which is ordinarily negligible.

the same motion), and appears to them under the guise of Time. If now we assume that we become conscious successively of one world after another, or, to use a poetic image, that the ego " moves " along the fourth dimension, in a regular manner, we shall interpret this experience to ourselves as *living* in a single material world which changes continuously in a regular manner. Really " we " are four-dimensioned objects, but we are conscious of a three-dimensional section of these objects (which we interpret as our material bodies located in space) in one way, while perceiving the fourth extension of our own bodies in quite a different way, namely, as a sense of duration.

Now to explain precognition we have to postulate the real " present " existence of, let us say, the " three-dimensional world in 1950," now somewhere outside our own present three-dimensional space ; and we have to postulate that the medium, instead of becoming conscious of the next adjacent world in the normal way, suddenly becomes conscious of the world of 1950. To say that the medium's mind " moves " along the Time dimension to the year 1950 is not allowable ; all we have is the fact that at a certain moment the medium is perceiving our present world, while at what we call the next moment his mind is perceiving a world which eventually we ourselves perceive after a lapse of what we call so many years. Admittedly it is difficult and tedious to attain an accurate description of this phenomenon, but the attempt may be worth the trouble in the end.

It will easily be granted that retrocognition, or the perception of events in the past, is the same phenomenon as precognition, though acting in the inverse sense. The past worlds, like the future worlds, exist " now," and both are subject to the medium's perception in the same manner. There is no ground for attributing a great quantity of the supernormal knowledge of the past which is shown by many mediums (e.g. Mrs. Piper and dozens of psychometrists) to telepathy from distant or discarnate minds, as is commonly done, when it is clear that retrocognition and precognition are two aspects of one and the same phenomenon and also that telepathy is wholly incompetent to explain precognition. When Spiritualists postulate telepathy from Spirits as an explanation of the facts of precognition they are simply avoiding this difficulty and adding an unnecessary factor. Merely to be discarnate does not give an intelligence the power to see an as yet non-existent future ; and so we are compelled to postulate that future events really exist in the present, that is to say, that the universe is really four-dimensional. Now if this is the case, it is just as easy for us to conceive that a living mind can, under suitable conditions of sleep or trance, perceive what lies for us in the future, as that a hypothetical spirit can do so. Here, as elsewhere, when we consider the matter closely, we find that the quality of discarnate-ness does not add anything to the powers of an intelli-gence ; that any attribute we can credit to mind as such must be attributable to incarnate minds ; and that since we do know the existence of the latter, whereas we do not know the existence of discarnate minds at all, the spirit hypothesis is not merely no explanation of the observed psychological facts, but is a quite unnecessary addition to them. Thus if acts of pre-cognition are possible to any mind they are potentially realizable in this life, and the same argument applies to acts of retrocognition ; hence none of those argu-ments for survival after death which are based on the revelation by a medium of private details in the past history of deceased individuals have the cogency which at first blush they seem to possess. Nor, of course, do similar arguments based on premonitory warnings and revelations of the future. In the search for direct evidence of the survival of the personality we are con-tinually checkmated in this fashion ; for whenever we fix our finger on some alleged phenomenon, such as ghosts or previsions, and say " prove this to be a fact, and then no one will be able to deny Spiritualism," we find, on following it up, not that the alleged facts are unfounded (as our sceptical friends averred) but that such facts, although demonstrable up to the hilt, never prove survival, but always extend our knowledge of the powers of the incarnate mind.

If we accept the theory of a four-dimensional universe, we may derive from it a clue towards the interpretation of the observed experimental fact that a psychometrizing medium requires some material object, it hardly matters what, which has been in contact with the person about whom information is sought.   In the classical case of the clairvoyant Marie (Dufay and Azam) quoted in our chapter on Cryptæsthesia, it was the neckerchief with which the murderer had strangled himself that the doctor gave Marie, and with that as rapport-object she was able to get in touch with the crime.   Again, it was a necktie that enabled Mme. Morel to find the corpse of M. Lerasle—in this case, be it noted, a necktie which was never present at the scene it was to reveal.

It has been suggested by occultists that all objects have their appropriate " etherial effluvia," and that they carry with them magnetic influences from their previous environment, etc. ; also, by persons not classed as occultists, that every object has its whole past history in some obscure way impressed upon it ; and various other vague ideas of " radiations " and so forth have been invoked with the purpose of explaining the part played by a material object in provoking clairvoyance.

If, however, the material universe has four dimensions then every object, such as the necktie in the Lerasle case, is merely a three-dimensional section of a four-dimensional *thing*, what the Relativitists call a World-line.   This Thing is joined to all the other Things that the necktie has been in contact with,[6] one of which is

[6] More strictly, " this Thing is joined to all other Things, any of whose three-dimensional sections has been in contact with one of its own three-dimensional sections."

the World-line of M. Lerasle's body. The medium, when asked to look for the missing man, could do

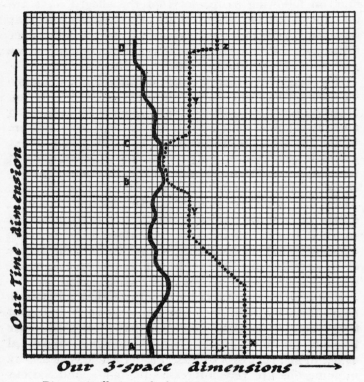

Diagram to illustrate the function of an evocatory object in Psychometry.

———

A B C D = World-line of M. Lerasle
X Y Z = World-line of Necktie
B C = M. Lerasle wearing Necktie.
D = Corpse of M. Lerasle in Wood.
Y = Necktie in Wardrobe.
Z = Necktie in hands of Medium.

nothing by roaming at random in an uncharted se
but when given the necktie she was thus brought in
contact with a World-line which intersected the Worl

line of M. Lerasle. With this to guide her, like a railway line leading to a junction, she could trace its past history until M. Lerasle had last touched it, and then change and follow *his* history forwards, until he was found a corpse.

In our railway line and junction image we have necessarily fallen back on our conventional ideas of time, so perhaps we might do well to express the matter differently, and say that in these cases the medium *lives in another direction*. This may sound like one of the ideas of " The Other Professor " in *Sylvie and Bruno* ; but if we recall Eddington's phrase about slicing the continuum in the direction along which the observer is travelling, and our comment that this means in the direction along which he is *living* it may be easier to follow the idea. Suppose that the medium ceases to slice the universe in such a way that he chooses the same Time axis as we choose, he would then be *living sideways!* One must imagine, I think, that if the medium began to live in a direction greatly inclined to our normal one he would get an aspect of Reality so unlike anything perceived in our familiar world that it would make no impression on his mind at all, in which case he would simply be unconscious. With a slight angle of inclination perhaps his consciousness would be less intense and much less precise than on waking. Now suppose further that in his trance the medium lives sideways for say five minutes of our time while we look on ; this will not be five minutes of his new time, and his mind will have vacated our world and temporarily penetrated into one of the adjacent worlds which must exist in our four-dimensional complex. At the end of our five minutes let him re-orient himself, and owing to the force of habit and innate human constitution, recommence to live in the usual direction again. He will then become aware of a world which he perceives in the same manner as we perceive ours, but it will not be the identical world that he left or that which we have reached; it may be the world as perceived by someone at some place in 1732 or in 1999, or it may be our world *now* at a different place. There is absolutely no telling what it would be in any one case, but the *probability* on *a priori* grounds and as a deduction from observation, is that it will be relatively near, both in our space and in our time, to the world the medium left in his trance. The vast majority of predictions and retrocognitions relate to events which are near in time, and the majority of clairvoyant perceptions (e.g. reading sealed notes which are held in the medium's hand) relate to objects which are quite close in space.

As the subject is so complex we may be permitted to summarize shortly the salient ideas which have somehow to be grasped.

1. The real Universe is a four-dimensioned complex consisting of an infinite number of worlds of three dimensions; just as a solid body may be regarded as consisting of an infinite number of planes.

2. Every material object is thus merely the three-dimensional section of a four-dimensional Thing, which is often called a World-line.

3. The process of Living appears to involve our automatically focusing our consciousness on successive three-dimensional sections, leaving the fourth extension to be felt vaguely in the background as a sense of duration. It is highly probable that most animals focus their consciousness on only a two-dimensional section, and apprehend all the rest as time.

4. Owing to our human constitution, and owing to the fact that, from an astronomical point of view, we all move, relatively to the heavenly bodies, with the same speed, our choice of the time axis is necessarily the same under ordinary circumstances, at least to a high degree of approximation.

5. In trance or sleep, however, our ordinary waking consciousness is partially or wholly destroyed, and replaced by another which seems determined by a

different choice of the time axis. We perceive worlds which, to our waking consciousness, lie in the ordinary past or future.

6. The problem of how our mind can perceive a future world is identical with the problem of how it can perceive the ordinary world ; both are inexplicable facts of consciousness, enigmatic attributes of mind ; and we must leave it at that. But as Sir James Jeans says : " It is always the puzzle of the nature of time that brings our thoughts to a standstill."

BIBLIOGRAPHY

OSTY. Supernormal Faculties in Man.
RICHET. Thirty years of Psychical Research.
HYSLOP. Enigmas of Psychical Research.
FLAMMARION. On Death. Vol. 1, Before Death ; Vol. 2, At the Moment of Death.
J. MAXWELL. Metapsychical Phenomena.
See also PROCEEDINGS, Society for Psychical Research, Parts 13, 29, and 72 for Articles on Prevision, and
GELEY. Ectoplasmie et Clairvoyance, for two cases.
EDDINGTON. Space, Time, and Gravitation.
JEANS. The Mysterious Universe.

CHAPTER TWELVE

CLAIRVOYANCE

1

THE study of clairvoyance, or the " occult " perception of objects by means other than the ordinary channels of sense perception, raises many difficult but highly interesting problems. But so, for the matter of that, does the study of normal sense perception ; and in the end the problems are much the same.

We usually assume that when we perceive something outside us, whether by touching, tasting, seeing, smelling, or hearing it, there is always some objective physical process which begins at the object perceived, travels across the intervening space to our end-organs, and is continued as a nerve-current in our nerves until it reaches the brain, which it excites in a particular manner ; and lo and behold ! the result of this physical excitation is a purely mental image ; something radically and totally different in nature from the physical processes which provoked it, and belonging to a different order of being from theirs, and from that of the object which set them in motion.

We have, of course, very good reason to believe in these physical processes—light waves and nerve currents and what not—but they obviously do not help us to understand the fundamental mystery of the act of perception ; and until this is understood we naturally shall not solve the kindred mystery of clairvoyant perception.

But we have first to show that clairvoyance exists ;

that mental images corresponding with real external objects do occur when we can eliminate all known intermediary physical mechanisms capable of provoking them. Moreover, since we know that telepathic inter-mental communication is a possible factor, we must eliminate this too ; which means that the object cognized clairvoyantly must be unknown to any mind, if the demonstration is to be absolutely unequivocal.

Of course, supposing that we demonstrate clair-voyance under these conditions, it is open to us to postulate that there is an intermediate physical process, such as highly penetrating short radiation, or a certain electro-magnetic condition in the intervening space, which impresses the seer, who is able to react to this just as we react to a retinal impression. Such a view obviously suggests itself in the first instance, and is to some extent supported by experimental observations. Reichenbach's experiments with "sensitive" persons, who described various coloured lights coming from magnets, crystals, the human body, etc., have never been properly refuted, or confirmed. De Rochas did something to confirm them, and satisfied himself that these people saw an objective reality by making them look through a spectroscope and himself verifying that the adjustment of the instrument corresponded every time with the colour they alleged that they saw. It would be extremely difficult for a subjective illusion to escape detection when tested in this way, unless the person had first learned by heart the positions of the telescope on the instrument which corresponded with given shades.

Many other researchers have adduced evidence to show that almost everything gives off rays or effluvia which are imperceptible to normal senses though they may be perceived by suitable sensitives—usually in hypnotic or mediumistic trance. But there is no general agreement as to the objective reality of all this, and, although the hypothesis in its vague and generalized form is at first blush extremely probable, there is a strong feeling that the descriptions given by these sensitives are quite untrustworthy and subjective. Moreover, no theory of rays or effluvia can explain the clairvoyant reading of folded and crumpled up letters, examples of which are given later, as in these cases the rays would form a chaotic jumble.

It has long been known that under certain conditions, particularly hypnosis, a person will develop a very greatly enhanced sensitiveness, which might be mistaken for clairvoyant faculties, but which is only a hyperæsthesia of normal senses. Good examples (not, perhaps, the most striking and extreme, but carefully controlled and measured) are given in Alrutz's paper on *Problems of Hypnotism.* An interesting instance is that of one of his subjects whose waking vision is quite normal, but who in the hypersensitive state of light hypnosis sees more of the spectrum than is normally detectable. His normal vision (tested by the spectroscope) ranges over wave-lengths of from 720 to 400 micro-millimetres ; under hypnosis he sees the red-brown and brown as far as 800 micro-millimetres, and with a different instrument (anomalscope) down to 900 micro-millimetres.

Similar results are obtained with other senses ; for example in one case where, in the waking state, a pressure of 0·8 grams with the needle of an algesimeter gave no pricking sensation, under hypnosis a pressure of 0·1 grams was felt as pricking.

Thus hyperæsthesia of the senses is a demonstrable fact, and must be taken into account when we are tempted to attribute many things to an occult clairvoyant faculty. But that the experimental and measurable facts of hyperæsthesia do not suffice for all the observed instances of apparent clairvoyance will, I think, be granted by everyone who familiarizes himself with them.

A sort of borderland class, between hyperæsthesia

and clairvoyance, is provided by the cases of what has been termed Autoscopy, and also by many curious instances of the transposition of the senses. Hypnotized persons or hysterical patients sometimes appear to see their own internal organs, and can describe accurately what is taking place in them, following, for example, the passage of a small foreign body, under conditions which seem to exclude normal sensation or external suggestion. The Indian Yoga training is said to involve the development of this power of acute consciousness of internal processes, as a preliminary step in the acquirement of voluntary control over the whole physical organism. And such a power is not intrinsically occult, but only demands a great degree of hyperæsthesia, or perhaps we should say a mental attention to sensations which we all have continuously, and therefore do not notice any more than we notice a smell or taste in ordinary water or pure air.

The instances of transposition of the senses are more suggestive of the occult, and indeed lead insensibly into instances of true clairvoyant perception. In these cases a hypnotized or hysterical patient will apparently see things with some other part of the body than the eyes ; or hear through the fingers, or otherwise confound our previous notions of proper behaviour. For example, Lombroso had a patient who was an hysterical young girl. At times she failed to see with her eyes, but yet saw with her ears ! With her eyes suitably bandaged she read print which was held to one of her ears. Similarly Boirac describes how one subject, bandaged and sitting in a dark room, could describe a photograph by merely running the fingers over its surface. This suggests tactile hyperæsthesia of a degree far and away beyond anything experimentally observed, or else it is pure clairvoyance.

Instances of what has been called travelling clairvoyance are numerous ; a typical trustworthy one is an account given by Prof. W. de Morgan and reproduced in

Hyslop's *Enigmas of Psychical Research*. In these cases the " spirit " or " etheric body " or " soul " of the seer (who is either asleep, or in trance) is alleged to travel away from the body and see things in the ordinary way, just as if this soul were the real seat of sensation. Such is the ordinary interpretation, and the very marvellous tales of this sort of clairvoyance certainly make it plausible. An hypnotized patient, for example, is told to project his soul to a certain place and see what is happening ; and the patient proceeds to describe step by step, for all the world as if he were actually present, the things he sees, which, in general, are in fact found to be true by inquiry afterwards.

But these cases are more complex than they appear on the surface. In spite of De Rochas' experiments it remains highly improbable that there is an etheric body, or that it is the real seat of the sensations. Probably there is a considerable amount of true clairvoyance in all these instances, together with much telepathy, and sometimes with the essentially irrelevant projection of an ectoplasmic phantom, which is mistaken by the patient, and often by his investigator, for a permanent vehicle of the soul. In any case it is difficult to estimate and eliminate what is purely subjective in these descriptions ; but what does remain is the fact that the subject becomes aware of material things at a great distance, presumably by a clairvoyance that is analogous to ordinary vision, although the extent of the factor of telepathy is usually impossible to determine.

2

We may now turn to cases of definite clairvoyance which cannot reasonably be attributed to telepathy or to hyperæsthesia. Such cases are a little difficult to find, since it is quite rarely that people have deliberately taken precautions to exclude telepathy ; they have usually been quite satisfied to get something supernormal without bothering about the scientific principle of the isolation of causes.

First we must mention the celebrated Alexis Didier. He was a professional " magnetic " subject a century ago, and specialized in clairvoyance. In 1847 the famous conjurer Robert Houdin confessed his inability to explain or compete with this marvellous man. Houdin played a game of cards with Alexis, using his own new pack, which he shuffled himself, and holding his own hand of cards under the table. Yet Alexis, without looking at his own cards, which were face downwards, first told Houdin which card he ought to play, and then played his own card without looking at it first—and at each step the card corresponded with that played by his opponent.

Another similar type, Reese, was apparently clairvoyant without needing any artificial trance state to help him. He specialized in reading sentences which were written on slips of paper and then crumpled or folded up ; generally they were questions which he answered appropriately, showing thus general psychometric powers. As the writers of the questions were usually present and often themselves knew, or at least could imagine, the appropriate answers, we cannot rule out the telepathic factor. Nevertheless it is probable that Reese (who convinced Edison and Schrenck-Notzing of his abilities) did work largely by direct clairvoyance.

In the similar case of Kahn (studied at the Institut Métapsychique) several persons would write sentences on slips of paper which were then crumpled up or folded into pellets, and mixed thoroughly. Each person then took a pellet at random (sometimes a few of them would be burned so as to lessen the probabilities of correct guessing) and Kahn, usually without touching the pellets, would read the contents of each in turn.

Crookes long ago recorded a simple, but quite good, example which excludes telepathy. He wished to decide whether the intelligence controlling a lady who wrote automatically by means of planchette was really, as it said, an independent spirit. His experiment does not decide the question in the least, but it does demonstrate the fact of clairvoyant perception on *somebody's* part.

" I therefore said to this intelligence, ' Can you see the contents of this room ? ' ' Yes,' wrote the planchette. ' Can you see to read this newspaper ? ' said I, putting my finger on a copy of *The Times*, which was on a table behind me, but without looking at it. ' Yes,' was the reply of the planchette. ' Well,' I said, ' if you can see that, write the word which is now covered by my finger, and I will believe you.' The planchette commenced to move. Slowly and with great difficulty the word ' however ' was written. I turned round and saw that the word ' however ' was covered with the tip of my finger.

" I had purposely avoided looking at the paper when I tried this experiment, and it was impossible for the lady, had she tried, to have seen any of the printed words, for she was sitting at one table and the paper was on another table behind, my body intervening."

Our next instance is one given by Dr. Gibier in his *Analyse des Choses*. It reads superficially like a case of hyperæsthesia or of transposition of the senses, but this is due to the accidentals of the experiments ; the essential feature is the reading of words placed outside the field of vision, and not previously seen by the experimenter himself. The subject was a young woman who was hypnotized, and then her eyes bandaged with wads of cotton, over which was tied a silk handkerchief. Gibier took at random a book from his shelves, opened it haphazard, and held it with the pages down and cover uppermost a short distance (2 centimetres) above the woman's hair, without himself first looking at the page. After a moment or two she succeeded in reading most of a given line of print correctly. It is evident that she did not do this with her eyes, and it is almost impossible to conceive that light reflected from the page down on to her head, without any focusing such as that given by the eye in ordinary vision, should impress her with a sense of the form of the words. Of course it is possible to invent *ad hoc* hypotheses for these cases ; such as that she projected a sensitive ectoplasmic feeler which read the page by touch, as a blind man reads Braille ; or that she materialized an ectoplasmic eye and read it with that. But these suggestions have no empirical support, and in any case are insufficient to explain many other instances where the circumstances are different.

The fact of clairvoyance has also been demonstrated by dealing out cards and making the percipient name them, without the experimenter seeing them first. This was done, for example, in a series of experiments by Professor Richet. Again, an obvious experimental method is that used by Tischner, who enclosed picture postcards in definitely opaque envelopes, mixed them all up so as to avoid knowing the contents in any given instance, and gave them, in random selection, to the medium who then proceeded to read or describe the contents. Several of his experiments in this direction were successful, and indicated that the medium perceived the visual form of the writing or the picture in the envelope. But this sort of experimentation, though necessary, never seems so fertile in positive results as the less exact, but more human, methods of consultation for general psychometry. So much depends, presumably, on the active interest of the medium, and this is usually not obtained by rigorous experimentation with cards or written words, whereas it is freely given in the ordinary course of consultation, for the purpose of finding a lost article for example, or obtaining messages from, and " proofs " of the survival of, deceased friends.

The success of the so-called " Book Tests," by which mediums produce evidence that they are really in communication with surviving spirits, illustrates this point.

Mrs. Leonard, studied by Drayton Thomas and others, was very good at this. The spirit communicators (i.e. in our view an unconscious personification on Mrs. Leonard's part) would indicate a page of a book in the shelves, where would be found a sentence, or perhaps a word, strikingly apropos of the occasion. The book was indicated by its position on the library shelves, not by its title, and it might be taken from amongst books not belonging to the consultant, or the medium, or the experimenter. On one occasion Drayton Thomas had some old books, chosen haphazard by a dealer, sent to him, without his looking at even the titles, and though they were put in a box Mrs. Leonard still managed to read out of them. Of course, the appropriateness of the lines read convinces many people of the genuineness of the spirits who thus showed their intelligence; but the inference is entirely the other way if we regard it as a case of clairvoyant reading by Mrs. Leonard herself; and in any case it is clairvoyance on somebody's part.

Among the very few first-rate mediums who have given of their best to scientific inquirers, and who have entered into the spirit of scientific demonstration, the Pole Ossowiecki ranks high. He has been studied by Geley, Richet, and others, and there is little doubt of his great powers of cryptæsthesia. It is, however, difficult in most instances to decide whether he works mainly through mind-reading or by means of a direct clairvoyance of objects themselves. Certain examples point one way, while others point the other way; and the great probability is that both are operative.

The best account of experiments with Ossowiecki is to be found in Geley's *Ectoplasmie et Clairvoyance*, from which I will select some examples.

In one instance the sentence, "*I consider you are wonderful*," was written on a piece of paper, which was folded and put into an envelope and sealed up. Ossowiecki took the letter in his hands, crumpled it up, and said : " It is in English ! I cannot read it, I do not know English. . . . I see a single letter, then a word of eight letters beginning with C O N S, then two short words, then a long word something like *vendredi*. But it cannot be vendredi, as it is in English."

It will be seen that this is a very close description, from a visual point of view, of the sentence. The letters are seen as such, and sometimes deciphered ; but the sense and meaning of the phrase (which was of course known to the man who wrote it, who was present) was not at all grasped, as it would indubitably have been in a case of telepathy.

Another example. A lady, who left Warsaw the same day, prepared a paper whose contents were unknown to any of the other experimenters, and put it into a tube of lead, which was sealed up. When Ossowiecki was given this to read he first said it was written by a woman, then that it was something about the creation—nature. Then, after a pause, that it contained a picture and some writing. " The picture represents a man with heavy moustaches and heavy eyebrows, but no nose—he has a military uniform—he is like Marshal Pilsudski. The writing is in French, it says : ' This man, he fears nothing, neither in the political world nor in any other sphere, like a chevalier.' "

The tube was then opened and inside was found a cartoon sketch of Pilsudski, with military coat and hat, but an entire blank for the face and head, with just the eyebrows and moustaches heavily drawn. Underneath was written : " le Chevalier sans peur et sans reproche."

In this example there is a certain amount of telepathy perhaps, and certainly an attempt to reconstruct the sentence written from a very partial perception of it. But the description of the sketch with its eyebrows and moustaches, and no nose, seems to indicate a direct clairvoyance of the sketch on the paper. Yet it is possible that the tube of lead acted as a *rapport* object, enabling Ossowiecki to get into touch with the lady and see the images in her mind at the time she designed the picture.

On another occasion Richet, taking the necessary precautions, wrote the word TOI in capital letters on a piece of paper, which he crumpled up into a ball and put into the palm of Ossowiecki's hand, which hand Richet held in his own. Ossowiecki, after a few minutes, said : " It is a number . . . it is very short . . . it is a word. . . . I see a T . . . there are two little tails on the horizontal bar of the T . . . (this was correct) . . . there is a number, a nought, . . . there is a figure 1 "— then in a low voice he added—" It isn't *moi* . . . give me some paper to write on." He then wrote TO1, making the final letter into a figure 1.

In this instance the factor of telepathy seems absent, and a visual reading of the paper, with a misreading of the capital letter " I " for a figure 1, seems the obvious interpretation. Again, in reading the sentence " *La vie nous semble belle, parceque nous le savons éphémère,*" Ossowiecki misread the fifth word as *humble*, with which it had a certain similarity in the handwriting, and he failed to read the last word (which was not in his vocabulary, he being a Pole with only an elementary knowledge of French) but said that it was composed of eight letters.

3

The problem of the nature of the processus in Ossowiecki's clairvoyance may perhaps be partially cleared up by considering his own account of the matter. In response to Geley's request he attempted to describe what happens in these words : " Whether I read a sealed letter, or find a lost object, or practise psychometry, my sensations are almost the same . . . a veritable lucidity possesses me ; pictures rise up, usually of the past. I see the man who wrote the letter, and I know what he has written. I see the object at the moment that it was lost, with details of the event ; or I perceive, I feel the history of whatever object I hold in my hands. The vision is cloudy, and it demands great efforts to see certain conditions or details in the scenes." Again, he says, " I find myself in a new state of special kind, in which I see and hear quite outside space and time."

This account tallies very well both with the details of his procedure and the things he says during his séances, and with our general theory of psychometry. It seems as if he becomes conscious of the fourth dimension, and is able to follow down the world-line of, let us say, the letter until he reaches the moment when it was written, and there he perceives the event of writing it, together with details of the person concerned. The only open question then is whether he perceives the things themselves, or whether he perceives mental images of them. The evidence of visual misreadings suggests that it is the thing, not the idea, which is seen ; and this is of course supported by all those cases when the thing perceived (e.g. a card chosen haphazard from the pack) is not previously known to any mind at all.

This mental act of clairvoyance, in which the mind perceives an object directly without any aid from bodily organs of sense and physical stimuli like light waves, is doubtless astonishing and deserves a technical name. But is it intrinsically any different from all other perception ? When I say that I see a table, and that this is caused by the light reflected from its surface striking my eye, and there stimulating certain nerves which stimulate the brain, I have done nothing to explain how or why my mind pictures the image of a table. Normal sense-perception, regarded as an act of the mind, is just as much a form of Cryptæsthesia as the clairvoyance we have been discussing ; in the end the mind seems to perceive the material world directly. Of course, though, this dualistic theory of mind and matter, which has always been unsatisfactory to the philosopher, is now being attacked from the point of view of physics ; more and more are we coming to the idea that all the things which we call material, and even the electrical ultimate particles, are essentially mental. The various links in the physical chain which joins the external object to the perceiving mind are themselves mental, as also is the object at the far end of the chain, so that from first to last mind simply perceives mental realities, and the whole process is purely psychological. If this is so, the curiosity of clairvoyance lies merely in the mental objects selected for perception, not in the intrinsic nature of the act.

That this view is not wholly a piece of unbalanced speculation may be seen if I quote a few lines from Jeans' *Mysterious Universe*. In his final chapter he suggests that the Universe may best be pictured as consisting of pure thought ; not that objective realities are non-existent, but that they are essentially mental. True, he chooses the word " Mathematical " as a label, but he expressly states that this is to connote the whole of pure thought, and not merely the studies of the professional mathematician. And later on we come to a passage which needs quotation :

" Mind no longer appears as an accidental intruder into the realm of matter ; we are beginning to suspect that we ought rather to hail it as the creator and governor of the realm of matter—not of course our individual minds, but the mind in which the atoms out of which our individual minds have grown exist as thoughts.

" The old dualism of mind and matter . . . seems likely to disappear, not through matter becoming in any way more shadowy or insubstantial than heretofore, or through mind becoming resolved into a function of the working of matter, but through substantial matter resolving itself into a creation and manifestation of mind."

BIBLIOGRAPHY

BOIRAC. Psychic Science.
ALRUTZ. Problems of Hypnotism, P.S.P.R., Part 83.
GIBIER. Analyse des Choses.
TISCHNER. Telepathy and Clairvoyance.
DRAYTON THOMAS. Some New Evidence for Human Survival.
GELEY. Ectoplasmie et Clairvoyance. (Eng. Trans., Clairvoyance and Materialization.)

PART FOUR

CHAPTER THIRTEEN

THE SURVIVAL OF THE PERSONALITY

THE evidence which points *prima facie* to a survival of the personality after death has accumulated so rapidly in the last half-century, largely as a result of the labours of the S.P.R. and similar societies abroad, that its adequate analysis and critique would occupy many large tomes. And yet the quality of this accumulation of testimony is not often sufficiently high to deserve the laborious analysis which is indispensable before we can accept the proffered proof of survival.

The first question to raise is as to the kind of evidence that might conceivably be held to indicate personal survival. Formerly, I suppose, an objective and complete proof of the appearance of a ghost would have been considered satisfactory, but to-day the known facts of ectoplasmic materializations, with their peculiar inherent tendency to dramatic personification, make evidence of this sort quite valueless unless it is associated with some other psychological feature. In many books dealing with supernormal phenomena one finds a separate chapter, or several such chapters, devoted to ghosts, apparitions at or after death, hauntings, and the projection of the etheric body. In fact such things appear to most people to be the essential and interesting phenomena of the science of metapsychics. It is popularly assumed that there is an " etheric " or semi-material body, which is a kind of attenuated double of the ordinary body, and which acts as the immortal vehicle of the personality and soul. At death, or in moments of great stress, this etheric body is supposed to be liberated, and sometimes to be made visible to other people, perhaps a thousand miles away. The etheric body, or soul, may be " earth-bound," and remain after death attached to some house, which it haunts, perhaps to re-enact periodically some crime or act of violence, as if wholly obsessed by one idea. This theory, loosely and variously as it is stated by different schools, seems to derive its support from two directions. In the first place there is the subjective ingrained materialism of people, which leads them to derive satisfaction and comfort from the idea of a quasi-solid soul which can be seen, felt, and weighed ; for if the soul is an entirely immaterial entity, which can never be a subject of sense-perception, it can only appeal as a concept to those who have a taste for intellectual abstractions. In the second place there are innumerable stories of ghosts seen and heard, and in addition some quite reasonably well-evidenced phenomena, which do, on the face of it, seem to point to some such etheric body as their cause.

Nevertheless, in my opinion, there is no definite ground for supposing that an etheric (or ectoplasmic) double is a permanent constituent of our being—still less for the multiplication of such bodies, each one less material than the last, which seems to be the hobby of some theosophers. We need, in metapsychics, an ever-present sense of the importance of Occam's principle of excluding unnecessary entities. It may be said that I have not excluded enough in this book ; that I have admitted an ectoplasm and a fourth dimension, each of which is a new entity. The only reply is that I do not see how you can explain the facts without them ; but I may point out that I have excluded the hypotheses of a permanent invariable personality, of a personal " spirit " which survives after death and influences

events in this world, of one or more special etheric
bodies, and am inclined to merge the various phenomena
of telepathy, clairvoyance, retrocognition, and precognition, into one general phenomenon of cryptæsthesia,
which again is only a generalized form of something
which, in one particular case, we know as Sense-
Perception.

I propose, therefore, to devote very little space to
what may be called the ghost department, and merely
to suggest that all such (objective) cases may well be
explained by the ectoplasmic theory, combined, when it
is necessary, with the theory of the fourth dimension.
This may seem to many readers to be a deliberate refusal
to deal with difficulties and with phenomena which, in
their opinion, would disprove my arguments. But this
book is as far as possible confined to a discussion of
known facts, and the fundamental facts of hauntings
are not really known. The multitudinous tales of
haunted houses and of ghostly apparitions, of spectres
of deceased murderers, and so on, are not well certified
as to the essentials, and nothing valuable can be gained
from any one of them except by means of an exhaustive
and detailed examination of every relevant feature.
Such analyses as have been made do not by any means
lead one to adopt the popular explanations, and it is
fairly safe to say that in any given instance of haunting
or of poltergeist phenomena there is present some person
who is acting as the agent (as a rule unconsciously) and
that the only supernormal actions probably involved
are telekinesis and perhaps materialization. In many
particular instances the medium has been discovered to
be a boy or girl at the stage of puberty—a period of stress
which often seems to release mediumistic faculties in
slightly hysterical or ill-balanced children. But it is not
theoretically necessary (although probably almost always
in fact the case) that the effective agent must be actually
on the haunted spot while the manifestations occur.
There is the possibility of action at a distance, since the

ectoplasm may be projected away from the medium ; to say nothing of the possible movements in the fourth dimension.

As to other evidences for the etheric double, we may mention that M. Baraduc photographed a white cloud escaping from a body at the moment of death ; that Dr. Kilner examined the auras of his patients through a screen stained with dicyanin ; that de Rochas and Lancelin made use of hypnotized " sensitives " who observed and described the stages of projection of the etheric double ; and that Dr. D. MacDougall weighed his dying patients and discovered that at the moment of death they lost half an ounce or so. But none of these observations are demonstrative of the existence of the supposed vehicle of the soul. It is even highly doubtful how far they correspond with reality at all ; but in any case they go no further than showing that ectoplasm may sometimes escape from the body, and perhaps that it normally drapes the body, like a cloak, giving the appearance of an aura.

To return to the ghost-proof, a very good instance which appears on the face of it to be a real visitation from the dead, and which has the kind of additional feature which makes it worth considering as evidence, is given in P.S.P.R., Vol. 6, and quoted again by Myers. The account has been investigated thoroughly and we may take the story as being quite true as to its facts. It is shortly as follows. A man one day saw the phantom form of his sister, who had been dead nine years. Much perturbed he at once went home and told his parents, who were naturally somewhat incredulous. He happened, however, to say that his sister's face appeared to have a bright red scratch on the right-hand side. At this his mother nearly fainted, and declared that this mark identified the phantom as being really her daughter, since no one living but herself knew that there was this scratch ; the mother had accidentally made it when arranging the dead body, and had been much distressed by the occurrence, which she had never mentioned to her husband or son, or to any other person. A few weeks later the mother died, happy to think that her daughter was awaiting her in the Beyond.

Myers, whose sound judgment entitles him to our greatest respect, considers that in this case the spirit of the daughter knew of her mother's approaching death, and appeared to the son in order to make him return home and at the same time console the mother's last moments with his testimony as to the survival of her daughter. It is a good interpretation, though a little ingenuous, but we might equally suppose that the phantom was projected by the mother herself. We do not know yet that the personality does survive, or that it can, after death, reappear in phantasmal form, or that it can apprehend coming events. But we do know that the living person may project an ectoplasmic phantom, may foreknow its own demise, and may unconsciously dissociate (temporarily) to enact a dramatic part with its ectoplasmic phantasm. Consequently it is more in accordance with hitherto proven facts to interpret this case in terms of a phantom projected from the mother.

I have given this case as the best example that I know of the evidence for survival based on ghosts. But it is really no evidence at all for survival of the *personality*, for in this instance the phantom gave no signs of mental or emotional life at all ; a mere physical simulacrum existed for a moment and then vanished. The survival of personality, however, cannot in any case be demonstrated by physical manifestations, for the whole concept is psychological. We are so used in daily life to meeting and recognizing people's bodies and finding that they are vehicles of personality, that we forget that a physical form, however recognizable, is no guarantee for the existence of a psychological personality. The argument for survival must finally be based on purely psychological evidence, and this at once brings the whole discussion on to a plane more akin to that habitually trodden by literary critics and classical scholars than that to which physical scientists are accustomed. It is largely a question, that is to say, of criticizing a given communication, obtained through some medium who speaks in trance or writes automatically, and of establishing that this communication contains internal evidence, in its style and thought-content, that it emanated from the mind of a deceased person. Now, in view of the uncertain nature of all literary criticism, in view of the examples of literary forgeries whose detection has been due to external rather than internal evidence, and especially in view of the known and suspected powers of the mediumistic mind to acquire information by clairvoyance, by telepathy, and by as yet unexplainable acts of retro- and pre-cognition, it is certainly a little daring to assert of any given communication that it must have come from the mind of the ostensible communicator. Dr. Geley, when discussing the spirit hypothesis, says that it should be adopted when the communications and general phenomena of mediumship show direction, knowledge, and abilities beyond those of the medium, either while conscious or when hypnotized. But we can set no arbitrary limits to the medium's powers while in trance ; we can simply observe their display. We may take it as established that ecto-plasmic projections do occur, that a phantom form is directed and controlled ; the question as to how this may be done is not simplified by ascribing it to the agency of spirits. On the contrary, this assumption complicates matters by introducing a new factor. So also we may accept as a fact that mediums do reveal supernormal knowledge of facts, whether these are in the historical past, or in the future, or are merely mental facts such as the thoughts of the sitter. But given the medium and his knowledge of the fact, how does the spirit hypothesis simplify our interpretation ? If the medium's mind (which at least is a real known factor) cannot in some obscure way apprehend a future event,

how are we any better off in postulating a spirit mind
which can apprehend it, and can also pass it on to the
medium's mind—not, be it observed, by a normal means
of communication like speech, but by yet another supernormal act of telepathy or of possession ? Let us insist
on this point, even to the extent of giving a prosaic
enumeration of the assumptions implied. On the one
hand we have a Medium A (given as a fact) and a piece
of information B (also given as a fact). Our one solitary
assumption—which is really only a statement of another
fact—is that A, by some unknown process which at
present we cannot understand, apprehends B ; or,
objectifying this, we say A has the *power* (cryptæsthesia)
of apprehending B.

Our spiritualistic friends, on the other hand, say that
A obtains B not directly by his own mental power, but
mediately through C, a spirit (1st assumption), who
apprehends B directly (2nd assumption) and who conveys B to A by telepathy (3rd assumption), or, alternatively, by displacing A from the control of his own body
and speaking or writing with A's organs. As a matter
of fact, where we simply assume cryptæsthesia as a
function of known real people, spiritualists assume
cryptæsthesia of the same people, plus the existence of
spirits, plus the cryptæsthesia of spirits, plus the communication of spirits with living people. And with this
quadrupling of hypotheses they are absolutely no nearer
a satisfactory interpretation of the mystery than we are
with our one hypothesis.

The question of course arises as to why an entranced
medium should show any powers greater than those of
normal waking persons. Whether we answer this
question or not does not affect the observed fact that
cryptæsthesia is shown during trance, but an answer
may make this observed fact more easily digested, and
therefore we will attempt one, though it can only be
given in quite general terms.

We have seen that the personality is a complex and

ever-shifting interplay of mental states and tendencies. Also we have seen that the reality at the back of our physical bodies is a four-dimensional thing, the world-line which is the sum of all our successive three-dimensional bodies at all instants of our lifetime. We have also seen that in the act of living our mind splits up the continuum into three directions which it apprehends as space and one which it feels differently as time. In our normal waking life we are aware of one three-dimensional world at a time (why, no one can tell), we perceive by means of the five senses (how, no amount of knowledge about electrons and photons can explain), and we (whoever " we " may be) achieve a certain degree of self-expression by checking some innate tendencies and giving others regulated exercise. What Life is, what Perception is, and what entity (if any) is behind our mental gymnastics, no philosopher has yet been able to say. But it would appear that during our waking life our perceptions are canalized and limited, in order that we may act efficiently, just as our personalities are canalized and limited for the same reason. The state of trance, however, appears to be one in which life is not lived in the same three dimensions, and perceptions are not canalized in the same manner. Presumably all the vagueness and incoherence of trance utterances are due to this very fact. It may well be that in trance we return to a primitive original mode of cognition, of which our sense perceptions are only highly specialized forms evolved for the purpose of three-dimensional life and adapted for daily use in the ordinary world. It is only to be expected that as one develops excellence in certain highly specialized forms of perception one should lose the power of exercising other more general, though wider, forms : that acute consciousness of the personal self and its present surroundings should prevent our being conscious of things remote in time and space. So it is not unnatural to find that more extended modes of perception and consciousness present themselves in conditions when self-consciousness and awareness of the immediately external real world are considerably lessened, as for example in sleep, in hypnosis, and in the mediumistic trance.

We asked the question, a little way back, what kind of evidence might be held to demonstrate personal survival ? Spiritualists generally seem to accept most of the ostensible evidence at its face value, but when driven to defend themselves against competent opponents they usually limit themselves to a few categories of phenomena which they claim to be absolutely inexplicable on any other hypothesis. We must here hold our ground, however, and point out that if phenomena a, b, c, etc., are produced, and are at present inexplicable by means of known factors, such as general cryptæsthesia, precognition, ectoplasmic projections, and the psychological tendency to assume fictitious personalities, we are not thereby reduced to an acceptance of the spirit hypothesis. We may not be able to prove that a, b, c, etc., are due to such and such causes, or we may even prove that these, and all other known causes, are inadequate to explain the phenomena ; and yet the spirit theory is not thereby proved, nor even rendered more probable than before, if we consider it to be in itself an unsound hypothesis. As to the categories a, b, c, etc., which are in dispute, they are summarized by Bozzano[1] as follows :

(a) Cases of the identification of deceased persons who are unknown to the medium and the sitters.

(b) Cases of the apparition of deceased persons at a death-bed.
Special cases of telekinesis at, and after, a death.
Cases of " transcendental music " heard at, and after, a death.

(c) Cases where the medium talks or writes fluently in languages unknown to him, and sometimes unknown to the sitters.

[1] Bozzano, *A propos de l'Introduction à la Métapsychique.*

Also cases where a medium writes fluently with the handwriting of a deceased person.

(*d*) Cases of bilocation just before death.

(*e*) Cases of materialization of a living, speaking phantom.

(*f*) Certain cases of " cross-correspondences."

(*g*) The existence of supernormal faculties, which are independent of the laws of biological evolution.

It will be readily understood that to deal adequately with these various categories a long book would be required. One would have to reproduce many instances of each type of case, giving full details, discussing all the evidence as to the facts, and then critically examining all the data and all the alternative explanatory hypotheses. Here we can only give a few bare general ideas, and cite a few cases which illustrate them.

Let us begin by considering the last category (*g*). We admit the reality of supernormal faculties, such as clairvoyance and precognition, and we would also admit, though this is by no means so self-evident as is commonly assumed, that these faculties have not been evolved in accordance with any biological law of natural selection. But why should we conclude, with Podmore and Bozzano, and others, that this logically leads us to infer that these faculties demonstrate the existence of a higher, spirit world, in which they are to be freely used ? This seems very curious reasoning, for if one accepts the laws of evolution by natural selection, it would be far more logical to regard such a spirit world as being anterior to our life here, and to look on these supernormal faculties as being the residue of those belonging to us before incarnation on earth, instead of as being a sort of magical anticipation of our future life. But I confess that the existence of faculties not produced by natural selection or biological laws does not give me the same difficulty that it appears to present to Bozzano. I think it is hard enough to demonstrate the efficiency of

such laws even in purely physiological matters, without
going any further; and no one has yet given us any
adequate reason for supposing that natural selection has
had much to do with the appearance or development of
rational thought, of musical appreciation, of literary or
artistic abilities, or of moral or religious instincts, among
humanity.

With regard to the various classes of phenomena taken
to demonstrate the action of spirits, consider first
class (*a*). Cases of the appearance during a sitting with
a medium of a spirit who claims to be a deceased person,
gives his name and personal details, and is quite unknown (or, at any rate, seems so) to the medium or the
sitters, are very common. They are held to constitute
proof of survival, and indeed the spirit very frequently
appears for the express purpose of convincing one of the
sitters that the dead do survive. Usually in such cases
the sitter is communicating with some deceased relative,
or with the medium's Control, and is trying to convince
himself that they are not fictitious pseudo-personalities
created by the medium. He asks that other inhabitants
of the spirit world be allowed to communicate, people
unknown to any of those present, so that telepathy may
not be introduced. If only some verifiable communication is then produced, how convincing a proof is
obtained ! But one difficulty in all these cases lies in the
proof that these deceased persons who appear are in fact
unknown to the medium and sitters. It is easy to say
that you have never heard of some obscure person who
lived and died in a remote part and with whom you had
no conscious contact. But in fact the newspapers make
most of your statements a little uncertain. The majority
of cases cited enable us to say that there is the distinct
possibility of either the sitters or medium having heard,
or read in a paper, some details of the decease of the
person in question. Occasionally the source of this
information has been traced successfully, and the
fictitious character of the spirit demonstrated. For

example, Mr. Soal's case of " James Miles " (in **P.S.P.R.**, Part 96) is a neat instance of the creation of a fictitious communication as the result of a newspaper paragraph casually read and completely forgotten. But there is a second, more fatal, difficulty for the adherents of Spiritualism, which consists in the fact that it is by no means necessary to assume always a normal source of information, such as a paragraph in a newspaper. It is obvious that telepathy and clairvoyance, and still more, retrocognition, make the possible sources of information far greater, and reduce the strength of this argument for spiritism very considerably.

Moreover, it sometimes happens that a spirit is demonstrably fictitious—for example, the case, previously cited, of M. Til, and Mr. Soal's case of John Ferguson (**P.S.P.R.**, Part 96). In this last case the personality, John Ferguson, who communicated, was invented, unconsciously and piecemeal, by Mr. Soal, the sitter, out of recollections and scenes connected with himself, and was telepathically communicated to the medium, and reproduced by her as a veritable spirit. Towards the end of the sittings in which John Ferguson communicated, when Mr. Soal had realized his fictitious character and had disproved most of his statements, the following instructive conversation took place between Mr. Soal and the spirit of his brother Frank, who also communicated during the sittings, and who took John Ferguson to be a real spirit :

Soal : What do you think of John Ferguson ?
Frank : Think he got mixed up, Sam. Mistook your thoughts for his own.
Soal : How do you mean ?
Frank : His mind was blank. He caught at any thoughts flying round—he'd have believed he was Jonah if you had told him so.
Soal : But I didn't tell him he was anything.
Frank : You thought it—no difference. . . . You see,

John had forgotten all about himself—clutched at any straw in the wind . . . couldn't bear to think he was nobody.

It is the last phrase that I would like to emphasize ;— only apply it to the mobile uncrystallized part of the medium's subconscious mind, and we have the clue to all these personifications, their motive power. The comparatively recent " Gordon Davis " case, which bids fair to become a classic example, clearly demonstrates the possibility that the most intricate and ingeniously persuasive " evidential " communication may be fabricated, and that the medium may acquire almost any information supernormally and from it build up a personification which seems, on the face of it, indubitably genuine.

It appears that Mr. Soal, who was sitting with the medium, Mrs. Cooper, had heard of the death of a man whom he had once known slightly, and that during his sittings this man, Gordon Davis, communicated by the " direct voice " (i.e. it was apparently the voice of the spirit which spoke). The mannerism and intonation were convincingly true to life, and many personal statements were made which Mr. Soal verified. It looked, in fact, like one more instance of the familiar type of evidential cases of personal survival. But Mr. Soal discovered, to his astonishment, that Gordon Davis was *not* dead, and that at the time of the sittings he had been well, engaged in his business, and blissfully unaware of his supposed communication ! When he read the account of the sitting he clearly recognized his own personality therein, the only false item being that he was dead. This idea, however, had been previously in Mr. Soal's mind, so that we must assume that Mrs. Cooper obtained by telepathy the general notion of a dead Gordon Davis, and then, in some hidden manner, got in touch with the real man and " psychometrized " him, and finally (of course unconsciously and in all good faith) manufactured the communication and delivered it with consummate histrionic skill. It is difficult to understand how this might be done, certainly, but it is obvious that the fact that it *was* done justifies us in suspecting all the other apparently evidential cases, and withholding, for the present, our assent to their claim to constitute a proof of survival.

A very persuasive case of communication is that contained in Mr. G. W. Balfour's paper (P.S.P.R., Part 69), dealing with Mrs. Willett's scripts, which emanated ostensibly from the classical scholar, Dr. Verrall. By means of apparently disconnected literary allusions involving Gray, Dryden, Dante, and the Roman poet Statius, as well as an obscure (in the sense of being narrowly circulated) essay by Dr. Verrall, a seemingly incoherent script is shown to be the work of a mind which is either Dr. Verrall's own, or else an exceedingly clever imitation of it ; and this latter alternative seems improbable by reason of the range of knowledge shown as well as on account of the fidelity to the manner of the original. Mr. Balfour demonstrates at least that the mind which produced the communications worked in the same way, and on the same materials, as Dr. Verrall was wont to work in life. On the other hand, the case is made less persuasive when we remember that both Mrs. and Miss Verrall were mediumistic, and wrote automatically, and that they were known to Mrs. Willett. Moreover, they were anxious to get just this complicated type of evidence for survival, and did in fact produce it in their own scripts. Further, when one of Mrs. Willett's scripts was written, Mr. Balfour, a friend of Dr. Verrall, was present, and on another occasion Miss Verrall was present—thus the opportunities and conditions for involuntary telepathic collusion (of the type which produced " John Ferguson " but far more efficient, since the basis was a real and familiar person) were certainly present ; and since such collusion is a known possible cause we must suppose it in preference to the hitherto undemonstrated one of spirit action.

The second class (*b*) of death-bed cases includes four sorts which Bozzano deals with separately, but which I have grouped together, on the ground that it is extremely difficult to get any precise, well-attested evidence, observed by competent persons in a detached frame of mind, to enable us to distinguish between real and hallucinatory phenomena, or to sort out the various possible factors. This may appear to be a shelving of awkward material in order to prejudice the case, but really the material is too uncertain to be of much value until sifted and analysed to a degree which is beyond the scope of this book. The conditions of a death-bed are not conducive to cool judgment and observations of supernormal facts ; they allow none of the control which is possible at a séance, and they tend to produce a state of emotional credulity which prevents one from distinguishing what is real from what is apparent. In the same way class (*d*), cases of bilocation just before death, will not be considered here, because they are not sufficiently well attested by competent persons to be admitted as indisputable facts, and also because (and this applies also to class (*e*), cases of materializations, as, for example, the case of Katie King), even if the fact of bilocation be admitted, it is equally easily explained as a projection of a materialized ectoplasmic structure—in this case taking the form of the dying person.

Let us pass to class (*c*), of cases where the medium talks or writes in a language unknown to him. Let us remark at once that here again much of the evidence adduced is rather unreliable. However, the mediums Valiantine and Kluski are both quite credibly reported to have spoken to sitters of various nationalities in the appropriate languages, to the extent of a dozen tongues or so, all of which were unknown to the medium. In these cases, however, it is perfectly possible that an unconscious telepathic collusion between sitter and medium is the sole and sufficient cause of this dramatic phenomenon. Consequently the Spiritualists make great play of some cases where the language spoken by the spirits is unknown to the sitter also.   But such cases obviously are open to the suggestion that the unknown language is in fact not any language at all !   For example, Kluski materialized a phantom of an old bearded man, whom the circle called " The Assyrian Priest."   He spoke a guttural language, unknown to everyone, and not yet identified.   But then, what evidence have we that it was not mere gibberish, or an infantile language created by the medium, like the Martian tongue created by Helen Smith ?   In the only case where such an unknown tongue has been carefully examined (at least, so far as I am aware), namely, in the case of Helen Smith's " Martian," the spirit hypothesis has not received much support from the analysis, and the powers of the subconscious mind have been demonstrated to be considerably greater than was formerly supposed.

The Case of Helen Smith.

Helen Smith was a young, intelligent and capable woman, quite normal in health and behaviour, and occupying a responsible position in a business house in Geneva, who held remarkable séances in which, among other things, her spirit was conducted to Mars and there saw many strange sights.   She was studied by Professor Flournoy, whose book *From India to the Planet Mars* is a masterly psychological analysis of her quite typical spiritualistic adventures.   Concluding one of his chapters, Flournoy points out one or two striking features of Helen's description of life on Mars.   In the first place, the Martian world combines complete identity with our world in all essential points, with puerile originality in a host of minor details.   For example, the bridges there slip under the water to allow boats to pass, instead of being drawn up as ours are ; and the people there eat off square plates which have a furrow for the gravy.   Secondly, the complexions, features, costumes of the Martians, their houses and

the vegetation, have a strong flavour of the sham Orient
—it is pseudo-Japanese. Thirdly, the Martian language
which Helen spoke is found to be an original creation
based on French—being, in fact, superficially quite
unlike it as to the actual words, and yet identical
with it in syntax and grammar. For example, the order
of words in the two languages is identical, and idiosyn-
crasies such as the divided negative (*ne . . . pas*) or
the euphonic " t " in *reviendra-t-il* are copied faithfully.
For example :

Martian. cé *ké* lé nazère *ani.*
French. je *ne* me trompe *pas.*
and
Martian. kévi bérimir-m-hed.
French. quand reviendra-t-il.

The Martian vowels are five and correspond exactly
with the French vowels. The Martian c and s have the
same character as in French ; e.g., s is generally hard,
but between two vowels it is soft. Every Martian word
corresponds exactly to one French word ; so that we
have the remarkable fact that the Martians speak a
language which, though its words have a certain quasi-
Oriental look, yet corresponds more closely with French
than do German or English, or other European
languages. The following passage will show the close
correspondence, especially in the smaller points of the
language, such as the omission of " pas " after the
verb " puis " :

Martian. cé ké mache radziré zé tarvini na nini nini—
French. je ne puis prononcer le langage où nous nous—
Martian. triménêni ii adzi. . . .
French. comprenions si bien. . . .

There is no resisting Flournoy's conclusion that this
Martian language is simply an infantile creation made
up by a mind which naively supposed that a new
language could be evolved by simply substituting un-
couth words for each word of the mother tongue ; and

that the whole Martian romance is a piece of subliminal imagination, based mainly on childish ideas about the Orient, and fabricated by an infantile Helen Smith who survives in the background of the adult lady, and who comes to the fore when she goes into a trance. This interpretation is also supported by his analysis of her other romances—as when she incarnates Marie Antoinette or a Hindu princess—and of the various spirits who in turn appear in her séances. Her spiritualistic incarnations, as a matter of fact, are simply a special and intense form of compensatory day-dreaming, by which she achieves romance and a grandeur which the circumstances of her daily life have denied her.

But the remarkable point which we wish to bring to notice here is that this infantile subconscious personality which enacted these romances was able to invent a kind of language (creating words at first, no doubt, on the spur of the moment, but probably also elaborating it at leisure between the séances) and to maintain this language consistently throughout about forty séances, covering a period of three years, so that words used in the earlier séances are used again correctly in later séances, only very few and small errors occurring. The waking conscious personality of Helen Smith could have had little to do with the language, as it was either spoken during trance, and taken down phonetically by Flournoy, or written by her in trance in a special Martian calligraphy ; in both cases the texts were taken away by Flournoy, and the translations, which were given during her trance by her spirit control, were kept out of her sight until practically the end of the series. Then Professor Flournoy, having come to the conclusion that he could prove to her that Martian was really her own invention, discussed the texts with her and criticized them adversely. The result was unexpected, for she shortly afterwards produced an ultra-Martian language, extremely rich in *a* sounds, whereas Martian had been over-rich in *i* and *e* sounds, and having no discoverable grammar or syntax at all ! The language, in fact, avoids the charge of earthliness only by becoming chaotic.

A more recent, and well-known, example of the phenomenon of speaking in an unknown tongue is Valiantine's production of the voice of Confucius. At some sittings with him in New York various Oriental tongues were spoken, and so a noted Oriental scholar, Dr. Whymant, was invited to be present. During his sittings a spirit announcing himself as Kung Fu Tzu appeared, and on being questioned at some length by Dr. Whymant in Chinese he gave various proofs of his knowledge of remote and obscure points—such as the popular name of Confucius when he was fourteen years old, the usage of archaic Chinese phrases and sounds, and the interpretation of a doubtful passage in the philosopher's writings.

Moreover, at later sittings, in the absence of Dr. Why-mant, gramophone records of this Chinese voice were made which, in spite of being faint and blurred, were recognizable as the same voice. Nevertheless we cannot avoid recognizing the possibility that all this Chinese was obtained from the mind of Dr. Whymant himself. Mere physical propinquity, though indubitably an aid to the initial establishing of telepathic communication, is by no means essential for, and even perhaps quite irrelevant to, its continuance when once established. Telepathy across six hundred miles is no more difficult to understand than across six feet, since space is apparently quite irrelevant to it. The proximity of the sitter simply facilitates the establishment of " rapport " ; it does nothing to facilitate the actual mental exploration or transmission involved in telepathy.

It will, I think, be agreed now, that the phenomenon of writing or speaking in unknown or unfamiliar languages is not so convincing a proof of spirit possession as is commonly assumed, and with this we may pass on to the remaining category of Bozzano's incontrovertible proofs.

Class (*f*) includes certain cases of " Cross-Correspond-ences." Evidence based on cases of " *cross-correspond-ence* " is plentiful enough and occupies many parts of the Proceedings of the S.P.R., being perhaps the Society's chief contribution to the subject.[2]

These cases reveal the general fact that two different mediums may obtain the same message, or that what is said by one automatic writer may be amplified or illustrated by what another writes ; so that we are ultimately forced to conclude that one and the same mind is dominating the two mediums. In view of the apparently deliberate concealment of meaning which marks many of these scripts, so that only a person who reads both messages and compares them is able to see any sense in either, we are compelled to admit that if a single mind produces both messages it does so either because it is in a state of helpless oscillation, or else because it wishes to demonstrate the fact that a single mind, above and beyond the minds of the two auto-matists, is communicating. To take an instance of a simple type. On a certain day a Mrs. Forbes received a script purporting to come from her dead son Talbot. This ended by his saying that he was looking for another medium through whom he could send a message to confirm this one—i.e. to demonstrate that what Mrs. Forbes had written did not emanate merely from her own subconscious mind. Now on the same day Mrs. Verrall, another automatist, wrote of a fir tree planted in a garden, and signed this with a sword and bugle. She could attach no meaning to this, but Miss Alice Johnson, who, as an officer of the S.P.R., read both scripts, found that a sword and bugle were in Talbot's regimental badge, and that Mrs. Forbes had in her garden some fir trees which had been grown from seed given to her by her son. The sword and bugle and the fir trees, then, were identificatory signs of Talbot's personality, given to Mrs. Verrall (who was apparently

[2] See especially P.S.P.R., Parts 53, 55, 57, 60, 63, 67, and 68.

ignorant of their significance) for the purpose of convincing Mrs. Forbes of her son's present existence. But it may legitimately be objected that here we have another wish-fulfilment phantasy, enacted this time on the mental plane, and through the mechanism of telepathy. I do not say that this must be the explanation ; nevertheless, I think it is the correct one. As a matter of fact, Mrs. Verrall was a friend of Mrs. Forbes, and on several occasions her automatic writings corresponded with those produced at the same time by Mrs. Forbes. On October 16, 1909, for example, Mrs. Verrall's script gave details as to what Mrs. Forbes was doing at the time, and these were subsequently verified. On the same day, Mrs. Verrall had a mental impression of Mrs. Forbes and her son standing in the former's drawing-room at Cambridge ; at the same time Mrs. Forbes received a message (by automatic writing) from her son, saying he was present, and that a test was being given for her at Cambridge. On another occasion (November 26th and 27th, 1902) Mrs. Forbes obtained references to the Symposium of Plato, which Mrs. Verrall had been reading on those two days. Now all these facts, and countless similar ones, are suggestive, and are certainly likely to constitute in many people's minds the most convincing proof of continued existence after death. Myers, Dr. Verrall, and their circle thought that this kind of evidence excluded telepathy, since the separate parts of a message were unintelligible to each of the recipients, and only achieved intelligibility when put together by some third person. But in the light of what we now know of dissociated personalities, and of fictitious personalities created by one part of the subconscious mind in order to gratify itself or the normal personality, in the light of what we have learned both as to telepathy and as to cryptæsthesia, does it not seem rather that all these cross-correspondences are highly special instances of telepathy ? All these recondite classical illusions, so characteristic of Myers and Dr. Verrall, are they not equally within the scope of Mrs. Verrall, herself a scholar, who seems to have been involved in the production of so many of them ? It is not a little significant that the chief contribution of the S.P.R. to psychic science, namely, the production of cross-correspondences, should have been something so characteristic of the scholarly minds of their chief leaders, and something, too, which seems to have been practically invented by the fertile genius of F. W. H. Myers. In most departments of thought one runs the risk of finding what one is looking for, but in psychic science the risk is doubly great, for the mere act of desiring a certain kind of evidence sometimes creates that very thing.

In his book *And After* Mr. Dennis Bradley describes a recent case of cross-correspondence which was arranged to occur simultaneously between " Margery " in Boston and Valiantine in Venice. Briefly, the Boston Circle arranged to sit on May 27, 1929, at 5 p.m. (American time), and Mr. Bligh Bond had with him nine leaves torn from a block calendar which, without seeing their faces, he had signed at the back and placed in a sealed envelope in his inside pocket.

During the séance, in absolute darkness, the spirit control " Walter " told him to take out three leaves and place them on the table, and then to pick them up and put them together in his pocket. At 5.45 p.m. " Walter " said good-bye, and the séance ended.

Meanwhile, at the same hour (11.30 Italian time) a sitting was in progress in Venice with Valiantine as medium. The control " Walter " appeared here, too, and greeted two of the sitters whom he knew. At 11.45 a luminous clock stopped, and Valiantine woke from his trance and immediately wrote down on a paper three numbers—3, 5, 10. Finally, the Boston Circle sat again at 9 p.m. (American time) and Margery began to write a short message descriptive of the sitting in Venice, and including the words : " Write 3, 5, 10." At 9.5 the sitting ended, and Mr. Bligh Bond showed everyone the envelope and the three selected leaves bearing his signature on the back. The leaves read May 5, May 3, and May 10.

Now this is not really such a scientific test as it seems at first glance. Many objections might be raised, but I am only concerned here with its use as a proof of the Spiritualist theory, so I am prepared to accept all the facts as given without any dispute, and concentrate on their explanation. The Spiritualist explanation involves (1) the existence of the spirit " Walter," (2) his power of " possessing " or entering into the living medium [alternately, his power to captivate their minds, or some equivalent], (3) his cryptæsthetic ability to read the numbers in absolute darkness, and (4) his ability to act simultaneously in Boston and Venice ; or, alternatively, the existence of a fourth dimension whereby these two places may be brought into immediate proximity. The chief point of the experiment was the synchronization of the times, and Bradley insists that 5.45 p.m. in Boston corresponds exactly with 11.45 p.m. in Venice.

Thus Cryptæsthesia (of somebody) and something equivalent to a four-dimensional theory of the world are necessary to the spirit theory.

But with them the extra hypotheses of the existence of the spirit Walter and of possession are at once superfluous.

Margery in Boston could read the numbers, and so for the matter of that could Valiantine, although his body was in Venice. We have seen that the world is four-dimensional, and that clairvoyance and telepathy function independently of distance. Perhaps one of them " saw " the numbers (clairvoyance) and communicated them to the other (telepathy) ; or perhaps both of them saw the numbers. We must remember that the séances were arranged by agreement for the purpose of synchronized cryptæsthesia, so that Margery, or Valiantine, may as well be supposed to pull their weight as " Walter."

Moreover, the conditions were ripe for a wholesale telepathic collusion. Valiantine knew the Americans (being one himself) and the control " Walter " greeted two of the Venice sitters whom he knew—i.e. they had previously sat with Margery. Two of the Venice sitters (Mrs. Hack and Mrs. Bradley) were themselves mediumistic, and may certainly be presumed to act as favourable influences for an unintentional telepathic collusion. When two or three mediums are gathered together, with the express purpose of trying to " get in touch " and obtain cross-correspondences, it is hard to say what limits should be set to the reasonable possibilities of telepathy. Thus while this case is an interesting one of Cryptæsthesia in general it is quite inconclusive as a piece of evidence for Spiritualism, and is more economically interpreted without any reference to spirits at all.

I am aware that it is impossible to prove that all these various categories enumerated by Bozzano are *not* due to the actions of spirits. The point, however, is that they do not, either separately or together, compel one to the spirit hypothesis, because in the first place there are alternative hypotheses which at least have the advantage of having been previously demonstrated by other phenomena ; and, in the second place, the spirit hypothesis in itself conflicts with our ideas as to the nature of human personality ; while in the third place the spirit hypothesis is entirely *additional to* the other hypotheses and does not enable us to do away with any one of them, nor does it even make it easier to explain the phenomena—that is to say, it is wholly superfluous.

NOTE TO CHAPTER THIRTEEN

HAUNTINGS AND POLTERGEIST CASES

Numerous instances of hauntings and poltergeists are given by Flammarion in his book *Haunted Houses*, from which I will summarize briefly one good case, as follows.

In September 1903 a Mr. Grottendieck was sleeping one night in a jungle hut in Sumatra, accompanied by a Malay boy. The hut was unfinished and " made of beams stuck together and covered with large dried leaves plastered over with *kadjang*."

At 1 a.m. he was awakened by the falling of black stones, about one inch long, from the ceiling. They fell in a parabolic curve. He wakened the Malay boy, and both went outside to explore with an electric torch, but found nothing. Meanwhile the stones continued to fall. He found it impossible to catch any of them in their descent, as " they seemed to jump in the air as I grabbed at them " (1).

When he examined the roof he found that, though the stones had emerged from the ceiling, yet the leaves composing it had no holes in them (2).

He then fired his rifle five times out of the window, in order to scare away anyone who might be there. The noise had the effect of waking up the Malay boy completely—for up to this moment he had been somnolent and abnormally slow in his movements (3). Now, however, he seemed first to notice the stones falling, and was terrified by them and ran away out into the jungle. With his disappearance the stones ceased to fall (4).

Further observations by Mr. G. showed that the stones were in no way abnormal, except that they were rather warm (5). In describing their flight through the air he says :

" The stones fell with astonishing slowness, so that if fraud must be assumed there would still be a mystery to explain. It seemed as if they went slowly through the air, describing a parabolic curve, and hitting the ground with force. Even the noise they produced was abnormal, for it was too loud relatively to the fall " (6).

Now this case is quite typical of scores of others, and we have no reason to doubt the justness and general correctness of Mr. G.'s observations. But at what point does the Spirit hypothesis help us to explain the facts more easily than the more naturalistic theories outlined in this book ? Points 1 and 6 show that the stones were carried rather than simply projected, for otherwise they would have had the usual gravitational acceleration, and could not have eluded his grasp by jumping. Point 3 shows that the Malay boy was in a semi or full trance state, and point 4 proves that he was the immediate cause of the phenomenon. Points 2 and 5 both suggest an apport.

We may therefore interpret the whole as a case where a

young person falls into a trance (while asleep, in this instance)
and projects ectoplasmic structures with which he apports
stones into the room.   When he is roused by the shock of
the gunshots his ordinary personality becomes aware of the
unusual fall of stones and he is frightened and runs away ;
and so the phenomenon ceases.

Some of the numbered points in the above account recur
in another case given by Flammarion, who quotes it from
P.S.P.R., Vol. 7, p. 383.   It is an account of spontaneous
movements of bits of wood in a carpenter's shop by a certain
Mr. Bristowe.   Two quotations may be given.

" It is remarkable that in spite of innumerable attempts
we could never catch a piece in movement, for it cleverly
eluded all our stratagems.   They seemed animated and
intelligent . . . sometimes the direction taken by the projec-
tiles was a straight line, but more often it was undulating,
rotatory, spiral, serpentine, or jerky."

" Nobody ever saw a missile at the time it started.   One
would have said that they could not be perceived until they
had travelled at least six inches from their starting-point."

From the first quotation we conclude that the bits of
wood were not thrown, but *carried*, presumably by an ectoplasmic structure ;   and from the second that they travelled
at first in the fourth dimension, and reappeared in our space,
where they were perceived coming as it were from nowhere.

BIBLIOGRAPHY

F. W. H. MYERS.   Human Personality and its Survival after
     Bodily Death.
BOZZANO.   A Propos de l'Introduction à la Métapsychique.
SUDRÉ.   Introduction à la Métapsychique.
SOAL.   Report in P.S.P.R., Part 96.
BALFOUR.   Scripts affording Evidence of Personal Survival,
     P.S.P.R., Part 69.
FLOURNOY.   From India to the Planet Mars.
Various cases of cross-correspondence are given in Parts 53,
     55, 57, 60, 63, 67, and 68 of P.S.P.R.

CHAPTER FOURTEEN

TRANSCENDENTAL CONSCIOUSNESS

IT is now time to collect together the main ideas which may be gathered from our all too rapid and superficial survey, and to attempt to weld them into a consistent and coherent point of view. As it seems to me, there are four main themes in the theory by which all metapsychic phenomena may be related, and we will consider them in turn.

1. First comes the theme of *Personification*.

From an analytical point of view a personality is a complex of various psychological factors—memories, desires, instincts, interests, habits of thought and behaviour, and so on. This complex may be radically altered, either temporarily or permanently, by various influences, among which our daily experience in life is the most universal, disease the next commonest, and hypnotic suggestion the most striking and immediate. But not only is a personality an unstable, continuously changing, and relatively transient phenomenon ; not only can it change abruptly and profoundly, as the hysterical alternations and multiplications of personality bear witness, but it is also a phenomenon which has meaning and significance, at any given time, solely in relation to this world. The general common instincts (which are *ipso facto* not specifically personal) might have meaning in another world ; but the characteristics which distinctively differentiate one man from another (for example his personal interests, habits, and memories) are dependent upon life in this world for their existence, their meaning, and their value. As Keyserling has put it : " Precisely those tendencies which seem to be particularly personal, demonstrably do not lead to infinity." This sentence gives the best single refutation of the philosophy of Spiritualism that I have seen. The mistake of the Spiritualists, as I understand it, is that they confuse the personality with the soul (assuming there is a soul) and consequently they invest it with a value and significance which, *sub specie aeternitatis*, it simply does not possess. The Platonic argument for immortality, that the soul is indivisible and therefore eternal, cannot apply to a personality which is composite.

We have said that a personality derives its meaning from this world. To say this does not imply that personality is of little value ; on the contrary, from the point of view of our present life in this world the achievement of a harmonious and effective personality seems to be of the very highest value and significance ; it is even possibly the chief object of human life, if we can admit that there are purposes apart from and above the individual and transient aims of living things. But although the achievement of an ideal personality may be the supreme aim in this life it has no significance with respect to other possible future lives in immaterial worlds ; nor can one unchanging personality even be conceived of as living for ever, since it would have to exist without undergoing any more experience (for experience would necessarily alter it), and existence without any experience hardly constitutes living.

And if we demand that the personality should be immortal, and undergo an eternity of continuously changing experience, we cannot at the same time expect it to be always recognizably the same. In an infinite time there would have to be an infinitude of experiences, which necessarily involves an infinite change in any one personality. The idea of a static never-changing person living at all, let alone living for ever, is in the last analysis self-contradictory, since living involves change. No experience is simply passively received, it is always actively lived ; and every action involves a reaction which modifies the agent. We are thus on the horns of a dilemma : either we must arrest all development and perpetuate for eternity a personality which, at the moment of its death in this world, is obviously imperfect and only of value in relation to its life in this world, or else we must allow the personality to undergo an infinite variety of experience in its eternal life, and reconcile ourselves to the fact that it will very quickly cease to be recognizable as the one we knew on earth. As far as I can see the only escape from our dilemma is to recognize that an individual personality is not an eternal entity at all, but a transient manifestation, in terms of space and time, of something of a different order of being, and of higher dimensions, which includes the essentials of all living things (and probably of non-living, if anything is really non-living) in one unity. This inner and eternal self which is the same within us all is, as one of the Upanishads says, " the only one free from qualities." In other words it is the antithesis of what we would call an individual personality, which is personal and individual only because of qualities that differentiate it from others.[1]

---

[1] Schopenhauer expresses many of the essential ideas which I have tried to bring out in this book. Had he lived a century later he would indubitably have written in terms of the fourth dimension, and would probably have come near a true exposition of the nature of time and of personality. Thus in Section 54 of his *World as Will and Idea* he writes :

" For every individual is transitory only as phenomenon, but as thing-in-itself is timeless and therefore endless. But it is also only as phenomenon that an individual is distinguished from the other things of the world ; as thing-in-itself he is the will which appears in all, and death destroys the illusion which separates his consciousness from that of the rest ; this is immortality."

And in further explanation, the following sentences culled from his essay *On the Indestructibility of our Nature by Death* may be quoted :

" The more clearly one is conscious of the transience, nothingness, and dream-like nature of all things, by so much the more clearly is one conscious also of the eternity of one's own inner nature. . . . Life may certainly be regarded as a dream and death as an awakening. But then the personality, the individual, belongs to the dreaming, and not to the waking, consciousness ; for which reason death presents itself to the former as an annihilation. . . . For in death the consciousness assuredly perishes, but not by any means that which till then had produced it."

In any normal healthy person there is an approach towards the harmonious synthesis which constitutes an effective personality, however imperfect the result may be. True it usually entails the neglect and suppression of many valuable factors, and an imperfect control of many others, but nevertheless a sufficiently stable synthesis of the main psychological components is achieved, making a complex which is adapted to life, and is recognizable by others as approximately the same unit throughout life.

But there are many people who do not achieve a practical and useful working synthesis, and in whom large and important tracts of very active psychological components are not brought under the domination of the central main personality. In these persons the personality is not even apparently unified ; it is manifestly dissociated (and this is the crux of the matter) into two or more alternating or co-existing secondary personalities. In other words, the unassimilated factors which do not come into the empire of the main reigning personality do not remain detached, ineffectually languishing for lack of use, but seem to unite together, co-operating like an association of outcasts, and conspire to produce between them another personality which tries to usurp the throne. There is a fundamental urge for psychological matter to organize itself into a personality, or, as we may say, mental factors are characterized by a tendency to personification.

In the case of the madman and the hysteric the split in personality is grave and more or less lasting. In the hypnotized patient it may be very trivial and temporary, and the case of the medium, considered simply as a medium and without any reference to any hysteria in particular individuals, is essentially similar. The factors of personality are in a labile condition, and under the appropriate influences of auto-suggestion and the séance the normal " worldly " personality of the medium dissolves, more or less as the case may be, and new and

fleeting syntheses are made. In general the medium
will create fictitious spirit personalities—and the greater
the degree of dissociation the more full and rich will be
the pseudo-spirit created. The more or less habitual
" Controls " usually represent the medium's own secondary personalities and imply an approach towards the
condition found in hysterical cases of multiple personality such as Miss Beauchamp or Léonie ; but the
ephemeral spirits who communicate on demand are
special and transient *ad hoc* dramatic personifications,
and derive their substance largely from psychological
materials supplied by the sitters or consultants. The
factors of telepathy and clairvoyance obviously play an
important part and enable the medium to produce
strikingly " evidential " results, which convince the
majority that the communicator is an independent
spirit ; but everything tends to indicate that it is merely
a pseudo-personality elaborated by the medium when
in a state of mental dissociation essentially similar to
that of hypnosis, and that it derives its content largely
from the sitter's subconscious mind.

2. Our second main theme is the principle of *Ideoplasticity.*

Accepting the common-sense dualistic terminology
we say that an essential attribute of mind is that it
has the power to direct and mould matter. This is
familiar to us in the case of the voluntary movements
of our limbs, though the essential mystery is here as
patent as in the unfamiliar examples. The mind can,
and does, move and control the physical body belonging
to it ; and the examples where this control is demonstrated in all sorts of unfamiliar and striking ways prove
that this is ultimately the essential fact about the living
body. The blisters suggested to the hypnotized patient,
the amazing wealth of physical symptoms shown by
hysterical patients, and due to purely mental factors,
and the phenomenon of stigmatization, all illustrate the
fundamental ideoplasticity of the living organism ; and

we have no need to doubt the truth of any of the stories about the control that Indian yogis acquire over their internal functions ; for they are at least theoretically possible in principle, which is all that matters to us here.

When we deal with the materializations of the séance-room we find this ideoplasticity is greatly enhanced. This is just what ought to be expected, since the ecto-plasm is not, like the body, a crystallized, almost petri-fied, structure, canalized through centuries of habit and heredity, but is still amorphous and amenable to the slightest organizing influence.   What is gained in stability is necessarily lost in plasticity.

It is a principle of Yoga philosophy, and of Western occultism, that the mind can influence external matter directly, just as it can the body or the ectoplasm. This, of course, is not justifiable as an inference from facts discussed in this book, nor does there seem to be any independent experimental evidence to support it. But yet it is not improbable in theory, although in practice such an effect would presumably be a work of great intrinsic difficulty ; because, as we have already men-tioned, matter is in all probability itself mental. The effect of mind on matter is probably really an effect of mind on certain other stable and crystallized forms of mind. Moreover, since individual minds are apparently in constant communication under the surface (as tele-pathy reveals), and since a mind is in any case not bounded by space and time, it is not inherently absurd to suppose that every individual mind is connected, not merely with all other individual minds, but with every object in the external world, and can thus influence it. It would appear to be simply a question of degree, and very likely the yogis are right when they assert that, with a sufficient amount of the proper training in con-centration, one can acquire the power to influence external objects at will by a pure act of thought. Whether the result to be achieved is worth the necessary training is of course another matter.

3. Our third theme concerns the *Four-dimensional Nature of the Universe*.

The evidence of Physics, both from the standpoint of Relativity and from that of Wave-mechanics, shows that the phenomena studied by modern physicists cannot be explained satisfactorily with less than four dimensions ; whether more are needed has hardly been settled yet. It also shows that the Time dimension is qualitatively of the same nature as the three space dimensions, our conception of it as something quite different being a psychological and private interpretation of our own, not justified by anything in the continuum itself.[2]

The facts relating to Apports and the tying of knots in endless cords also lead us to deduce the existence of a fourth dimension, and the possibility of displacing objects in it.

Again, looking at the matter from the point of view suggested by the facts of precognition, we deduced the four-dimensional nature of things and the unreality of our popular notions about Time. And this enabled us to explain, in vague general terms, the facts of Clairvoyance and Psychometry, and in particular the hitherto puzzling rôle of the evocatory object. This last is a point of capital importance.

Osty has established that psychometric clairvoyance is very greatly facilitated, and even initiated by contact with any sort of object connected with the person concerned. The efficacy of the object is the greater the longer it has been in contact ; and contact with many other people in no way weakens its power to assist the clairvoyant except by bringing in a number of irrelevant connections. It is simply a means of communication between the medium and the other person, and it is just as effective if the other person is already dead. The supposition that the object is " impregnated " with the

---

[2] I am here taking the view that the difference between Time-like and Space-like separations is not real and noumenal, but only phenomenal.

memories of the persons it has touched is on the face of it absurd, and all the occult theories of personal fluids and effluvia are totally inadequate to explain how the medium gets his information from the object placed in his hands.   Much of the mystery disappears at once when we remember that every object is a four-dimensional " worm " and that in consequence the World-line of the object still intersects the World-line of the person who is being psychometrized, so that there is a permanent connection between them.   Even if the person is dead, the medium can still journey down the object's World-line until he arrives at the junction where it meets the World-line of the person about whom information is sought.   The evocatory object simply acts like a railway line, leading the medium direct to another railway which is the World-line of the person.

4.   Finally our fourth theme is concerned with what may be termed *Four-dimensional Consciousness.*

The problems presented by our normal waking life and the mystery of perception are themselves at present insoluble.   But we may say that our ordinary life is characterized by the fact that, out of the continuum presented to our mind, we select three aspects which we relate together in a special way and call space ; while we sense the fourth aspect vaguely and differently, calling it time.   But though everybody thus chooses axes of space and time the Relativity theory demonstrates the highly important fact that we do not, in actuality, choose exactly the same axes ; and that if a man should move with a very high velocity relative to another, their respective axes would be greatly different.   In other words the external world as we perceive it is once more, and this time in a new and disconcerting manner, shown to be not " reality " but " appearance."

The question naturally arises as to whether our normal waking consciousness is the only, or the best, or the most accurate mode of consciousness ; and whether other modes of consciousness, if they exist, do not carry with them new values, new sorts of logic, and new inherent possibilities. And of course we have plenty of evidence that states of consciousness do occur in which the external world is cognized differently, and a word like *Reality* has a new meaning. Such states (apart from Sleep) are the various degrees of hypnotic trance, the mediumistic trance, and the mystical ecstasy, and though they have received various different names derived from the varieties of action and behaviour resulting from them, they are, in my opinion, essentially mere variants of one and the same state of four-dimensional consciousness.

We have already seen how the hypnotic trance is induced, and with what phenomena it may be associated ; but the problem of what exactly is the state of consciousness of the hypnotic patient has not been adequately solved by academic psychologists. We may say, however, that it involves a considerable degree of withdrawal of attention from the multitude of sense perceptions coming from the external world, together with, at least as a preliminary, a kind of immobilization of the mind so that it is almost wholly occupied with one idea or image, not however by any voluntary act of concentrated attention, but by an involuntary state of fascinated fixation. The " upper," conscious, voluntary, and, we may add, essentially *personal* aspects of the mind are held in abeyance or temporarily demolished ; and the unconscious mind then dominates the situation. There is apparently a state of mental blankness, but when the operator commands or suggests something, whether it is a feat of arithmetic or a physiological *tour de force* like creating a blister in a certain pattern, the unconscious mind is found to attack the problem with accuracy and certainty, as if the whole inner powers were concentrated efficiently on the task.

The mediumistic trance is essentially similar, differing mainly in two respects ; first, that it is usually self-induced, by auto-suggestion, and secondly, that it is almost always dominated (indeed created) by the desire to produce specifically spiritist manifestations—either to communicate with spirits, or to let them manifest physically through the medium. Instead of a case of hypnotic personifications produced at the conscious suggestion of an operator, we have here auto-hypnotic personifications produced by auto-suggestion arising from the whole spiritualist faith, and, in former days, from popular superstition. But though the pseudo-personalities are, considered in themselves, worthless, the mediumistic trance often reveals a state of consciousness which is in many respects capable of more than our normal one is ; for example it has extensive powers of telepathy, clairvoyance and precognition. Its essentially four-dimensioned character is illustrated by the two following quotations.

Ossowiecki, who once gave Dr. Geley an interesting description of his own feelings in trance, says :

" I begin by stopping the process of reasoning, and I throw myself, with all my internal powers, into spiritual sensation. I then find myself in a new and special condition, in which I see and hear *quite outside space and time*." (Italics mine.)

Another self-description, more elaborated and imaginative perhaps, but still worth noting for its four-dimensional implications, is that given by Andrew Jackson Davis.

" The sphere of my vision now began to expand. At first I could only see clearly the walls of the house. At the start they seemed to me dark and gloomy ; but they soon became brighter and finally transparent. I could now see the objects, the furniture, and the persons in the adjoining house as easily as those in the room in which I sat. But my perceptions extended further still ; before my wandering glance—the broad surface of the earth, for hundreds of miles about me, grew as transparent as water," etc.

The various forms of mediumship are closely related,

and would appear to be different applications of one and the same original faculty. Thus we find that, although each medium tends to specialize in one or only a few effects, and to work always under the same limited conditions, yet none of the best mediums have been totally barren of any of the forms of mediumship, and in most mediums several forms show themselves at one time or another. There may seem, on the face of things, no conceivable connection between the power to materialize an ectoplasmic phantom and the power to read someone else's mind, or the power to foresee the future. Regarded from any ordinary common-sense philosophy there *is* no connection between them. Yet it is a matter of observation that anyone who produces physical phenomena can be trained (if it does not happen spontaneously) to produce the mental phenomena, and vice versa ; and further, that when a medium is occupied mainly in one direction his powers in the other directions grow weaker.

Now in the two branches of mental and physical phenomena of mediumship which we have studied in the previous chapters there seem to be only two common fundamental factors ; subjectively, a particular state of consciousness, characterized largely by loss of ordinary awareness of the " real " external three-dimensional world and also by a temporary dissociation of personality and an emergence of the " unconscious mind " ; and objectively, the four-dimensional nature of the universe. I say, then, that the medium is in a state of transcendental consciousness, in which he perceives, more or less clearly as the case may be, the universe as a four-dimensional structure. If we add to this statement the fact that the universe is essentially also a mental structure we may, I think, find ourselves ultimately able to integrate the whole set of apparently disparate, yet demonstrably inter-related, metapsychical facts.

The hypnotic and the mediumistic trances are then

states of four-dimensional consciousness; but by no means in the sense that the continuum is apprehended clearly and its essential nature understood. Rather are they states in which the mind is not vividly conscious of three dimensions, but vaguely conscious of four; or conscious first of one three-dimensional section, then of another. In a word, we are only on the threshold of the study of this subject, and cannot yet define the varieties and shades of consciousness which may occur.

CONCLUSION

But it will perhaps strike the reader that the state of mystical ecstasy might well be one of almost complete four-dimensional consciousness, and it is worth our while to examine the matter.

Mysticism may be regarded as a religious, or even a poetic, attitude of mind: but the mystical ecstasy, which is the practical goal aimed at by the mystics, is a state which may be studied from the psychological point of view. Such studies as have been made by, for example, R. M. Bucke, William James, Evelyn Underhill, and Professor Leuba, give us a good quantity of interesting data, without exactly revealing the actual psychological realities involved, and we will briefly summarize the most relevant facts.

Regarded from the point of view of psychology, a mystic is a person who experiences a particular type of trance, largely analogous to sleep, epilepsy, inebriation, hypnosis, and the mediumistic trance, but distinguished from these by certain features. Vivid visual and auditory hallucinations are usual, and there is a strong subjective feeling of intense joy, peace, or beatitude which, by universal consent, is an unutterable rapture. With this is usually associated a strong feeling of conviction that some hitherto concealed idea is now revealed and known with a certainty that transcends all other knowledge. This is felt as a deepening, rather than a widening, of knowledge, and is usually not amenable to exact intellectual expression. Doubtless much of this depends often on auto-suggestion based on the religious convictions of the mystic, but there is nevertheless an underlying sameness in all mystical experience, independent of the religious preconceptions and interpretations of the individuals concerned, which leads us to suppose that there is a constant factor in this state of consciousness which corresponds with some objective reality. Moreover, in contradistinction to the allied but pathological states, the mystic seems usually to be a better and deeper person after the experience than he was before ; from the ecstasy he derives steadfastness of purpose, and a strength which, in the exceptional cases, may make him a world force. He gains a realization of, and the power to pursue, some vital mission in life, and a calm indifference to the usual petty personal aims and desires.

As to the psychology of the actual ecstasy, there are remarkable coincidences in the descriptions by mystics in all ages and of all races, which indicate that it is a state in which the sense of time is lost, in which the sense of personal identity and separation is also lost, and in which a sense of wider, divine, or universal personality and of permanence and immortality is gained. The formulæ and expressions vary, and the emphasis is laid now here and now there, but there is a fundamental uniformity in the teachings of all mystics, whether we take Buddha, the *Bhagavad Gita*, the gospel of Jesus, Plotinus, Boehme, or William Blake as examples.

The Hindu mystics practise first of all extreme concentration of thought, and then the obliteration of all thought from the mind, in order to arrive at an ecstatic state in which, according to one formula, " The knower and the thing known are one," or according to another formula, one " beholds within the body of the God of Gods the whole universe in all its vast variety." An essential condition of attainment is to " detach oneself from the objects of sense," to cultivate indifference as to all worldly actions and results ; and the consequences of attainment, according to the Yogis, are first a complete mastery over one's own body, and secondly the mastery over all the range of what we call metapsychic powers.

In the Chinese classic, *Tao-Teh-King*, the chief emphasis is laid on the doctrine of inaction and detachment from desire. Buddha laid more stress on the essentially evil nature of desire and the illusory nature of personality. " The illusion of self originates and manifests itself in a cleaving to things. . . . There is self, and there is truth ; where self is, truth is not ; where truth is, self is not. Self is individual separateness . . . it is the yearning for pleasure and the lust after vanity. Truth is the correct understanding of things, it is the permanent and everlasting, the real in all existence. . . . The attainment of truth is only possible when self is recognized as an illusion."

The Hindu form of the same doctrine is that the self and the not-self are identical, being both, fundamentally, manifestations of the universal Self, Brahm. Or, in more Christian terminology, the same idea is expressed by Boehme's dictum : " Not I, the I that I am, know these things ; but God knows them in me." And the final goal of Christian mysticism has always been recognized as the complete absorption of the individual self, with consequent loss of the limitations of personality, in a union with the infinite Deity.

Sometimes the mystic vision crystallizes into an hallucination of the accepted form of the deity, as in the case of those who, like St. Theresa, see a vision of Jesus. But where the religious auto-suggestion is less definite and anthropomorphic, or where the vision itself is perhaps deeper, a sort of general clairvoyance, analogous to that described by A. J. Davis, may ensue. For example Boehme says : " In this light my spirit suddenly saw through all, and in and by all the creatures, even the herbs and grass, it knew God, who he is, how he is, and what his will is ; and suddenly in that light my will was set on by a mighty impulse to describe the being of God."[3]

Boehme's style of writing is not very lucid ; Blake's, however, is a marvel of clarity in places, as in the following :

" I saw no God, nor heard any, in a finite organical perception ; but my senses discovered the infinite in everything."

As a single phrase to express a state of four-dimensional consciousness, " my senses discovered the infinite in everything " can hardly be bettered.

Suppose, if we can, that a state may be reached in which we are conscious of the four-dimensional nature of the universe absolutely and completely. Would it not be a pure ecstasy, such as the mystics have alleged ? Would it not necessarily involve the complete loss of personal individuality and the attainment of a sense of one's identity with all the mind in the universe ? Would it not also involve complete loss of the sense of time, so that all action, which involves motion, would be meaningless ? Yet it would not be a blank, but rather a state akin to godhead while it lasted. In fact, does it not correspond closely with the Nirvana of Eastern mysticism ?

It would be going too far to answer all these questions definitively, but it is well to let them suggest themselves ; and this much at any rate I think we may say, that ultimately all the problems of the universe are problems of consciousness, and will only be solved, if at all, by an expansion of our consciousness.

" *If the doors of perception were cleansed, everything would appear to man as it is, infinite.*
For man has closed himself up, till he sees all things thro' narrow chinks of his cavern."

W. BLAKE.

[3] See note at end of chapter.

NOTE TO CHAPTER FOURTEEN

The similarities between various descriptions of mystical visions are interesting. In the Bible this similarity may, of course, be due to the prevailing religious ideas common to the various seers. Compare, for example, Isaiah vi, 1–8 ; Ezekiel i, viii, and x ; Daniel vii, 1–15 ; x, 4–9 ; and Revelation i, 1–15, and from chapter iv onwards.

But the following vision by Arjuna, in *Bhagavad Gita* (Ch. XI, Judge's trans.), is essentially similar.

" I behold, O God of Gods, within thy frame all beings and things of every kind ; the Lord Brahma on his lotus throne, all the Rishees and the heavenly Serpents. I see thee on all sides, of infinite forms, having many arms, stomachs, mouths, and eyes. But I can discover neither thy beginning, thy middle, nor thy end, O universal Lord, form of the universe. I see thee crowned with a diadem and armed with mace and chakra, a mass of splendour, darting light from all sides ; difficult to behold, shining in every direction with light immeasurable, like the burning fire or glowing sun."

And again, Blake's " first vision of light," described in his letter to Thomas Butts, though not of the same poetical or religious depth, is distinctly analogous.

> " In particles bright
> The jewels of Light
> Distinct shone and clear.
> Amazed and in fear
> I each particle gazed,
> Astonished, amazed ;
> For each was a Man,
> Human formed. . . .
>
> .   .   .   .
>
> My eyes more and more
> Continue expanding,
> The Heavens commanding,
> Till the jewels of Light,
> Heavenly Men beaming bright,
> Appeared as One Man."

The imagery used by the mystics to translate the contents of their visions into three-dimensional language, to express it and communicate it to others when they have returned to normal consciousness, must of course not be regarded as adequate, or exact. But although the images used necessarily differ, and depend on the previous mental background of the visionaries themselves, they nevertheless contain common elements; and the chief impression made by a comparative study of many of them is that the vision itself is a four-dimensional experience.

BIBLIOGRAPHY

R. M. BUCKE. Cosmic Consciousness.

W. JAMES. Varieties of Religious Experience.

E. CARPENTER. A Visit to a Gnani.

OUSPENSKY. Tertium Organum.

BOEHME. Dialogues on the Supersensual Life (e.g. in The Signature of all Things, Everyman's Library).

JUDGE. Trans. of Bhagavad Gita.

CARUS. The Gospel of Buddha.

GILES. The Sayings of Lao-Tsu.

PARKER. Trans. of the Tao-Teh-King.

INDEX TO PROPER NAMES

Aksakoff, 90
Alexis (Didier), 201
Alrutz, Dr. S., 23, 25 *et seq.*, 163, 165, 198
Azam, Dr., 44, 143, 191

Balfour, G. W., 223
Baraduc, 213
Beauchamp, Miss, 44 *et seq.*, 240
Beraud, Marthe. *See* Eva C.
Bergson, 70, 103, 171
Bernheim, 23, 24
Bidder, 41
" Bien Boa," 91, 96, 102
Binet, 33, 38, 46, 48, 51
Bisson, Mme, 85, 87, 98
Blake, 7, 8, 43, 248, 250, 251
Boehme, 28, 248, 249, 250
Boirac, 23, 25, 26, 31, 32, 163, 199
Bond, Bligh, 231
Bottazzi, 70
Bouillard, 8
Bozzano, 50, 138, 218, 219, 224, 228, 233
Bradley, D., 231, 232
Braid, 21, 23, 24, 27
Bramwell, Milne, 21, 23, 29, 31, 32, 33, 42, 52, 156, 157, 158
Buddha, 248, 249

Campbell Holmes, 135, 137
Carrington, 69, 70
Casimir-Périer, election of, 175, 176
Charcot, 23, 30
Chevreuil, 62
Cook, Miss, 80 *et seq.*, 90
Cooper, Mrs., 222
Courtier, 70
Cox, Serjeant, 137
Crawford, W. J., 19, 64, 68, 72 *et seq.*, 84, 85, 88, 90, 96, 110
Crookes, Sir W., 11, 64 *et seq.*, 80 *et seq.*, 130, 201

D'Albe, E. Fournier, 74, 116
Dase, 41
Davis, A. J., 245, 249

Davis, Gordon, case of, 222
Delboeuf, 99
de Morgan, 11, 199
de Rochas, 23, 24, 25, 110, 163, 197, 200, 213
D'Esperance, Mme, 83, 91
Didier (Alexis), 201
Dingwall, 145
Dostoevsky, 49, 107
Draga, Queen, case of, 140 *et seq.*
Drayton-Thomas, Rev., 204
Dufay, 143, 144, 191
Dufferin, Lord, case of, 168, 177, 188
Dunne, 182, 185
Dunraven, Lord, 64

Eddington, 185, 186, 193
Eglington, 134
Einstein, 172
Elliotson, 21, 23
Esdaile, 21, 23, 29, 30
Eusapia Palladino, 14, 68 *et seq.*, 85, 90, 106, 110, 111, 130, 136
Eva C., 14, 84 *et seq.*, 91, 94 *et seq.*, 110, 136
Everett, 137

Faraday, 62
Felida X, case of, 44, 46
Ferguson, John, case of, 221, 223
Flammarion, 8, 11, 104, 161, 177, 233, 235
Fleurière, 148, 149
Flournoy, 18, 44, 54, 59, 225 *et seq.*
Forbes, Mrs., case of, 229, 230
Forthuny, Pascal, 181
Fox, Kate, 61, 130
Fraya, Mme, 106
Freud, 9, 33, 34, 38, 39, 40, 165

Gallet, prevision of, 175, 176
Galloy, 146
Geley, 40, 64, 68, 88 *et seq.*, 91 *et seq.*, 94, 99, 106, 175, 204, 206, 215, 245
Gibert, Dr., 30, 163, 164
Gibier, Dr., 79, 137, 163, 202

Goligher, Miss, 72, 90, 96, 106, 117, 136
Grottendieck, 234
Gurney, 23, 33, 38, 153, 168
Guzig, 96

Hack, Mrs., 138, 233
Hall, Dr. Marshall, 22
Hall, Stanley, 112
Hanna, Rev., case of, 47
Hare, 63
Hart, B., 49
Helen Smith, case of, 44, 59, 106, 225 et seq.
Hillprecht, Assyrian dream, 43
Hinton, C. H., 122, 185
Home, D. D., 64 et seq., 106, 136
Houdin, 201
Husk, case of, 135, 136
Hyslop, 155, 172, 200

James, W., 11, 247
Janet, Pierre, 23, 30, 38, 44, 48, 52, 163 et seq.
"Jean," case of, 149, 150
Jeans, Sir J., 120, 140, 195, 208

Kahn, 201
Karamazov, Ivan, 49
"Katie King," case of, 79 et seq., 90, 102, 224
Keyserling, 236
Kilner, Dr., 213
Kluski, 14, 91 et seq., 96, 106, 224, 225

Lancelin, 213
Lankester, Prof. Ray, 122, 123
Lenormand, Mme, prophecy of, 173, 176
"Léonie," case of, 44, 52, 240
Leonard, Mrs., 204
"Leopold," control, 59
Lerasle, case of, 147, 191 et seq.
Liébault, 23, 24, 172, 173
Lodge, Sir O., 11, 12, 19, 58, 177
Lombroso, 11, 68, 199
Lowes-Dickenson, 38

M'Dougall, Dr. Duncan, 213
Maeterlinck, 125
"Margery," 231 et seq.
"Marie," case of, 143, 144, 191
Marryat, Miss F., 82
Maskelyne, 136
Maxwell, 178
Melzer, Herr, case of, 128 et seq.

Mesmer, 20, 21, 23, 24, 29
"Miles, James," case of, 221
Miles, Miss (and Miss Ramsden), 157
Morel, Mme, 146, 147, 191
Morselli, 11, 69, 130
Moses, Rev. Stainton, 55
Myers, F. W. H., 30, 36, 41, 43, 163 et seq., 168, 213, 214, 230, 231

Neumann, Therese, case of, 100 et seq.

Ochorowicz, 25, 30, 71, 107, 112, 161 et seq.
Ossowiecki, 106, 107, 204 et seq., 245
Osty, Dr., 18, 68, 76, 118, 146 et seq., 166, 173, 179 et seq.
Ouspensky, 9, 122

Palladino. See Eusapia
Peyroutet, Mme, 179, 180, 182 et seq.
Pilsudski, 205
Piper, Mrs., 55, 57, 106, 112, 143, 189
Podmore, 219
Prince, Dr. Morton, 38, 44, 45, 52
Przybylska, Mme, predictions of, 179

Queen Draga, case of, 140 et seq.

"Rector," control, 55, 58
Reese, 201
Reichenbach, 197
Richet, 11, 18, 23, 24, 51, 64, 70, 79, 84, 91, 96, 138, 139, 158, 165, 173 et seq., 203, 204, 206
Rudi Schneider, 76, 77, 106, 118

"Sally" Beauchamp, 45, 46, 108
Salmon, Mme, 79, 137
Schiller, Prof. F. C. S., 67
Schopenhauer, 238
Schneider. See Willy and Rudi
Schrenck-Notzing, 15, 18, 23, 71, 85 et seq., 91, 95, 98, 107, 109, 110, 130, 146, 201
Schubert, Prof., 124
Scotto, Marquis C., case of, 138
Sidgwick, Mrs., 18, 56, 58
Slade, 122, 130 et seq.
Smith. See Helen
Soal, 221, 222
Sonrel, predictions of, 173 et seq.
Stanislawa P., 89, 98, 130
Stanislawa Tomczyk, 71, 107
Sudre, 50, 165

Tardieu, 173 et seq.
Thurston, Rev., 100

Til, M., case of, 54, 221
Tischner, 144, 145, 203

Valiantine, 224, 228, 231 *et seq.*
Verrall, Dr., 223, 230
Verrall, Mrs., 177, 223, 229 *et seq.*

" Walter," 231 *et seq.*
Warcollier, 167

Ward, 22
Whymant, Dr., 228
Wilkinson, Dr., 33
Willet, Mrs., 223
" Willy " Schneider, 71, 98, 106, 109, 110
Wyld, Dr., 135, 136

Zollner, 11, 19, 122 *et seq.*, 127, 130 *et seq.*

SUBJECT INDEX

Alternations of personality, 44 *et seq.*, 51 *et seq*, 236
Anæsthesia, 27, 32, 33, 112
Apports, 126 *et seq.*, 234, 242
Asana postures, 27
Aura, 213
Automatic writing, 42, 44, 48, 167, 229, 230
Autoscopy, 199

Bilocation, 224
Blindness, monocular, 33
Blisters, 100, 240, 244
Book tests, 203, 204
Brain and thought, 103, 104, 154

Calculating prodigy, 41
Clairvoyance, 23, 24, 139 *et seq*, 153, 159, 172, 191, 196 *et seq*, 212, 221, 232, 240, 249
Collusion, telepathic, 223, 224, 233
Confidence, need for, 64, 112 *et seq.*
Confucius, voice of, 228
" Controls," 54 *et seq.*, 105, 220, 227, 240
Cross-correspondences, 229 *et seq.*
Cryptæsthesia, 105, 139 *et seq.*, 153, 158, 191, 204, 207, 212, 216, 230 *et seq.*

Death-bed phenomena, 212, 213, 224
Dematerialisation, 82, 90, 126, 136, 138
Determinism, 183, 184
Dissociation, 44, 48, 50, 99, 105 *et seq.*, 239, 246
Dreams, 39, 40, 43, 44, 155, 156, 181, 182

Ecstasy, 244, 247 *et seq.*
Ectoplasm, 74 *et seq*, 84 *et seq.*, 94, 102, 105, 110, 111, 115, 116, 118, 119, 126, 142, 152, 211, 241
analysis of, 89

Errors, due to telepathic suggestion, 111, 148 *et seq.*
Etheric body, 200, 210 *et seq.*
Experimentation, principles of, 114 *et seq.*
Exposures of mediums, 17, 83, 112, 118

Fictitious spirits, 54, 220 *et seq.*, 240
Flat materialisations, 94 *et seq.*
Fourth dimension, 120 *et seq*, 142, 147, 172, 182, 184 *et seq.*, 207, 211, 217, 232, 235, 238, 242, 245 *et seq.*, 250, 252
Fraud, 12 *et seq.*, 86, 87, 95, 111 *et seq.*, 117, 118, 123, 128, 143

Ghosts, 79, 111, 210 *et seq.*
Great War predictions, 173, 174

Hallucination, 12, 32, 49, 100, 168, 177, 247
Hauntings, 210, 212, 233 *et seq.*
Heredity in mediumship, 106, 107
Hyperæsthesia, 27, 31 *et seq.*, 198, 199, 202
Hypnosis, 20 *et seq.*, 51, 53, 110, 161, 163 *et seq.*, 198, 218, 247
telepathic, 163 *et seq.*
Hysteria, 39, 44, 47, 48, 99, 106, 107, 110, 165, 199, 239, 240

Ideas :
affecting materialised forms, 96 *et seq.*
influence on the body, 34, 99 *et seq.*, 240
Ideoplasticity, 94 *et seq.*, 111, 240, 241
Impossibility, meaning of, 7
Incontrovertible proofs of survival, 50, 190, 191, 218 *et seq.*

Infra-red light, 76, 119
Insanity, 49, 106

Knots in endless string, 126, 132 *et seq.*, 242

Levitation of the medium, 66, 69
Light, action of, 115, 116, 118, 119
Lights, psychic, 134, 135
" Living sideways," 193

" Marmontel " prediction, 177
Martian language, 225 *et seq.*
Materialisation, 79 *et seq.*, 94 *et seq.*, 210, 212, 224, 241
Matter, mental nature of, 140, 208, 241
Mediumship, 105 *et seq.*, 215, 245, 246
Memory, 31, 33, 34, 38, 39, 103
Motion as shape, 186 *et seq.*
Mysticism, 169, 172, 247 *et seq.*

Occam's principle, 211

Pendulum, Moutin's, 25
Penetration of matter, 126, 133 *et seq.*
Perception, 123 *et seq.*, 140, 195, 196, 207, 208, 212, 217, 243
Personal character of mediums, 108 *et seq.*
Personality, 36 *et seq.*, 105, 107, 211, 214, 216, 217, 230, 233, 236 *et seq.*, 248, 249
Personification, 44, 53, 210, 222, 236, 239, 240, 245
Photographs, automatic, 76
Poltergeists, 212, 233 *et seq.*
Post-hypnotic suggestion, 33, 42, 52
Precognition, 106, 121, 139, 140, 142, 153, 171 *et seq.*, 212
Psychic rods, threads, etc., 71, 73, 88, 98
Psychometry, 142 *et seq.*, 169, 191, 207, 242

Rapport, hypnotic, 31, 32, 34, 161, 169
Rapport-object, rôle of, 146, 147, 169, 191 *et seq.*, 205, 242, 243
Relativity, 185, 186, 242, 243

Regurgitation, 15, 86
Retrocognition, 139, 142, 146, 189, 194, 212, 221
Ring, on medium's arm, 135 *et seq.*
Rings interlinked, 132, 134

Shock, influence of, 30, 106, 235
Sleep, 29, 105, 167, 189, 194, 218, 244, 247
Spirit hypothesis, 19, 60, 120, 127, 132, 152, 190, 204, 215 *et seq.*, 232 *et seq.*, 237
Stigmatization, 100 *et seq.*, 240
Suggestion, 23 *et seq.*, 28 *et seq.*, 32, 34, 98, 110 *et seq.*, 163, 172, 173, 236, 248
Survival of personality, 190, 213 *et seq.*, 236 *et seq.*
Symbolism, 148, 149, 167, 177, 178
Sympathy, need for, 112 *et seq.*

Telekinesis, 61 *et seq.*, 107, 110, 128, 212, 228
Telepathy, 139 *et seq.*, 152 *et seq.*, 190, 200, 205, 212, 221, 222, 230, 240
Time, 121, 125, 171, 172, 182, 184 *et seq.*, 217, 242, 243, 248, 250
Trance, 44, 105, 110, 112, 129, 161, 167, 189, 193, 194, 216 *et seq.*, 234, 244 *et seq.*
Transfiguration of medium, 83
Transportation of medium, 137, 138
Transposition of the senses, 199, 202
Travelling clairvoyance, 199, 200

Unconscious mind, 33, 36 *et seq.*, 167, 170, 178, 225, 244
Universal mind, 170, 250
Unknown languages, 224 *et seq.*

Vital fluid theory of hypnotism, 25 *et seq.*

Wave theory of telepathy, 153 *et seq.*
Wax gloves, 91 *et seq.*
World lines, 188, 191, 192, 194, 207, 217, 243

Yoga, 27, 199, 241

A SELECTED LIST OF TITLES AVAILABLE IN SENATE

☐	Aborigine Myths & Legends	ISBN 0 09 185039 8	£1.99
☐	Ancient Man in Britain	ISBN 1 85958 207 9	£1.99
☐	The Buddha & His Religion	ISBN 1 85170 540 6	£2.99
☐	Calendars & Constellations of the Ancient World	ISBN 1 85958 488 8	£1.99
☐	Celtic Britain	ISBN 1 85958 203 6	£1.99
☐	Epigrams of Oscar Wilde	ISBN 1 85958 516 7	£2.99
☐	The Folklore Calendar	ISBN 1 85958 040 8	£1.99
☐	Handbook of Folklore	ISBN 1 85958 157 9	£1.99
☐	History & Lore of Freaks	ISBN 1 85958 485 3	£1.99
☐	History of Dreams	ISBN 1 85958 168 4	£1.99
☐	Gestapo	ISBN 1 85170 545 7	£2.99
☐	Immortality	ISBN 1 85958 487 X	£1.99
☐	Lore of the Unicorn	ISBN 1 85958 489 6	£1.99
☐	Mysteries of Britain	ISBN 1 85958 057 2	£1.99
☐	Mythology of the Celtic People	ISBN 0 09 185043 6	£2.99
☐	Phallic Worship	ISBN 1 85958 195 1	£1.99
☐	Who's Who in Shakespeare	ISBN 0 09 185144 0	£2.99

ALL SENATE BOOKS ARE AVAILABLE MAIL ORDER IN THE UK

Please send cheque, postal order, Access, Visa or Mastercard (NOT CASH):

☐☐☐☐☐☐☐☐☐☐☐☐☐☐☐☐ CARD NUMBER

Expiry Date: .... Signature: ....

Total amount of order including p&p: £ .... (INSERT AMOUNT)

UK POST & PACKING:
Allow £2.00 each for first two books and £1.00 each for any books thereafter

ALL ORDERS TO:
Grantham Book Services, Alma Park Industrial Estate, Issac Newton Way,
Grantham, Lincolnshire, NG31 9SD, England
Tel: (01476) 567421   Fax: (01476) 567314

NAME: _____

ADDRESS: _____

Please allow 28 days for delivery
Prices and availability subject to change without notice